Changing Trends of Indian Cinema

CHANGING TRENDS OF INDIAN CINEMA

Editors

DR. SUSMITA BALA

DR. PARUL MEHTA

PRAMOD KUMAR PANDEY

KANISHKA PUBLISHERS, DISTRIBUTORS

NEW DELHI 110002

KANISHKA PUBLISHERS, DISTRIBUTORS
4697/5-21A, Ansari Road, Daryaganj
New Delhi -110 002
Phones: 2327 0497, 2328 8285
Fax: 011-2328 8285
E-mail: kanishka_publishing@yahoo.co.in

Changing Trends of Indian Cinema

First Published 2019

ISBN: 978-81-937070-8-1

PRINTED IN INDIA

Published by Madan Sachdeva for Kanishka Publishers, Distributors, 4697/5-21A, Ansari Road, Daryaganj, New Delhi-110 002, Typeset by Sunshine Graphics, Delhi, and Printed at Rajdhani Printers, Delhi.

Foreword

Cinema and television have long held mainstream entertainment appeal. From a mass media perspective, the content in movies or cinema can be classified vis-à-vis the status of society. There have been those that, upon release, mirror the life and times of the audience. Also present have been both regressive and progressive productions. There are in fact considerable themes into which productions can be categorised and various lenses through which they can be understood.

India produces numerous films in many languages every year. There is also endless hours of television programming churned out, day in and day out. Indian films have been widely recognised as a tool for soft power diplomacy too. Their reach and appeal have transcended borders and left a indelible impression on even India's fiercest foes. From my travels across South-East Asia I have also seen firsthand how Indian soap operas have a loyal and dedicated audiences well beyond India's borders. Add to this the heady mix of new networks that have aggregated content and are also producing Indian originals– Netflix, Amazon Prime Video, AltBalaji etc., and the playing field has just expanded exponentially.

Given the scale and reach of Indian cinema and the nuances of the developing TV and networks platform, a study of the journey, direction and impact of these is very much in order. In fact the lack of periodic and systematic analysis of what we are watching, is simply astounding. This series of four books tries to fill this gap, and is a first in what should be a regular inquiry into the state of Indian productions.

These books contain research articles that analyse the various facets and developments in this field, and were presented at DME's second international ICAN– Indian Cinema & Alternate Networks Conference. The Conference, partnered by Deak in University, Australia, and inaugurated at the India Habitat Centre on 16th November 2018, received exceptional support and contributions.

It is indeed heartening that we are sharing the spirit of inquiry and awareness with leading academicians of Australia, which is emerging as one of India's more prominent foreign connection.

An enormous amount of hard work has gone into organising of the conference as well as release of these books, and the ably led DME Media School must be congratulated on this feat.

I am hopeful that these papers contribute positively to the study of an industry that, while understandably acknowledged as a commercial giant, is often intellectually ignored.

Aman Sahni

Vice-Chairman, DME

Acknowledgement

This book has come out with the institutional support of Delhi Metropolitan Education (DME), and the motivation for this entrepreneurship came from the leaders of this institute i.e. Mr. Vipin Sahni, Chairman, Ms. Kiran Sahni, Chairperson and Mr. Aman Sahni, Vice Chairman. The academic guidance came from Honourable Justice Bhanwar Singh, Director General of DME, Dr Ravi Kant Swami, Director, DME and Dr. Manjula Batra, Director – Research, DME. Converting the research papers to produce a book on Indian Cinema and Alternate Networks was a big task which could not have been accomplished had the visionary leadership not been there by my side.

DME Media School has witnessed progress leaps and bound in a short period of its existence. The school is known not only for curricular but also for co-curricular and extra-curricular activities, but holding an international conference in collaboration with a foreign university i.e. Deakin University of Australia is the first mammoth task that the school has taken up. The first international conference ICAN organized in 2018 only in the month of March witnessed huge participation and the second edition is expected to be momentous again.

For us the objective of a conference is creating storehouse of knowledge for the use of media educators, trainers, researchers and the students. In the first edition of ICAN we produced four books, three in English and one in Hindi. This time also, we have planned the same number of books.

The idea of organizing an international conference on Indian cinema and alternate networks as a collaborative venture churned out during a discussion with Dr. Vikrant Kishore, experienced filmmaker and Course Director – Film, Television and Animation at School of Communications and Creative Arts, Deakin University. It was also decided to take out publications so as to make a permanent contribution to the knowledge world.

ICAN^2 is the outcome of the hard work that the faculty members of DME Media School has undergone for more than three months. Right from inception of the idea to drafting the plan and from making the strategy to execution on the ground, the faculty members have been working day and night. Under the supervision of two conveners, Dr. Vikrant Kishore and Dr. Susmita Bala, the energetic team members carried the things forward.

I owe a lot to my faculty members without whom this conference and the publication of books would have never happened. When I decided to steer the ship of ICAN^2 2018 (***International Conference on Indian Cinema and Alternate Networks***) as Advisor to the conference along with Dr. Vikrant Kishore and Dr. Susmita Bala in August 2018, Dr. Parul Mehra, Dr. Atul Arora, Ms. Manmeet Kaur, Ms. Neelam Nanda, Ms. Divya Rastogi, Ms. Sanchita Chakraborty, Mr. Pramod Kumar Pandey and Mr. Mohammad Kamil joined hands as Co-Conveners. Mr. Sumantra Sarathi Das, Ms. Kritika Sati, Ms. Deepika Dhawan, Mr. Harjeet Singh Kukreja, Mr. Rahul Joshi, and Ms. Tulika Arora made significant contribution as members of the Organizing Committee of the conference.

I would like to make a mention here of the team of Deakin University which proved a backbone to the conference under the leadership of Professor Matthew Allen, Head, Dr. Sean Redmond, professor in Screen and Design, Dr. John Cumming, Senior Faculty – Film and TV, School of Communications and Creative Arts.

I would also like to thank and appreciate all my friends and colleagues who always motivated and helped me during all the stages of this mammoth task. Special thanks to Dr. Mansavi Maheshwari, Assistant Professors in K.R. Mangalam University, Mr. Hemant Kaushik, senior faculty of TV Today Media Institute and Ms. Deepa Zutshi, visiting faculty, ZIMA.

I cannot forget the immense contribution made by Dr. Aman Vats, Associate Professor and Coordinator, Research Division, Amity School of Communication, Amity University, Noida as Reviewer. Along with him, the task of reviewing was handled by Dr. Parul Mehra as internal member of the team.

The galaxy of media educators, researchers and professionals provided an unconditional support to this endeavour. To name a few from the long list, Dr. Devesh Kishore, Professor Emeritus, Makhanlal Chaturvedi Rashtriya Patrakarita Avam Sanchar Vishwavidyalaya, Bhopal, Prof. J.S. Yadav, former Director of IIMC, Prof. K.G. Suresh, Director General, IIMC, Prof. Ashok Agora, Director, Apeejay Institute of Mass Communication, Dr. Shahid Rasool, Director, CEMCA (Commonwealth Education Media Centre for Asia), Mr. Anirban Sarma, National Program Officer, UNSECO, Dr. Dhruv Joyti Pati, Dean, India Today Media Institute, Prof. Subhash Dhuliya, Dean, Sharda University, Prof. Jaishri Jethwaney, former Course Director of Ad & PR in IIMC, Prof. Gita Bamezai, Head of Research in IIMC, Prof. Shambhu Nath Singh, Director School of Journalism and New Media Studies (SOJNMS), IGNOU and Dr. Kiron Bansal, Associate Professor, SOJNMS, IGNOU.

The distinguished scholars of cinema who agreed to support in various capacities like experts of plenary sessions, chairing technical session and conducting workshops include Mr. Nimish Kapoor, Scientist 'E' and Head, Science Films Division *Vigyan Prasar*, Department of Science & Technology, Government of India, Dr. Asad Nizam, Deputy Director, Electronic Media Production Centre (EMPC), IGNOU, Dr. O.P. Dewal, Associate Professor, SOJNMS, IGNOU, Ms. Shubhra Gupta, renowned film critic associated with The Indian Express, Dr. Namrata Joshi, Head, Journalism and Mass Communication Department, Guru Nanak Dev University Regional Campus, Jalandhar, Dr. Gauri Chakraborty, Joint HOD, ASCO, Amity University, Noida, Mr. Iqbal Rizvi, Senior print and broadcast journalist and author of *Poster Bolte Hain*, Mr. Alok Verma, senior broadcast journalist and media entrepreneur, Prof. Kiran Bala, Dean, School of Journalism and Mass Communication, K.R. Mangalam

University, Gurugram and Mr. Aditya Seth, Academic Consultant for the University of South Wales in Cardiff, Wales, U.K.

At my work place, I received exceptional support from all the schools of DME. Mr. Anmol Ratan Mehta helped with his designing skills and Mr. Pawan Saxena provided valuable logistic support. Mr. C.M. Anand, Administrative Officer and Mr. Abhishek Yadav, Technical Head were instrumental in facilitating the smooth conduct of the conference. Mr. Sunder provided support in critical areas of creativity and execution.

In the last, I must make a mention of documentary ***Me Too*** which has been produced by the journalism students for screening in the conference. Some students have also initiated graffiti on the walls as a prelude to the conference.

Prof. (Dr.) Susmita Bala
Head, DME Media School

Preface

Cinema makes a lasting effect on viewers' mind. It not only entertains but enlightens too. It is the real documentation of the culture, history, heritage and societal issues in a country. Cinema fascinates, it is alluring and captivating, and that is how it draws crowd to theatres all across the globe.

For the creative people cinema is a craft and not an academic subject. Learning the craft may be easy with an ingenious approach and skill friendly attitude. But, academics has its own importance. It gives a depth, an understanding to the producer of cinematic content. Educational institutions perform this job either through prescribing the subject in curriculum or organizing film appreciation workshops.

Besides academic and creative aspect, film making also involves technology and marketing. The arrival of OTT signals the departure of satellite age and internet based promotional tools have changed the dynamics of business. There is an earnest need to appreciate and comprehend these changes in whichever capacity we are associated with cinema whether as producer of content or merely consuming the content as viewer.

ICAN^2 held on November 16, 17 and 18, 2018, at DME provided a platform for all those who love cinema and want to live with cinema. Technical sessions (8), plenary sessions (3) and workshops (3) during International Conference on **Indian Cinema and Alternate Networks** delivered ample opportunities to film academia and film makers.

This conference looked at various aspects of Indian cinema while looking into how its reception and consumption, collaboration and distribution have changed over the years. Various aspects of Indian cinema were researched, analysed and discussed by scholars and filmmakers in different sessions of the conference.

ICAN^2 provided ocean of knowledge in terms of research based writings by eminent and emerging scholars from India and abroad. The research papers presented in this international conference are being published in the form of four books, three in English and one in Hindi. This book **Changing Trends of Indian Cinema** is one of these books. The other two books are titled "Bollywood Women and Indian Society" and "World Cinema and Alternate Networks".

This book **Changing Trends of Indian Cinema** discusses the effect of urbanization on films right from themes to emergence of multiplexes. Some authors talk about the commercial aspects in filmmaking business. Some other authors have focused on the real lifeline of Indian cinema – romance, music and dance in the write ups published in this book.

This book comprises many articles written on biopics and period drama in Indian cinema. While biopics have been interpreted as tools of motivation and promotion, period dramas are accused of distorting history. Freedom of filmmakers and the issue of censorship has also been discussed in some articles.

Film reviews incorporating analysis and criticism is an important component in film studies and many scholars have chosen this subject for writing articles. Many eminent media scholars, researchers and film experts have contributed to this book by penning down the outcome of their research and analysis. Hope, this book will benefit the cine lovers.

Prof. (Dr.) Ambrish Saxena
Dean, DME Media School

Contents

Foreword *v*

Acknowledgement *vii*

Preface *xi*

PART 1

Urban Phenomenon and Marketing Trends in Indian Cinema

1. Changing Trend of Indian Cinema Revisit 1
   Yogita Swami
2. Multiplex Oriented Indian Cinema 8
   Shruti Sharma
3. Indian Cinema: A Study of Promotional Trends by Bollywood 16
   Gurwinder Singh
4. Indian Cinema and Covert Advertising: A Study of Symbolic and Technical Elements 22
   Nitya Dhingra

PART 2

Romance, Music and Dance in Indian Cinema

5. Transition of Romance in Hindi Cinema from 'Swiss Alps' to Dingy Lanes of Small Town India 30
   Kanika Arya

6. Punjabi Cinema: Changing Trends Over the Years 42
Muskan Sidana

7. Changing Trends of Indian Cinema Music: A Study of Remix Songs 54
Samiksha Sharma

8. The Utilisation of Indian Folk Dance Forms in Bollywood – Hybridisation or Exploitation? 62
Dr. Vikrant Kishore

PART 3

Biopics and Period Drama in Indian Cinema

9. Biopics as Source of Motivation amongst Youth: A Study in Noida amongst Students at UG Level 89
Mohd. Kamil

10. Role of Biopic Films in Promoting Sportsmen and Sports in India 99
Annu Sangwan and Dr. Manasvi Maheshwari

11. Distortion of History in Bollywood Period Drama (Films) 115
Kritika Sati

12. Studying Approach of Indian Community towards Indian Cinema of Different Periods 127
Nidhi Suryavanshi

PART 4

Regulation and Antagonism in Indian Cinema

13. Freedom of Speech and Expression of Filmmakers/Artists and Censorship 133
Kush Kalra

14. Indian Cinema: Role of Censorship in Indian Society 145
Dr. Radhika Mehta and Divya Khera

15. Dissecting Director G. Aravindan's Classic-Kanchana Sita (1977) 152
Adv. Anand Kumar. V.

16. Antagonists the New Emerging Heroes of Bollywood 166
Shikha Sharma

17. Alluring yet Mysterious: Representation of Femme Fatal in Hindi Noir Films 178
Neema Negi

PART 5

Film Analysis and Criticism Evaluation

18. Indian Art Cinema: The Sinking Ship 187
Sudhanshu Maheshwari

19. Effect of Watching 'A' Certified Movies on Children: A Study 197
Smriti Bajaj

20. Film Analysis through a Web of Networks: A Paradigm Shift on Writings about Regional Films 205
Manish Prakash

21. Through the Freudian Lens: Zindagi Na Milegi Dobara 212
Deepika Dhawan

22. Film Review: Elements of Film and Style of Writing 218
Dr. Ambrish Saxena

List of Contributors 227

Index 232

PART 1
Urban Phenomenon and Marketing Trends in Indian Cinema

1

Changing Trend of Indian Cinema Revisit

Yogita Swami

Hindi film industry, popularly known as Bollywood produces more than 1200 films every year and is considered to be the world's largest film industry. Ever since, the first film of silent era Satya Harishchander was produced in 1913, the Indian film industry has seen several ups and down in its development history. Although, till 1931, until the first talky Alamara was produced, the films were mostly focusing the mythology and magic shows with some moral messages. Picking mythology and magic gave an easy hand to the producers for publicity as the stories were well known to the audience and, hence not much money was needed for bringing the spectator to the theaters. Moreover, keeping the political activities going on in the country, the mythology, religion and magic were the safe subjects for the entertainment of the people. I would like to quote the comment of R.K. Narayana here that:

> *"Almost every individual among the five hundred millions living in India is aware of the story of Ramayana in some measure or other. Everyone of whatever age, outlook, education, or station in life knows the essential parts of the epic and adores the main figures in it - Rama and Sita. Every child is told the story at bed-time".*

The lines of the writer underline the popular Indian psyche to remind us that everyone in this country knows the story very well and loves to listen it again and again. Yearly performances of Ramlila are the best example, which performed in evey corner of the country with large crowds of every class attends them. Pointing out the importance of mthology and its use in Indian cinema, the comment given by Tapan Kumar Ghosh are also very significant, which are still relevant and haunt the Indian psyche. Discussing the role of villains in Indian films, he points out that:

> *This gives us a lead to understanding why Bollywood films which show the trouncing of the villain over and over again has kept the audience glued to their seats. The spectacles of the villain pummeled and destroyedby the hero are associated by the psyche with Ravana being crushed by Rama. The ugly and monstrous rakshasa abducted Sita, and in spite of repeated warnings issued to him by his well-meaning brothers, he wasn't prepared to hand Sita over to Rama, repenting his misdeeds.*

Undoubtedly, mythology have always played their role to create fixed imaged in the mid of everyone, which helped the film makers to produce their works with such fixed images for good and the bad and the victory of the good over the bad.

However, from the time Alam ara was produced by Ardesher Irani in 1931, the cinema industry of India has produced films showcasing the variety of people life picking the themes from every aspect of the life irrespective to the theme and treatment like comedy, tragedy, thriller, horror, dram, etc. With the introduction of sound in cinema, it seems that every film maker had something to talk about the life and the society in his own way, reflecting their restlessness, or an inner pressure to comment, to speak and to express his own ideas. The scene was not much different from what the social and political activists of that period were doing, who desperately wanted to contribute in the socio-political stream of the country with their own ideologies and agendas.

In the present study, it has been tried to underline that the trends of Hindi film industry have kept on changing on a regular basis incorporating the changes taking place in the society, politics, technology, international relations, cyber impact, globalization, etc. These changing trends could be studied and explained into five sub categories.

As discussed earlier, the first phase was of the period from early twentieth century to 1940, where the films were mainly exploring the mythological themes. Major portion of this phase was of the silent films until 1931, when Alamara was released. This was a new beginning in Indian cinema, when suddenly the cinema started speaking. This was an exciting experience to the audience, when the saw the moving images on the screen speaking like real human beings. This magical impact of the technology was so well taken that the people started taking deep inspirations from the imaginary character. Suddenly the actors, who were real human being in their routine life, became larger than life on the screen with added glamour to their persona. Well, whatever was the reason, but suddenly the cinema personalities became very effective communicator of the message they wanted to give to the society at large.

The second phase could be traced from 1940 onwards till 1960, which is called "Golden Era of the Indian Cinema". The thematic aspect of the cinema shifted from mythology to the social reformist movement, political awakening, national movement for freedom, and dream of socialist society based on the right of equality, etc. This phase gave some critically acclaimed films of the history of the Indian Cinema. During first 10 years started from 1940 to 1050, the film industry saw some significant productions like Zindagi (1940), directed by Pramathesh Barua and produced by Birendranath Sircar with K.L. Saigal, Jamuna Barua, Pahari Sanyal, Shyam Laha, Sitara Devi, and Nemo as main actors. The story is about an unemployed university graduate Ratan, and his relationship with Shrimati, who is on the run from her cruel husband. Another important film of this era Bandhan (1940) was directed by N.R. Acharya with actors like Leela Chitnis, Ashok Kumar and Suresh. It was the second highest grossing Indian film of 1940, produced by Bombay Talkies.

Another most important film of the era was Achhut (1940), supposedly made to "promote Gandhi's movement against untouchability". The film was initially released in the Gujarati on 23 December 1939. This premier show was attended by Sardar Vallabhbhai Patel on 23 who stated: "If the picture helps India to remove this curse, it can be said to have helped India to win Swaraj as untouchability is one of the chief obstacles in the road to freedom". Another important film of 1940 was Pagal. It was the fourth highest grossing Indian film of 1940. The psycho-social melodrama was directed by A.R. Kardar for Ranjit Movietone. The story and dialogues were also by Kardar. The film had Prithviraj Kapoor playing a doctor with psychological problems, working in a "lunatic asylum". The rest of the cast included Madhuri, Sitara Devi, Noor Mohammed Charlie, Khatoon, Trilok Kapoor and Sunalini Devi.

The decade of 1950 also saw some extraordinary films of Indian cinema history. To name a few *Awaara* (1950), *Shree 420* (1955), *Mother India* (1957) are the productions of this era. The most important aspect of these films is that the story revolves around the common man, whose life is full of struggle for every minor facility for the survival. The audience easily could relate with these character that finally comes out with the right morals. The hero of these films is generally a common man, whose life is full of struggles but he is a man of right morals and fights to restore them in the general interest. At some point, he falls in the trap due to some greed, or due to some kind of pressure, but realizing his mistake, he comes out of such situation at the end. The end could be tragic with the end of the life, or could be happy with the reunion, and be a better person, overcoming his troubles at the end. Summarily it could be said that Indian cinema in its initial days focused on mythological stories and great epics such as the country's first feature "Raja Harishchandra directed by Dadasaheb Phalke in 1913. Cinema was used as a medium to show anger and voice the opinion of nationalist leaders and parties demanding independence from British colonial rule during the freedom struggle. Later, after Independence, it became a vehicle for addressing social evils. Bollywood portrayed a society which was both desired and achievable. In the golden era of Bollywood films, from the 1950s to the late 1960s, an India which was rural but had rich and vibrant traditions was portrayed through the films and showcased the relationships, customs, norms and ethics of Indian society.

However, the burning issue of poverty and the unemployment became important after 1960 and by the early phase of 1970, growing feelings of restlessness, anger and violence became the front runner among the youth of the country, which started reflecting in the cinema. Some fairytale like romantic films were produced in this era, where the hero is poor and the heroin is rich, but they fall in love, not accepted to the parents, later in a highly melodramatic situation, the relationship is exposed. The stories are full of melodrama, charged emotions, violence, role of underworld forces, car chase, and son. I would like to endorse the argument of Brototi Roy in her article *'A Bollywood Then, A Bollywood Now: Changing Trend of Indian Cinema'* that:

> *'This phase saw a distinctive shift in the general storyline of the movies. Movies like Aradhana (1969), Anand (1970), Bobby (1973) and Sholay (1975) mark this period. These movies were more action based and romantic in nature. Violence became an integral part of the movies, and a lot of emphasis was given on villains, who were basically underworld mafias. The image of the "angry young man" was introduced here, a brooding hero who was very good at delivering his punches and kicks, would destroy the villains and win the lady's heart in the end. A lot of films during this time revolved around this basic theme.'*

From late 1980s to the early 2000, Indian cinema saw the phase of diverse shift in film making procedure. Advance technology was widely introduced in the film making. Bony Kapoor's film Mr. India was full Si-fi Hindi film, released in 1987, which was a runaway hit film. However, romance was still main theme of the film. Comedy films were also hit trend of the phase. Almost more than 75% movies of this period were shot at the abroad location during this phase.

The ongoing phase of the 21st century introduced a lot of technical advancement in movie making. The movies put greater emphasis on the visual effects rather than the story during this period if we look at the film like *Koi Mil Gaya (*2003), to Ra One (2011). Several movies were shot abroad with only some mention of India.

The main reason behind the shift of various trends was the change in the character of the audience. The gradual changes in the politics of the country and introduction of globalization made a distinctive change in the character of the audience. The new economic policy and the new education system made the entire country a part of the global village. The sign of development were seen with growing speed everywhere. The frequent journey to the foreign countries also created a new taste among the audience. The growing relation with the Hollywood also made a significant change in the movie making in India. As a result some of the big industrial houses have started collaborating with the Hollywood producers and making film. Films like *Chennai Express* were made with the collaboration of Red Chilly Production of Shahrukh Khan with the Disney Production of USA. Likewise Ambanis also collaborated with French company to produce the films. However, Stephen Alter in his article *Fantasies of Bollywood Love Thief* rightly says that:

> "*It is impossible to compare Bollywood to Hollywood. Instead of being two sides of the same coin, they are separate currencies al together with a widely fluctuating rate.*"

Introduction of multiplexes has also changed the trend in movie making industry of India, subsequently bringing Indian cinema industry close to the American taste. Arvind Adiga writes in his article *White Tiger* that:

> *Now, PVR Saket is the scene of a big cinema, which shows ten or twelve cinemas at the same time, and charges over a hundred and fifty rupees per cinema - yes that's right, a hundred and fifty rupees! Thats not all: you've also got plenty of places to drink beer, pick up girls, that sort of thing. A small bit of America in India.*

While discussing any aspect of Indian cinema, one should not forget that this is the legacy inherited from Sanskrit theatre and the Parsi theatre, which runs in the nerves of Indian audience. Whatever, influence the Indian cinema reflects in its technology of its making; realistic treatment of its theme, or any other mechanical jugglery, the audience cannot leave it basic taste for the lyrical conversation, musical scores and whirling dances. Classical Sanskrit theatre's ultimate achievement lies in the culmination of the Rasa, the taste of enjoyment. Cinema in India cannot be separated from that taste.

REFERENCES

Narayan, R.K., *The Ramayana: A Shortened Modern Prose Version of the Indian Epic, Penguin, 1977, lx*

Ghosh, Tapan K., *Bollywood Baddies,* Sage, New Delhi, 2013, p.19

Roy, Brototi, *A Bollywood Then, A Bollywood Now: Changing Trend Of Indian Cinema*', in www.youthkiawaaz.com/2011/11/(last retrieved on 30/10/ 2018)

Alter, Stephen, *Fantasies of Bollywood Love Thief*, quoted by Nitin Govil in Orienting Hollywood, Speaking Tiger Publication, Delhi 2017, p.77

Adiga, Arvind, *The White Tiger,* New York Free Press, 2000, p.173

Govil, Nitin, Orienting Hollywood, Speaking Tiger Publication, Delhi 2017, p.77

2

Multiplex Oriented Indian Cinema

Shruti Sharma

Introduction

Multiplexes: Multiplex is a complex or a mall which houses several movie theater. The rise of multiplexes in India was witnessed in 1997, which at that time was a medium to spread mass culture. Mostly these multiplexes are situated in shopping malls or privately owned centers for entertainment. Multiplexes have not only bought a revolution in globalization but also provided a platform to the regional cinema to grow and come out with flying colors. By 2016 multiplexes which account for about 25% of the total screen contributed up to 60% of the total box office collection. One of the chief advantages of multiplex is that it offers customers with a lot many choices of movies according to their comfortable time zone.

Indian Cinema

Indian film industry is the oldest and the largest film industries in the world. In 1913 the film named Raja Harischandra directed by Dadasaheb Phalke was the 1st film to receive public screening for which he also got life time achievement award. Following this big success many more films came up for public screening. Later the directors realized that Indian is a large country with diversed culture so they have good scope in regional cinema. Soon Indian cinema welcomed regional like Hindi, Punjabi, Tamil-Telugu, Kannada, Bengali, Malayalam, Marathi, Bhojpuri, Gujarati, Assamese, Rajasthani & Garhwali and so on. Even regional cinema has trumped Bollywood in 2017 by dubbing the spectacular success of war epic 'Baahubali 2: The Conclusion' a Tamil-Telugu bilingual into Hindi. This has given people a sentimental touch of culture and language through cinema. Indian cinema is also regarded as vibrantly growing industry with a variety of sub cinemas.

Multiplexes and Indian Cinema

Multiplex has contributed enormously to the growth of Indian cinema and also helped regional cinema touch new heights. Since the Indian society and system has started following western culture, they have started living a comfortable and relaxing life. The youth of now works from Monday to Friday and spends its weekend watching movies and going out. On Saturdays and Sundays most of the shows go houseful. The Indian cinema is growing at 10% per annum driven by the comfortable multiplexes, which are flourishing well in metropolitan cities and the cities marked as 2nd tier and 3rd tier. The earning of Indian cinemas depending on Multiplexes is favored by demographics in cinema crazy nation and the variety of shows and timings which is customer friendly. Multiplexes have provided the people with a pocket full options of movies and timings.

Since film exhibition is most important component of Indian film industry and its run through. According to ICRA estimates it was found that India was having 2,200 multiplex screens. According to FICCI-KPMG report of 2017 multiplexes have grown at a steady rate of over 10% over last 3 years which was a result of urbanization. This increase in no. of screensled to larger number of audience watch the films in multiplexes.

The contribution of Multiplexes to the Box office collection of Indian Cinema is also important aspect showing the dependency of Cinema on Multiplexes. According to a research conducted by Vishnu Parashar, findings show that the PVR, one of the leading chain of Multiplexes in India has made handout contribution All India BO collection. The net box office earned by PVR till 27th April 2008 for the top 5 films was 173 million and the all India box office collection for the same was 1456 million. This data clearly indicates that 12% contribution was made by PVR cinemas alone.

The multiplexes views either the big banner movies of prominent starts like Salman Khan and Shah Rukh Khan and many more who are loved and cherished across the nation or the movies belonging to their region, like Punjab views Pollywood movies and South Indian Multiplex are full when Tollywood movies are out. Similarly Rajasthani Multiplexes exhibit movies of big bollywood starts or Bollywood productions.

Review of Literature

1. The Multiplex revolution and beyond (Published in livemint by Lata Jha on July 06, 2018) says "Within the luxury segment, it's one of the cheapest forms of entertainment and gives you an opportunity to spend time with the family. If you compare the ATP of our multiplexes with any other economy with the same target audience, we will be one of the lowest given that our investments are the same. It is a luxury form of entertainment, it comes at a price and if the returns on investment are not justified, the experience will not be upgraded," pointed out Devang Sampat, director (strategic initiatives) at Cinépolis India.
2. From Cinema hall to Multiplex: A public history (Published in Journal South Asian Popular Culture on July 06, 2011) states that as such, the multiplex has powerfully altered the nature of cinema as public space and thus, crucially, what it means to be in the cinema hall. While the reconstitution of the cinema crowd within the multiplex might be seen as constitutive of the 'globalizing' trends now at work in Indian

cities, this article seeks to demonstrate that the particular dynamics of the Indian multiplex at the present time must also be understood within the historical trajectory of the Indian cinema hall and the political struggles that have been played out within its confines.

3. How multiplexes are trying to strike gold in Bollywood-crazy India (Published in first post on Dec 21, 2014) mentions that Multiplexes account for just 8 per cent of India's 12,000 screens but rake in a third of total box office receipts, according to the Single Screen Association of India and a report by consultants KPMG and the Federation of Indian Chambers of Commerce and Industry (FICCI).

Objective

Since the Multiplexes have a vast impact and contribution to the vibrantly growing Indian Cinema and handsome Box office collections, this research has been taken up to study wether really Indian cinema has great dependency on multiplexes. If yes then what is the reason. Are multiplexes looking after the regional cinema too or not? What are the qualities in multiplexes that people prefer watching movies there?

Methodology

To conduct this research a Questionnaire was structured. The questionnaire consisted of 5 objective and 2 subjective questions related to the topic. A sample size of 50 participants from Film and Visual Arts Department of Chandigarh University were taken. The survey area was Chandigarh University because Universities cater students from different geographical extents/region. The age group of the participants was 18-30.

Data Analysis and Findings

Ques.1. Do you prefer watching movies at multiplexes?

Yes	No
47	3

In Favor: Since it a good alternative to relax after busy week. Multiplexes usually are situated in malls where a person can have kingly feeling. It is pocket friendly paisa vasool destination for weekends. Watching a movie and window shopping makes a perfect hangout with friends and family.

Not in Favor: After a busy week, it is very difficult to step out and go to Multiplexes. The tiring schedule doesn't allow to go to multiplexes.

Ques.2. Do you feel movies in multiplexes have a vital role in uniting people to their regional culture?

Agree	Disagree	I don't know
39	6	5

In Favor: It is an undeniable fact that very rarely a movie from regional cinema gets the nationwide screening. But for the younger generation it is very important to know there regional culture. In this case the directors and producers approach the multiplexes and cinema halls to earn and showcase their art piece. Many regional movies show antique and old Punjab, the people and culture which unites people to their regional culture.

Not in Favor: Many movies show the man stocking a woman, drug intake and rapes etc. which is not at all part of regional culture. Also films hardly focus on culture, the person viewing cannot focus on culture because his/her attention is taken away by story and cast.

Ques.3. Do you find any change in entertainment's quality at multiplexes in comparison to cinema halls?

Yes	No	I don't know
47	0	3

In Favor: With its variable time slots and numerous options in shows, it makes the quality of entertainment better in comparison to cinema halls. Cinema halls are single screened and do not provide so many options. Also the multiplexes have comfortable seats, air conditioned halls and snack shops too, which maximum cinema halls do not have. The most favorable thing is the location.

Usually multiplexes are centered in malls where a person can roam around before the movie or after it too. Cinema hall do not have such advantage.

Not in Favor: People go in cinema or multiplexes just to watch the movie. Once the movie starts, people hardly look around. So there is no role of Multiplexes in providing better quality of entertainment. It all about the script.

Ques.4. Do you feel regional cinema's success is dedicated to multiplexes?

In Favor: (50) Yes hardly regional cinema gets national platform so Multiplexes are a good option to screen the movie and earn profit. Since the regional cinema is limited to a particular culture and geographic extent. Apart from that geographical area, only few people view it.

Ques.5. Do you think multiplexes contribute to the box office collection?

Agree	Disagree	I don't know
50	0	0

Since the net box office collection is calculated by adding the contribution of multiplexes so it is very much admitted fact that Multiplexes contribute to the box office collection. Also if there is no contribution of multiplexes in BO collection then why how multiplexes are surviving. There are so many screens across the nation, how are they being used?

Ques.6. Multiplexes are replacing cinema halls. Do you agree to this statement?

Agree	Disagree	I don't know
44	5	1

In Favor: Yes the multiplexes are replacing the cinema halls due to their customer friendly service. The modern infrastructure is also the major reason behind the disappearing cinema halls. Multiplexes are the luxurious one stop destination to spend a whole day.

Not in Favor: Still there are less developed areas where Cinema exists, which has hardly got affected with the entry and expansion of multiplexes.

Ques.7. Multiplexes are the back bone of entire Indian Cinema. Rate the statement.

0%- 25%- (3)	51%- 75%- (3)
26%- 50%- (0)	76%- 100%- (44)

0%- 25%- (3)

Reason: Before the entry of the multiplexes too the Indian cinema was earning big bucks.

51%- 75%- (3)

Reason: If multiplexes do not exhibit movies they will have to suffer loss because mostly people approach multiplexes to watch movies as they are comfortable.

76%- 100%- (44)

Reason: Since entire India Cinema is not only about Bollywood, it includes the regional cinema too. So the low budget movies and regional cinema earns most out of multiplexes. Even the big banner movies earn the most out of multiplexes. Many times it is seen that the shows go housefull, which means the box office collection goes high. This also means that people go there to watch and contribute to the BO collection. Hence Indian Cinema relies on multiplexes.

Conclusion

The survey shows that Indian Cinema is oriented to Indian Cinema. Without multiplexes, the cinema can suffer unbearable loss. Since the Indian Cinema apart from Bollywood caters the regional cinema like Pollywood, Tollywood, Rollywood too. It contributes to the Box office collection. This shows that multiplexes act as the backbone of Indian Cinema.

The multiplex culture is highly accepted across the nation due to its customer friendly characteristics. These qualities attract them to the better quality to entertainment. The location of these multiplexes add up as 5 stars to their business. All these qualities are rapidly replacing the cinema halls.

REFERENCES

https://www.livemint.com/Consumer/VbhDs0dHTLmOdID8J1u6ZM/The-multiplex-revolution-and-beyond.html

https://www.tandfonline.com/doi/abs/10.1080/14746681003798037?src=recsys&journalCode=rsap20

ICRA report service rating

FICCI KPMG Report of 2017

http://www.filmreference.com/encyclopedia/Independent-Film-Road-Movies/India-NATIONAL-CINEMA-AND-REGIONAL-CINEMAS.html

https://www.firstpost.com/business/how-multiplexes-are-trying-to-strike-gold-in-bollywood-crazy-india-1239851.html

Research paper titled 'A study of impact of Multiplex Cinema's in India' by Ashwin B. Sonone.

A project report titled 'Impact of Multiplex' by Vishnu Parashar.

3

Indian Cinema: A Study of Promotional Trends by Bollywood

Gurwinder Singh

Introduction

Promotion of Bollywood movies is not at all a new concept, but the techniques and strategies of its promotion have changed over the past many decades. From the early days till the later, radio, television, newspapers and magazines have always remained the tools of promoting the films. But with the growth in the film industry and digital media, the Bollywood film makers are now trying to use more innovative methods of promoting their films.

The Indian film segment grew 27% in 2017 on the back of box office growth – both domestic and international – coupled with increased revenues from sale of satellite and digital rights. The Hindi films comprise the majority component of the Indian film segment. They contribute almost 40% of the net domestic box office (BO) collections annually, despite comprising only 17% of the films made. (Re-imaging India's M&E Sector, 2018)

Digital media has grown significantly over the past few years, and continues to lead the growth charts on advertising. Subscription revenues are emerging and are expected to make their presence felt by 2020. (Re-imaging India's M&E Sector, 2018)

India provides a large user base to social media platforms. India has already become the second largest market for social networking giants such as Facebook (with over 200 million users) and LinkedIn (with over 42 million users) and is expected to surpass the US to lead the global tally of the largest Facebook user base on mobile devices in the next couple of years. In addition, Instagram has 30 million users and Snapchat has reached 10% penetration. Many social media platforms have begun to stream short videos, and we expect the trend to increase in the near future. Research by Omidyar Network suggests that Indians spend 200 minutes a day on mobile apps, 40% of which is spent on social media apps. (Re-imaging India's M&E Sector, 2018)

India is a country where social media has brought a storm in the media sector. It is one of the most commonly used media amongst all the sections of the society. The Bollywood film makers have therefore started using a very unique way of promoting their films at a large and mass level. Also, the films are not being promoted in a direct way, rather they are being creatively done so as to leave an impact on the audience.

Working Definition of Key Terms:

1. **Indian cinema:** It is the cinema of India that includes the films produced in the country. The paper defines the Indian cinema as Hindi cinema or mainly Bollywood.
2. **Promotional trends:** The techniques and strategies used for the promotion of the Bollywood films.
3. **Bollywood:** The films of Hindi cinema from the year 2017 and 2018.

Objectives

1. To know how social media is used as a tool of promoting films by Bollywood film makers.
2. To find what kind of new promotional strategies are being used for promoting these films.

Research Methodology

The Research Methodology taken into consideration to study the promotional techniques in Bollywood cinema is quantitative as well as qualitative. The research method is Content Analysis.

Content analysis: Walizer and Wiener (1978) define content analysis as "any systematic procedure devised to examine the content of recorded information. Kerlinger (2000) defines it as a method of studying and analyzing communication in a systematic, objective and quantitative manner for the purpose of measuring variables. Use of content analysis is to describe communication content and compare media content to the "Real World"". (Wimmer & Dominick, 2003, p. 127)

The study is based on the innovative promotional strategies of Bollywood films that are prominently used by the film makers today. The style and the way of endorsing the movies in a different method have been analysed.

Data Analysis and Interpretation

Bollywood film makers always try to bring out some innovative and new methods of promoting their films in order to cater the largest number of audience possible. With the growth of digital media, these film makers take the help of social media and other such platforms to promote the films. The years 2017 and 2018 have shown various such activities.

Padman was one of the hit movies of the year 2108 that had a totally different storyline. The film was based on the short story "The Sanitary Man of the Sacred Land". The film was inspired by a social activist, Arunachalam Muruganantham, who introduced the low cost sanitary pads. It was promoted at a huge level by a very different idea. The actors who acted in the film and those who didn't were found holding the sanitary pads in their hands. Not only the Bollywood actors, but also the sports persons were found accepting the challenge on social media. Even the fans took it up. The challenge was so successful that it taught the public about menstrual hygiene and that it is a natural process. The social media had a large number of followers and fans accepting the challenge and the film got promoted on a large scale.

Itefaq is a 2017 mystery-thriller film that is inspired from the film of the same name from the year 1969. The later is directed by Abhay Chopra. While most of the Bollywood movies are promoted on different print and electronic media in the reality shows, etc., Itefaq was one of the movies that didn't get promoted in any such manner. May be the makers didn't want to reveal any further information about the intriguing *mystery* thriller. Instead, a social media campaign was launched to keep the storyline under wraps, #SayNoToSpoilers, urging the fans to not reveal any spoiler after watching the movie.

Lipstick under my Burkha is 2017 controversial movie produced under the banner of Balaji motion pictures. The movie which talked about gender biasness in our society fought legal battle with censor board before it was cleared for screening. Although the movie acclaimed 10 international awards, but that was not enough to convince the panellists of censor board. After the release of this movie, a social media campaign was started by the producers, the #LipstickRebellion to break gender barriers in the society. Soon this online campaign was trending with lots of celebrities and fans who posted photos with lipstick in their middle finger.

Phillauri is again one such movie of the year 2017 that had stirred up a storm on social media. Memes of Anushka's character, Shashi, from the movie have been digitally inserted into many iconic photos and that has become a rage. Bollywood films have occasionally managed to add an edge to their promotions. There are occasions when the stars go the extra mile and extend their talent and charisma to the real-world, doing things they wouldn't usually do, so that their film gets a stellar opening. It is a unique strategy where the social media platforms have been used to create a funny and engaging promotional strategy keeping in line with the comedy theme of the film.

The film makers these days have started more innovative techniques of promoting the movies. The social media has come up as a most prominent tool in the act of promotion.

Conclusion

The study "Indian Cinema: A study of promotional trends by Bollywood" has revealed very strong results. After analyzing the methods of promoting films by Bollywood film makers, the study has reached to the conclusion that there are innovative and more effective ways to promote a film.

The film makers have very smartly promoted the films. The movie "*Padman*" has been promoted by bringing a challenge to hold the pad and promoting it on social media. The directors, actors and producers of the movies like *Lipstick under my Burkha*, *Phillauri* and *Itefaq*, have taken social media as a tool of promoting the films. Social media is a most prominent and growing media these days. It has brought a storm in the media industry with its penetration in every household and individual. Unlike the traditional media, whether it be radio, television and newspapers, social media is the most common used media amongst all the sections of the society.

Therefore, it can be concluded that the Bollywood film makers use a very unique way of promoting their films at a large and mass level. Also, the films are not being promoted in a direct manner, rather they are being creatively done so as to leave an impact on the audience.

REFERENCES

(2018). *Re-imaging India's M&E Sector.* FICCI.

(2018). *Re-imaging India's M&E Sector.* FICCI.

Wimmer, R. D., & Dominick, J. R. (2003). *Mass Media Researh, 127.* Boston, USA: Wadsworth.

Bibliography:

- **Books:**

1. Berger, Arthur Asa. (2011). Ads, Fads, and Consumer Culture Advertising's impact on American character and society. New York: Rowman and Littlefield Publishers.

2. Chunawalla, S.A and Sethia, K.C. (2005). "Foundations of advertising-Theories and practices ". Nagpur. Himalaya Publishing House.

3. Cortese, Anthony. J. (2008). Provocateur: Images of women and minorities in advertising. New York: Rowman and Littlefield Publishers.

4. Dines, Gail, and Jean M. Humez, eds. (1995). *Gender, Race, and Class in Media*. Thousand Oaks, Calif.: Sage Publication.

5. Jhally, Sut. (1990). Image-Based Culture: Advertising and Popular Culture. *The World and I*: New York. Media Education Foundation.

6. Sutton, Robbie and Douglas, Karen. (2013). "Social Psychology". New York: Palgrave Macmillan.

7. Wimmer, Roger D. and Dominick, Joseph R. (2003). "Mass Media Research", USA, Michael Rosenberg.

- **Reports:**

1. *Re-imaging India's M&E sector. (FICCI Frames)*. March 2018. FICCI.

- **Links:**

1. https://www.cosmopolitan.in/celebrity/news/a12489/7-times-bollywood-used-social-media-promote-their-movies

2. https://www.filmfare.com/features/10-times-bollywood-movies-had-quirky-promotions-19405-1.html

4

Indian Cinema and Covert Advertising: A Study of Symbolic and Technical Elements

Nitya Dhingra

Introduction

Indian market has an extensive brand proliferation that has forced the Indian marketers to select a different sort of communication. Indian cinema is one of the most prominent medium of entertainment in the country. It is a larger than life medium and the impact it creates on the audience lasts for a longer time. Marketers, with the help of Bollywood, have been using the technique of embedding their product or brand in the scenes of films. The product so placed in it is done so successfully that it seems to be a part of the storyline of the movie.

The Indian film industry is the largest in the world in terms of number of films produced with around 1,500 to 2,000 films produced every year in more than 20 languages. The industry also had the second highest footfalls in the world in 2015 (over 2.1 billion) following China (almost 2.2 billion). Historically, the film industry in India has grown at a CAGR of over 10%. Currently, the film industry grosses total revenue of INR 138 billion ($2.1 billion). Going forward, the industry is expected to grow at 11.5% year-on-year reaching total gross realization of INR 238 billion ($3.7 billion) by 2020. The Indian film industry is dominated by Bollywood, the Hindi film industry, contributing 43% of the revenue. (Indywood: The Indian Film Industry, September 2016) The films fall into the categories of commercial and art cinema. The films are made to entertain the masses. Film makers try to appeal the audience emotionally and humorously and the marketers introduce their brands and products in them. Different products, such as, automobiles, health drinks, soft drinks, detergent powders, cosmetics, etc. are being placed in the movies so successfully that they seem to be the very essence of that storyline.

The Indian film segment grew 27% in 2017 on the back of box office growth – both domestic and international – coupled with increased revenues from sale of satellite and digital rights. All sub-segments, with the exception of home video grew and the film segment reached INR156 billion in 2017. (Re-imaging India's M&E Sector, March 2018)

The Hindi films comprise the majority component of the Indian film segment. They contribute almost 40% of the net domestic box office (BO) collections annually, despite comprising only 17% of the films made. (Re-imaging India's M&E Sector, March 2018)

Covert advertising is an advertising technique where the branded products are placed in the scenes of a film. The products are so placed that they are visible to the audience without any distraction. It has always been a hot trend in promoting the products. Both the cover advertising and celebrity endorsement are all together different techniques. In the covert advertising, the audience get exposed to the product in a very natural manner while the other technique lays emphasis on the celebrity to introduce the product to the audience intentionally.

Different product placement styles are used in the films. At times, the active placement of product is done, i.e., the product is talked about or used by the character in the film, and at the other time, passive placement of the product is seen, i.e. the product or its logo or poster is just kept in the foreground or background in a scene and it is not used.

As the Indian market is globally growing at a pace and Bollywood films have made their presence all around, marketers have continued to follow the trend of placing their products within the films so as to leave a bigger impact on the minds of the audience. The act is done so well that it seems to be a very natural process that is consumed by the audience while watching the film.

Working Definitions of Key Terms

1. **Indian Cinema:** It is the cinema of India that consists the films produced in the country. Here, in the paper, the term can be defined as the Bollywood films that contain the brands and products so as to advertise them in their storylines.
2. **Covert Advertising:** This type of advertising technique is the one where a product or brand is placed in a movie or a television serial so as to advertise it.
3. **Symbolic Elements:** The symbolic elements are those elements that represent a particular idea, belief, notion, etc. They can be the signs, symbols, objects, pictures, words, etc.
4. **Technical Elements:** These elements supplement the symbolic elements thereby raising the effectiveness and impact of the advertisement. They can be the different camera angles, camera shots, camera movements, sound effects, visual effects, etc.

Objectives

1. To find out how covert advertising is used in the Indian cinematic films.
2. To know the technical and symbolic elements which support the existence of the product or brand in films.

Research Methodology

The Research Methodology taken into consideration to study the covert advertising techniques in Bollywood cinema is quantitative as well as qualitative. The research method is Content Analysis.

Content Analysis

Walizer and Wiener (1978) define content analysis as "any systematic procedure devised to examine the content of recorded information. Kerlinger (2000) defines it as a method of studying and analyzing communication in a systematic, objective and quantitative manner for the purpose of measuring variables. Use of content analysis is to describe communication content and compare media content to the "Real World"". (Wimmer & Dominick, 2003, p. 127)

The study is based on the Bollywood films that have the technique of covert advertising in them. The style and the way of embedding products in the storyline of the films have been analysed.

Data Analysis and Findings

The Indian film industry is the largest in the world in terms of number of films produced with around 1,500 to 2,000 films produced every year in more than 20 languages. (Indywood: The Indian Film Industry, September 2016) The Indian film industry is world's largest producer of films. The films fall into the categories of commercial and art cinema. The films are made to entertain the masses. Film makers try to appeal the audience emotionally and humorously and the marketers introduce their brands and products in them. Different products, such as, automobiles, health drinks, soft drinks, detergent powders, cosmetics, etc. are being placed in the movies so successfully that they seem to be the very essence of that storyline.

Bollywood, since its early phase, have been using the technique of product placements in them. Films like "*An Evening in Paris*", "*Bobby*", "*Awwal Number*", "*Prem Diwane*", "*Love k Lye Kuch*

Bhi Karega", "*Kaho na Pyaar Hai*" and many more movies have advertised the products and brands in them very well. In the movie "*Shree 420*", a Coca-Cola banner was visible right above the head of the actor, i.e. Raj Kapoor, when he enters the Mumbai city. "*An Evening in Paris*", a movie that was released in 1967, show casts the actress Sharmila Tagore, where she was seen having a sip from the bottle of Coke. The product was so used that its logo was very clearly visible. The shot was so artistically taken that the logo printed on the bottle was visible very clearly. "Bobby", a 1973 film, places the Rajdoot Motorbike so as to launch it on a big screen. Rishi Kapoor, the actor in the movie, makes use of the bike so efficiently so that its features are being noticed by the audience. (Kaur, 2014) The camera movement, camera angle and camera shot play a very vital role here.

In the later movies like "*Love k Lye Kuch Bhi Karega*", the letter "M" of McDonald's is placed on a ball. And also, the Domino's Pizza and Diet Coke is uttered by the actress when she says that she consumes these two things. "*Jo Jeeta Wohi Sikandar*" targeted the youth and college going students by advertising the BSA SLR bicycles. In the movie "*Taal*", the actress Aishwarya Rai is seen taking a sip from the glass bottle of Coke. She picks one from the many placed together on a table. Also, the actor, Akshay Khanna picks one of the bottles making sure that the logo on the bottle is clearly visible to the audience. In some of the films, multiple brands and products are advertised.

Movie like "*Baghban*" advertises Tata Tea, Ford Ikon, Archies and ICICI Bank in the sequence of the storyline. As soon as the actor Amitabh Bachchan steps at the door of his home after the morning walk, the packet of the Tata Tea is opened by the actress Hema Malini. While opening the packet, only her hands and the packet are being shown and this act is repeated several times in the movie. The senior actor is shown working in the ICICI Bank and therefore it is advertised many times in the film. During his farewell from the work, the screen was loaded with the banners, logo and posters of ICICI. Also, the product Ford Ikon is advertised twice in the film. The products so advertised in the film are so done that fits in the scene and the sequence of the storyline very well.

Another movie, "*Krrish*" included the brands like Singapore Tourism Board, Sony, John Players, Bournvita, Tide, Hero Honda, Boro Plus, Lifebuoy, HP Power, Hansaplast, Lays, etc. In the movie "*Dilwale Dulhaniya Le Jayenge*", the actor Shah Rukh Khan mentions the Stroh's Beer while having it with his dad late night. "*Dil to Pagal Hai*" again advertised several brands in it. They were Pepsi, Levi's, Killer Jeans, etc.

The Bollywood films are truly a promotional tool for the marketers to promote and advertise their products and brands in such a manner that they appear to be the very essence of the storyline of that particular film.

Conclusion

The study "Indian Cinema and Covert Advertising: A Study of Technical and Symbolic Elements" reveals very strong results after critically analysing the product placements in the Bollywood movies. The product placement field in the area of marketing is growing rapidly and consistently with the increase in the competition of the products and brands in the market. It has been widely used since the growing years of Bollywood film industry. Both the marketers and film makers get benefitted with this strategy of advertising and promoting brands.

The first objective was fulfilled by analysing the type of product placement made in the scenes of the films. It was found that various types of styles and placements are done to advertise a product. Few products were actively placed while the others were passively placed. The actively placed products were directly consumed and used by the characters in the film, i.e., *Coke* in *An Evening in Paris*, *Rajdoot* in *Bobby*, *Tata Tea* in *Baghban*, also *Coke* in *Taal*, etc. The passively advertised products were the ones which were not consumed rather they were placed in the foreground or background of the scene. Their posters, logo or some signage was used for the promotion. For example, the logo and posters of ICICI bank in the movie *Baghban* and the letter *"M"* printed on the ball in the movie *Love k Lye Kuch Bhi Karega* justifies the above type very well.

The second objective of the study was fulfilled by knowing how the technical and symbolic elements support the existence of the product in the film. Different types of camera angles, camera shots and camera movements support the very being of the brand in the film. The motorbike in the film *Bobby* is ridden by the actor and the camera focuses on the name of the motorbike, i.e. Rajdoot. The sip of *Coke* taken by the actress Sharmila Tagore in*An Evening in Paris* and Aishwarya Rai in *Taal* is very clearly shot by the camera taking in view that it does not gets distorted. The symbolic elements that support the technical elements and the advertising techniques are the dialogues, storyline and different non-verbal language. These symbolic elements play a vital role in supporting the very existence of the particular product in the storyline of the film.

Hence, the covert advertising techniques are being widely used in the Bollywood films and it has always remained one of the prominent tools for the marketers to promote their brands efficiently.

REFERENCES

(September 2016). *Indywood:The Indian Film Industry.* Deloitte.

Kaur, B. (2014). Product Placement in Movies: The Bollywood Experience. *Global Journal of Finance and Management*, *6*, 55.

(March 2018). *Re-imaging India's M&E sector.* FICCI.

(March 2018). *Re-imaging India's M&E Sector.* FICCI.

Wimmer, R. D., & Dominick, J. R. (2003). *Mass Media Researh, 127.* Boston, USA: Wadsworth.

Bibliography

- **Books:**

1. Batra, Satish K and Kazmi, SHH. (2008). "Advertising and Sales Promotion". New Delhi. Excel Books.
2. Chattopadhyay, Rohitashya. (2014). *Understanding India (1st ed.).* New Delhi. Sage Publications India Pvt. Ltd.

3. Chunawalla, S.A and Sethia, K.C. (2005). "Foundations of advertising-Theories and practices ". Nagpur. Himalaya Publishing House.

4. Hansen, Anders. (2004). *Mass Communication Research Methods*. London. Macmillan Press Limited.

5. Maurice J. Mandell. (1968). "Advertising". NJ. Prentice-Hall

6. Paivio, A (1986). Mental Representations: A Dual Coding Approach. Oxford. England: Oxford University Press.

7. Percy, Larry. (1983). Advertising and Consumer Psychology. Canada. D.C. Heath and Company.

8. S. Hecker and D.W. Stewart. (1988). "*Nonverbal Communication in Advertising*", Lexington, Mass: Lexington Books.

9. Shrum,L.J.(2004).The Psychology of Entertainment Media. Mahwah. Lawrence Erlbaum Associates,Inc.

10. Sutherland, Max. (2008). Advertising and the mind of the consumer: What works, what doesn't and why. Australia. Allen Unwin.

11. Wimmer,Roger D. and Dominick, Joseph R. (2003). "Mass Media Research", USA, Michael Rosenberg.

- **Journals:**

1. Kaur, B. (2014). Product Placement in Movies: The Bollywood Experience. *Global Journal of Finance and Management*.

- **Reports:**

1. Re-imaging India's M&E sector. (FICCI Frames). March 2018. FICCI.

2. *Indywood:The Indian Film Industry.* September 2016. Deloitte.

PART 2
Romance, Music and Dance in Indian Cinema

5

Transition of Romance in Hindi Cinema from 'Swiss Alps' to Dingy Lanes of Small Town India

Kanika Arya

Introduction

Romance has been an indelible part of Hindi Cinema, since, its early days. Somewhere it started with social romances and mythological and historical romances, and contemporarily it still is pinned on stories with a tinge of romance. Narratives might have changed, so the settings, costumes or even characters but romance as an inevitable ingredient has stayed. This phenomenon is very interesting to observe, thus, the researcher has taken the period of nineties till now, as this has been the time when romance as a genre has gone through most of the metamorphosis.

This observation might give us interesting trends of this journey, stories have changed, their portrayal, the characterization, the narrative, everything has changed and so have the audiences. Throughout the paper, these trends will be observed and reason for the same will be discussed.

Literature Review

Tejaswini Ganti in *Bollywood: A Guidebook to Popular Hindi Cinema* (2013) discusses ages of Bollywood. 'Phalke and the Silent era' was the first phase, he is credited with the making of first ever Indian feature film *Raja Harishchandra* (1913). Phalke is known as the father of Indian cinema, not only did he initiate an indigenous film industry but also created a genre which lives and continues to be popular 'the mythological' in Indian cinema.

It was the nineties for Hindi commercial cinema which brought a lot of exposure towards how international films, especially Hollywood creates and markets itself. With satellite television, arrived a lot of varied content with superb finesse, to keep up with those standards, commercial Hindi cinema improved production values 'that included digital sound, foreign locations, extravagant song sequences, and lavish sets' (Ganti, 2013). The global exposure that Bollywood was receiving due to liberalisation led to 'increased Salaries for stars, directors, and technicians, and distributors were willing to pay previously unheard-of amounts for distribution rights' (Ganti, 2013). Due to global competition filmmakers began to pay greater attention to marketing and promotion, also internet began to be used as an important tool for promotions.

Nineties was also the time when filmmakers looked seriously at the international market, and tried to earn profits outside India from their work. Production houses like Mukta Arts and Yashraj banner even made movies with Diaspora in mind, and reaped huge success also from various corners of the world. The film industry was also given industry status in nineties by Government of India, this led to big names like Birla, Reliance and Tata entering film industry as producers and distributors, also existing production houses like Mukta Arts going public by getting listed in stock market and even big names from TV industry like Balaji and UTV entering the cinema-scape. These changes led to much organized and corporatized work atmosphere in the film industry which till now was working in a very irregular manner. Another development was creation of multiplexes which led to better movie watching experience, higher ticket prices and more specialized moviemaking, as now the filmmaker could get fragmented specialized audience. Since 2000, big international players like SONY, Warner Bros and 20th Century Fox have coproduced and even distributed Hindi Films. Indian companies have also tapped into new markets around the world.

Yash Chopra's name is synonymous with romantic films; *Kabhie Kabhie* (1976) and *Silsila* (1981) exemplify his specialization in making romantic films and dealing with social and sexual life of India's rich and affluent. His cinema can be divided into three categories: social films, action films and romantic films. Romance is his specialization and something which has given him global popularity. Dwyer (1998) says, 'The situation is vastly complicated when dealing with India for which no history of love in its broader senses has been written'. She says in Chopra's movies though erotic love holds place, but romantic love dominates. Film studies have discussed love or the romantic aspect of love as woman's movie or a high dose of melodrama. Yet romance is one of the themes of films worldwide with, irrespective of their genre. She quotes Prasad who delineates feudal family romance of 1960's and 70's was overcome by melodrama and realism again subsumed under social genre. Yash Chopra's movies belonged to the social genre.

Hindi cinema was divided in the 1970s into three types: 'developmentalist state realism; identification-oriented realism of the middle class arena and the aesthetic of mobilisation' (Dwyer, 1998). *Kabhie Kabhie* and *Silsila* belong to the second segment, a close replica to B.R. Chopra and the Barjatyas oveure. Yash Chopra's success also lies in 'simultaneous appeal to the bourgeois and the plebeian'.

Ziya Us Salam (2015) writes:

> Kabhie Kabhie was that kind of film; it changed the way people romanced. It changed the way people dreamt of love. It changed love itself. And Sahir, he of the progressive writers' movement, he of the Leftist leanings, became the messiah of every heart that had experienced sorrow.

The film had a multi star cast: much popular Amitabh Bachchan, the suave popular Shashi Kapoor, the dynamic Rishi Kapoor with artistically impeccable Rakhee, Neetu Singh, chirpy and beautiful and Waheeda Rehman, graceful as ever. Sahir Ludhinavi's lyrics and Khayyam's music created history. 'Not to forget Yash Chopra, he of love atop the Alps, romance with maple leaves and sensuous chiffon. And a heart that sweared by love'.

Majority of the romantic movies from 1980 to 1990 (India Today, 2012) can be placed under the genre action and romance, few well known movies from the era include *Maine Pyar Kiya* (1989), *Ram Lakhan* (1989), *Chandni* (1989), *Tezaab* (1988), *Qayamat Se Qayamat Tak* (1988), *Nagina* (1986), *Ram Teri Ganga Maili* (1985), *Tohfa* (1984), *Hero* (1983), and *Silsila* (1981). 1990s to 2000, When we think Bollywood, it is chiffon sarees and salwars, hero and heroine dancing around in exotic locales, the immortal charm of SRK and Kajol, Madhuri Dixit and her elegance and beauty, the beautiful music of Nadeem-Shravan and Jatin-Lalit and the warm voices of singers like Kumar Sanu, Alka Yagnik, Udit Narayan and Kavita Krishnamurthy. It was undoubtedly a decade which celebrated romance like no other and Bollywood came up with some of its best love stories ever. *Dilwale Dhulania Le Jayenge* (1995), *Hum Aapke Hain Kaun* (1994), *Kuch Kuch Hota Hai* (1998), *Lamhe* (1991), *Hum Dil De Chuke Sanam* (1999), *Dil To Pagal Hai* (1997), *Rangeela* (1995), *Aashiqui* (1990), *Kabhi Haan Kabhie Na* (1994), and *Raja Hindustani* (1996) are the frontrunners which make this decade the decade of romance.

Maine Pyar Kiya is a 1989 musical directed by Sooraj Barjatya. It is a very special film for those who grew up in '80s. The film changed perspectives about friendship and romance in Bollywood. *MPK* was a trendsetter that led to creation of many more such films. 'Everything – from the film's costumes to its dialogue and the soulful songs – makes *Maine Pyar Kiya,* an epitome of romance' (TOI, 2015). Considered a cult romance, the film established Salman Khan and Sooraj Barjatya in Bollywood. The film was successful overseas when it was dubbed in English as *When Love Calls*. The dubbed film was the one of biggest hits in 'the Caribbean market at Guyana and also dominated the box-office at Trinidad and Tobago'. The film was later also dubbed as *Te Amo* in Spanish.

Qayamat Se Qayamat Tak (1988) is a landmark film which gave us two heartthrobs of the time Amir Khan and Juhi Chawla and a director who changed romance on screen Mansoor Ali Khan. The film though thoroughly successful is not given same amount of reverence as DDLJ, because the people associated with it did fairly different work. Masoor is remembered for *Jo Jeeta Wohi Sikander*, while as Amir is known for his versatility with movies like *Dil Hai Ki Maanta Nahi, Rangeela, Sarfarosh, 1947: Earth, Lagaan and Dil Chahta Hai* but with Shah Rukh Khan, everything revolves around DDLJ, as none of his works could recreate the magic of DDLJ. Ray (2016) explains that the chocolate boy next door image of the hero is testimony enough to its contribution. 'The film practically redefined the way the hero operated in popular Hindi cinema'. Hindi film music was in abysmal state in 1980's before the release of QSQT. Music legends like R.D. Burman, Khyyam, Kalyanji and Anandji and Lakshmikant Pyarelal were reducing their assignments as they were finding it difficult to work in a musical environment with songs like 'Mera dil tota ban gaya' or 'Taaki re Taaki' but Jatin Lalit's musical score for QSQT was reminiscent of old memories and changed musical ambience of Bollywood forever.

The IMBD list (2017) of romantic genre movies from 2000 to 2017 include *Dhadkan* (2000), *Mohabbatein* (2000), *Kaho Na Pyaar Hai* (2000), *Rehna Hai Tere Dil Mein* (2001), *Gadar: Ek Prem Katha* (2001), *Devdas* (2002), *Saathiya* (2002), *Tere Naam* (2003), *Kal Ho Na Ho* (2003), *Hum Tum* (2004), *Veer Zaara* (2004), *Jab We met* (2007), *Namastey London* (2007), *Rab Ne Bana Di Jodi* (2008), *Love Aaj Kal* (2009), *Parineeta* (2005), *Band Baaja Baraat* (2010), *Tanu Weds Manu* (2011), *Jab Tak Hai Jaan* (2012), *Ek Tha Tiger* (2012), *Cocktail (*2012), *Aashiqui 2* (2013), *Ye Jawani Hai Deewani* (2013), *2 States* (2014), *Humpty Sharma Ki Dhulania* (2014), *Tamasha* (2015), *Tanu Weds Manu Returns* (2015), *Bajirao Mastani* (2015), *Goliyon ki Ras Leela:Ram Leela*

(2013), *Dear Zindagi* (2016), *Ki and Ka* (2016), *Toilet: Ek Prem Katha* (2017), *Badrinath Ki Dhulania* (2017).

Sudhir Kakar (1981) emphasises that Hindi cinema is a prism that reflects conscious and unconscious psychological concerns of millions of people, who devotedly watch it. Thus, Hindi films are like a 'group daydream', they are not as complex as literature, painting or an art film, but like a children's fairytale and adult dreams, its ingredients are fantastical; fulfilment of wishes, defeat of enemies and simplified victory for hero. Many characters and plots are stereotypical and repetitive, which bring this cinema under a lot of critical scrutiny. Critics consider it unrealistic, where the paradigm of reality is factual and not the, 'psychically real'. But he continues, these films affect the culture in varied ways, though it itself is a cultural product.

Films determine the visual style of other popular communication products like calendar, magazine illustrations, advertisements and even 'traditional iconography of statues and pictures for religious worship'. It was Raja Ravi Verma, who contributed to films by giving his paintings to Phalke for use, but now, Hindi films are contributing to the imagery of popular painting. Be it popular music or popular theatre, Hindi films dominate everywhere.

The 'collective fantasy of family relationships' is central to the plot of this cinema; Kakar talks about 'the mother–son' connection which is characterized by a psychoanalytic term 'splitting', the good and bad of the same relationship kept at a distance. The splitting is used as a device in another set of relation, 'the good and the bad brother'; it helps to deal with 'anxiety generated by disturbed relationships'. The 'aggressive and violent' components of a family relation are so difficult to accept in an Indian setting, that they always have to be shown split from perfection and projected as bad family. The 'father-daughter' relationship also is based on pure fantasy; most of the times father is a widower and heroine is the only child so that the relationship is undisturbed and uncontaminated. Kakar delineates Hindi films are contemporary myths, a vehicle of fantasy to heal the stresses arising out of Indian family relations. They also act as modern version of familiar myths; in this process creating new myths offering answers to conflicts arising out of contemporary political, social and economic forces.

Romantic films point towards 'passion, emotion and affection between individuals (mainly the main characters of the Film)', such movies describe the 'journey these characters go through dating, courtship or marriage caused by their genuine strong, pure and true emotions for each other' (Dirks). Every Hindi movie has a love theme or love song and other themes of love which go beyond the romantic couple but 'it is not clear whether romantic genre exists in Indian Cinema as a specific and universally acknowledged category' (Dwyer, 1998, p.185). Hindi movies have only a few clearly defined genres like nationalistic, historical, mythological, devotional, stunt, social and action, however viewers also recognize or categorize a movie by the stars it has; or for e.g.– ''A Yash Chopra Movie'', for the first time, since 1990's, his movies have been recognized as a category by audience, distributors and put them in romantic genre (Dwyer, 1998, 185).

Dwyer in *Hindi Romantic Cinema* (1998, p.183) discusses how Yash Chopra has created a different brand of Romantic Cinema, which has unique visual aesthetic manifested through location and the way he presents his stars. Shots of misty valleys, snow capped mountains, lakes and rivers, women in chiffon and field of flowers. According to the writer, Yash Chopra is synonymous with genre of romantic Hindi movie. Another feature of his films is melodrama, emphasis on making all interiority exterior, role played by chance, importance of secrets, use of non verbal signs, especially music and misc-en-scene. Plots are largely concentrated around a single emotional question and develop in a linear manner (p.188).

Dwyer (1998, p.205) discusses that the enormous changes in the depiction of love and romance in Hindi movies from 1950 to present can be traced within the oeuvre of Yash Chopra. Another great director with his brand of romance was Guru Dutt (1925-1964), his films were emotional, somewhere between melodrama and poetry and the brand of romance that he propagated leads the protagonist to self destruction, *Pyaasa* (1957). *Silsila* is the story of love, let down by society's weight, which rises like a phoenix but dies down to greater cause of maintaining moral code within the society. Although this film did not work at the box office in India, it attracted huge response overseas, considered a classic contemporarily, and remained a personal favourite with Yash Chopra. Though Indian Cinema has depicted extra-marital love before but 'this was the first film, to show the consummation of adultery' (Dwyer, 1998). Even as some explanation for treachery is given by the couple having been lovers before, Amit gives up their love, 'the film raises the question: can adultery be romantic?', The film captures the quick degeneration of this love which breaks down when they realise their loyalties lie with their partners. Chandni realises Dr. Anand's life is at risk; Amit comes to terms with his wife's pregnancy. The innocent lovers become a sleazy couple, notably in the eyes of the state', presented through the policeman who is also Amit's brother-in-law; in front of Amit's friends; and in front of older people who should be respected (Gurdip's parents) and the ideals they have set should be followed by younger generation. Dwyer points out:

The sadness and silent suffering of the partners, who discuss the affair in riddles in the context of a medical examination, also make the lovers look shabby.

Yash Chopra's heroes and heroines fall in love often sometimes more than once, and even share sexual relations with more than one partner. However, one must be committed to 'the bourgeois nuclear family', one must be faithful to one's spouse and let go of the past, live in the present. Everyone needs considerate and pardoning environment, and the abdication of these qualities is praiseworthy. While *Silsila* was not an early hit but is still considered a landmark film, not only for the gossips that surrounded it, not also for the depiction of adultery but for the reason that its images of glamour and beauty were unconventional for its time and acted as a catalyst to evolve Yash Chopra's style of moviemaking. 'Yash Chopra pays careful attention to all the visual aspects of his films, including framing, lighting, use of colour etc'. Dwyer calls this style glamorous realism, outpouring with sensuousness. This can be observed in the way he portrayed his heroines. He specification through a scrupulous style of clothes which he selects in discussion with the top clothes designers and make-up artists of Bollywood. They wear a look with less make-up and jewelry; 'chiffon saris, *malmal salwar khamees, churidars, mogras* etc., to give a style which is tasteful, elegant, and fashionable'. For *Silsila,* Rekha's look was created by detailed work upon costume and make-up. Yash Chopra created a new blouse design for her, worn with chiffons or satin saris, pearl necklaces and loose hair. This style was very much inspired by look and demeanour of Gayatri Devi, suggesting a royal look.

Research Objectives

To understand how:

1. Romance has changed its trajectory since nineties till now
2. To understand the change w.r.t characterization, narrative and overall *mise en scene*

Research Methodology

To understand how the genre of romance in Hindi Cinema has changed through nineties till now, the researcher chose the most popular romantic movies from each decade, since nineties, the selection was based on the choice of well-known critical sites Rotten Tomatoes and IMBD. The researcher then planned two focus group sessions, one with some students (60) of Bachelors in Mass Media, 2016-18 batch, Mumbai University and the other focus group session was with women aged 35 to 40 years (20 in number) from one of the housing society in Thane (west), Mumbai.

Both the set of discussions led to some interesting observations, the BMM students were excited and jovial about discussion upon romantic movies, on the basis of collective choice the movies that were selected for discussion were *Mohabbatein* (2000), *Kaho Na Pyaar Hai* (2000), *Rehna Hai Tere Dil Mein* (2001), *Saathiya* (2002), *Tere Naam* (2003), *Kal Ho Na Ho* (2003), *Jab We met* (2007), *Love Aaj Kal* (2009), *Parineeta* (2005), *Band Baaja Baraat* (2010), *Tanu Weds Manu* (2011), *Cocktail (*2012), *Ye Jawani Hai Deewani* (2013), *2 States* (2014), *Humpty Sharma Ki Dhulania* (2014), *Tamasha* (2015), *Tanu Weds Manu Returns* (2015), *Bajirao Mastani* (2015), *Goliyon ki Ras Leela*: *Ram Leela*(2013), *Dear Zindagi* (2016), *Ki and Ka* (2016), *Toilet: Ek Prem Katha* (2017), and *Badrinath Ki Dhulania* (2017). These students could relate more to movies from like directors like Imtiaz Ali, Ayan Mukherji, and Aanand.L. Rai; reason that they cited was that they felt the characters and plotlines to be more realistic, the narrative was at a pace that they enjoyed; which movies from certain directors like Johar and Chopra lacked and made them dizzy, while watching. The choice of music and dialogues was also subtle and relatable compared to the nineties bandwagon (movies like *Mohabbatein* and *Kal Ho Na Ho*, these are much like the romances of nineties).

The second group was closer and emotionally tied up with romantic movies from nineties. Few of the movies that they chose to discuss from the sample were *Maine Pyar Kiya* (1989), *Chandni* (1989), *Qayamat Se Qayamat Tak* (1988), *Dilwale Dhulania Le Jayenge* (1995), *Hum Aapke Hain Kaun* (1994), *Kuch Kuch Hota Hai* (1998), *Lamhe* (1991), *Hum Dil De Chuke Sanam* (1999), *Dil To Pagal Hai* (1997), *Rangeela* (1995), *Aashiqui* (1990), *Kabhi Haan Kabhie Na* (1994), and *Raja Hindustani* (1996). This set of group was more vocal and emotionally charged during the discussion, they whistled upon certain male actor's name; they went into prolonged discussion upon female lead's dressing and makeup, and how they have emulated their dressing during special occasions of their life. They even revealed the songs that were played during their weddings were from many of these movies and how much nostalgic and emotional they feel with each repeated screening. This set of respondents were more involved in discussion and loved the dream like status (Kakar) of these movies. It was observed that they felt *catharsis* like state reminiscing about these movies. This set couldn't feel the same for movies discussed by the former group as their favourites; they felt the characters and stories where sans glamour and emotion, also the editing and pace of the movies were hard to follow for them.

Conclusion

The researcher observed that not only the movies but the audience has also gone through a paradigm shift. The romantic movies of nineties and early 2000's was overshadowed with the style of Yash Chopra (as mentioned by Dwyer) and post 2000 the portrayal of romantic movies changed, from characterization to narrative to complete *mise en scene*, depending upon the individual style of the director. The focus group sessions revealed how the choice of audiences has varied through the years, for different set of age group. Though it is not clear but maybe the audience response and the movies both influence each other.

REFERENCES

Bollywoods' Best Romantic Movies. (2017, Aug 29). Retrieved from: http://www.imdb.com/list/ls020659722/

Bollywood 80s: Mix of Action and Romance. (2012, May 29). Retrieved from: http://indiatoday.intoday.in/gallery/bollywood-80s-mix-of-action-and-romance/1/7206.html#photo30

Dwyer, Racheal.(1998). The Hindi Romantic Cinema. *Journal of South Asian Studies*.21:1. Retrieved from: http://www.tandfonline.com/loi/csas20

Driks. Tim. Romantic Films. *Filmsite.* Retrieved from: http://www.filmsite.org/romancefilms.html

Ganti, Tejaswini. (2013). *Bollywood: A Guidebook to Popular Hindi Cinema*. New York. Routledge.

The Ties that Bind: Family Relationships in the Mythology of Hindi Cinema Author(s): Sudhir Kakar Source: India International Centre Quarterly, Vol. 8, No. 1, Indian Popular Cinema: Myth, Meaning and Metaphor (MARCH 1981), pp. 11-21 Published by: India International Centre Stable URL: http://www.jstor.org/stable/23001932 Accessed: 14-03-2016 05:58 UTC

Maine Pyar Kiya: Lesser known facts. (2015). *Times of India*. Retrieved from: https://timesofindia.indiatimes.com/entertainment/hindi/bollywood/photo-features/maine-pyar-kiya-lesser-known-facts/Maine-Pyar-Kiya-is-25-Lesser-known-facts/photostory/45675028.cms

Salam, Ziya Us. (2015). Kabhie Kabhie (1976). *The Hindu.* Retrieved from: https://www.thehindu.com/features/friday-review/kabhi-kabhie-1976/article7109589.ece

6

Punjabi Cinema: Changing Trends Over the Years

Muskan Sidana

Introduction

Cinema in India needs no special mention, every Indian no matter of what caste, creed, gender, age, status, qualification has been associated with cinema, for some it has been luxury, for some it has been bread earner, for some it has been sheer entertainment, for some it has been a activity to spend leisure time, for some it has been an eye opener and educator. Cinema has been an effective tool of mass media, keeping that in mind it was launched at a ground level. What better to learn than in your own mother tongue? It has been entertaining audiences since the day of its inception. Punjabi cinema has outgrown in a way no other cinema has lately. It is making its mark worldwide. Be it content, revenue, technique, acting, sets, costumes, locations, storyline everything is giving competition to world media. You can take Punjabi out of Punjab but you cannot take Punjab out of Punjabi; that's the major reason that Punjabi cinema is earning good in Canada, Australia, Germany and all countries where Punjabi's reside.

Objectives

- To study the changing trends in Punjabi Cinema.

- To study the content of Punjabi movies before and after partition
- To study the revenue invested and generated out of Punjabi movies in recent years
- To know about the interest of audience in Punjabi movies
- To know the extent of impact Punjabi movies leave on the mind of the audiences
- To know about the story choices of audience

Hypothesis

- Youth of Punjab prefer watching Bollywood movies over Punjabi movies
- Adults watch Punjabi movies on TV, rather than going to cinema
- Audience gets attracted to a Punjabi movie just because it has their favorite singer in it
- Audience watches movies just for entertainment purpose
- Punjabi cinema leaves a major impact on the audience
- Audience chooses Punjabi movies on the basis of their content

Research Methodology

- A survey was conducted among Punjabi youth and Punjabi adults
- The sample size was of 200 (100 youth + 100 adults)
- Various books, newspaper articles and websites have been used to research on the topic

Journey of Punjabi Cinema

***Punjabi Films in Pre-Partition Era*:** The recognition of the production of the first Punjabi film goes to K.D. Mehra who made the first Punjabi film Sheila. It is also known as Pind Di Kudi and it was a super hit in his time. Noor Jahan made her first appearance as an actress and singer in this film. While Sheila was made in

Calcutta, it was released in Lahore, the capital of the unified Punjab. From a business perspective it was a huge success and it was a hit in the province. The success attracted many more producers for making films in the Punjabi language. K.D. Mehra joined forces with M.M. Billoo makes his second film Heer Sial.

While some regional cinemas started with flop films, the Punjabi cinema made its debut with banging success. As majority of Punjabi people lived in and around Lahore so suddenly it became a big market for Punjabi films and bread earning ground for film makers. They believed to make the most of this untouched field and audience for their business to grow. Studios were opened and many artists, producers, directors and technicians from Bombay and Calcutta moved to Lahore, including Noor Jahan, Mumtaz Shanti, Wali, Syed Attahullah Shah Hashmi, Shanta Apte, Motilal, Chandra Mohan, Hiralal, and Shanker Hussain.

Films like Puran Bhagat, Mirza Sahiban, Surdas and Mera Punjab. Zubeida made her debut in Mirza Sahiban were few films released in 1939 and around nine films were released in 1940. This fact states the speed of growth of cinema industry in Punjab. Chambe Di Kali was the debut film of Indira Billi and comedian Kharaiti. Other films made in this year comprise are Yamla Jatt, Laila Majnu, Alibaba, Jagga Daku, Matwali Meera, Ik Musafir and Dulla Bhatti.

Seven films were released in 1941. Noticeable among these were Sipahi, Pardesi Dhola, Sehti Murad, Kurmai and Mera Mahi. In the year 1942 films like Ravi Paar, Patwari, Pattola, Mangti and Gowandhi were released. Mangti was a hit film of the year. Three films titled Mera Mahi, Poonji and Papi were made in 1943. While Dasi, Panchhi, Koel and Gul Baloch completed in 1944, whereas Champa and Nikhettoo released in 1945. Gul Baloch can be glared as the most popular Punjabi film in the Pre-Partition era. The political glitches and increased freedom struggle cast their shadow on Punjabi cinema because Lahore was one of the major working grounds of intellectuals.

***Punjabi Films Post-Partition*:** The partition of Punjab in 1947 affected Punjabi cinema and it was a death-blow for the industry because most of the Muslim artists and directors moved to the other side named as Pakistan. Punjab lost its laudable film centre,but determinations of artists were high to keep Indian Punjabi cinema alive. Punjabi films had to start from the scrape and the stormy period did not let films settle down easily. Film-makers got some success through films like Posti, Do Lachhian and Bhangra.

In the 1950s, the trend of comedies was leading: Phooman, Balo, Baisakhi (1951), Jugni, Laralappa, Koday Shah (1952), Vanjara, Shah Ji, Ashtali (1954), Mulkh Raj Bhakhri's Bhangra (1958), Pingan, Muklawa, Hulare (1957), Nikki (1958), Jagga Daku and Bhangra (1959) these were the few films that released in 50's. Most of these films were flop. The songs of these Punjabi movies used to run for months on All India Radio.

In the era of 1960s, starting with year 1961 in which five films were released out of which Guddi and Vilayati Babu were immediate hits. In year 1962 films like Pardesi Dhola, Dhol Jani, Chann Mahi and Khedan De Din Char were released. Out of these Khedan De Din Char of Manohar Deepak achieved some success. Music continued to be the back bone of Punjabi films. Prem Chopra amused Punjabi audience in 1963 with Sapni and Eh Dharti Punjab Di.

As many as eight films were released in 1964. Satluj de Kande (1964) the big-budget romantic Punjabi film was made by director Padam Prakash Maheshwary, was a major hit and earned a National Film Award. Movies like Kiklee, Main Jatti Punjab Di, Satt Saliyan also got released in the same year. Kamail Singh (1963) and Fagga (1964) bagged the President's Silver Medal. Chambe Di Kali was the only hit of 1965. No worth mentioning film could enter the market in 1966. Though Indira Billi continued to enthrall the audience yet none of her two movies could leave any impact in the year 1967. In 1969 the religious film Nanak Nam Jahaz Hai became the first major successful Punjabi film in post-independent India. Its seen as a major contributing factor to the revitalization of the Punjabi film industry in India.

The Turning Point: In the 1970s, Hindi movie actors of Punjabi ancestry became interested in Punjabi films. The popular and noted films of the decade were Kankan De Ohle, Nanak Dukhiya Sab Sansar (1970), Mele Mitran De (1972), Man Jeete Jag Jeet (1973), a religious film. Do Sher (1974), Bhagat Dhanna Jatt, Sacha Mera Roop Hai and the very successful Dukh Bhanjan Tera Naam.

Daaj Giddha, Main Papi Turn Bakhshanhaar, Papi Tarey Anek, Santo Banto, Sardar-E-Azam, Sawa Lakh Se Ek Ladaun, Saal Solvan Chadya, Sat Sri Akal, and Shaheed Kartar Singh Sarabha were released in the latter half of the decade. Walayati Babu (1978) was the first ever remake in Punjabi cinema. The religious film Guru Manio Granth was an instant hit. Til Til Da Lekha won the Punjab State Government Award for Best Story Writer and the Second Best Feature Film of 1979.

In the 1980s, Chann Pardesi was the first Punjabi film to win the National Award. Fauji Chacha, Mulkh Raj Bhakhri's Bhangra (1958) and Jatti were a great success. Ucha Dar Babe Nanak Da (1985) was a religious film that established Gurdas Mann as a star. The other hit films of the decade were Sarpanch, Yaari Jatt Di, Mamla Garbar Hai, Mohammad Sadiq's Guddo, and Veerendra's Vairi and Long Da Lishkara. Gugu Gill and Yograj Singh took on leading roles.

In the 1990s, Qurbani Jatt Di, Dushmani Di Agg, Badla Jatti Da, Udeekan Saun Diyan, Sounh Menoo Punjab Di, won applause. Sukhdev Ahluwalia emerged as one of the most successful directors. Kachehri (1994) starred Gurdas Mann and won a National Award.

Tabahi, a blockbuster hit; Naseebo and Qahar in 1995; Sukha; the critically acclaimed Main Maa Punjab Dee (1998) that won a National award; and Jaspal Bhatti's Mahaul Theek Hai, an instant hit, were other major films of the decade. Raj Babbar's Shaheed Udham Singh did well towards the end of the decade.

The Era of Diaspora: The year 2003 witnessed the release of Jee Ayan Nu which gave a new life to the poor Punjabi cinema. The movie addressed the problems and life style of Indians settled abroad. It was the debut film of singer-turned actor Harbhajan Mann. It may appropriately be called the first diasporic film made in Punjabi language. The movie was made on a budget of 90 lakhs as normal movies just cost around 20-25 lakhs. Another release of the year Badla was a failure. Its utter failure does not leave any doubt that the era of Jatt-animosity based movies was as good as over. Then in 2004, again, singer-turned actor Harbhajan Mann acted in Asa Nu Maan Watna Da, it was another diasporic film and was a huge hit. Films like Pind Di Kudi (Sarbjeet Cheema, Rima), Mittar Pyare Nu Haal Mureedan Da Kehna and Khamosh Pani could not do much business. Khamosh Pani broke the ground with a serious type of artistic theme. It got critical acclamation.

In 2005 films like Jija Ji, Des Hoyaa Pardes, Main Tu Assi Tussi, Yaaran Naal Baharan, Nalaik were released. Gurdas Mann sprang a surprise with his Des Hoyaa Pardes. It gave an intense description of terrorism and the reasons of its spread in Punjab. It was a big hit. Yaaran Naal Baharan and Nalayak stand nowhere near the definite success of Des Hoyaa Pardes. The year 2006 saw movies like Dil Apna Punjabi, Ek Jind Ek Jaan and Waris Shah-Ishq Daa Warris. Waris Shah was so appreciated that it made its way to the Oscars in the best film category.

Rustam-e-Hind and Mitti Wajan Mardi (2007), Yaariyan, Mera Find, Lakh Pardesi Hoye, Heaven on Earth, and Sat Sri Akal (2008), Jag Jeodeye Deh Mele and Tera Mera Ki Ristha (2009), were produced. Chhevan Dariya, directed by Ish Amitoj Kaur, was released on September 2011. Ish Amitoj Kaur was the first Punjabi woman to have directed, produced and written a Punjabi film.

There is a lot of talk about the boom in Punjabi cinema, but going through the statistics of films released in last few year, the picture seems contrary to the belief. The total number of Punjabi films released in 2012 was 24, of which two were super hits (Jatt & Juliet and Carry on Jatta), about four did above-average business, and the rest suffered losses. So, the success rate comes out to be less than 25%.

Singers Turning Actors Era: Trend of singers turning actors in Punjabi movies has its own plus and minus. No other state in India has had as many singers as Punjab. Some singers are sensibly good actors, and their success has made other singers consider that being a singer is similar to being a good actor. And so, all those who were earlier making music videos are now making films. In such conditions, it is very difficult to even think about getting some serious cinema. Go to any investor and the first question asked is: 'Kehda singer hai' (Which singer is your hero?), no one has ever asked what the subject or story of the film is. Few to name are Gurdaas Maan, Babbu Maan, Harbhajan Maan, Sarbjeet Cheema, Gippy Grewal, Amrinder Gill, Ammy Virk, Amrit Maan, Diljit Dosanjh the most famous majorly has done comedy movies but later he did some serious movies on topics like 1984 and got appreciated. Youth of today prefer lesson giving movies with their favourite singer as hero and in entertaining form. Audience have become more critical nowdays, you cannot just serve anything and fool them. Lately Punjabi films have been giving a tough competition to Bollywood movies. And movies are surpassing the 100 crore clubs now which trend was started by Bollywood. Punjabi movies have animations, graphics, English artists to work in and modern technology is used and out of the country locations are chosen. In the last few years, the trend has been to make commercially successful films with Hindi stars in the lead. Hindi masala-type films have gained more fame.

Reasons for the success and failure of a film are many; if there was a known success formula, then no movie would ever fail at the box office. In reality, Punjabi cinema is passing through a critical phase; excluding a few, most films belong to one genre: situational comedy. Some films released recently were really good and enjoyable, whereas others forced you to believe that Punjab has no literature, history, culture or social issues. For overall growth of regional cinema, one needs films of different genres that thematically belong to the region.

Revenue Generated from Punjabi Movies in Recent Years

Punjabi, as a language, has achieved publicity on the national forum through representation in mainstream Hindi cinema and popularity of Punjabi music across India.

However, when it comes to Punjabi films, there was a time when Punjabi movies used to come and go and people remained unaware about them. Later, the trend changed and the industry is on the rise and things of the past are no more same, as more and more Punjabi films are making a mark in the industry.

A recent example of this is movie '*Qismat' which got released in September, 2018* which proved to earn strong collections. In four days of its release, it minted over Rs 6 crore. *It* has emerged as a major earner amongst Punjabi films. Movies which are able to do business of Rs 1 crore or more is tagged as a major grosser.

The Punjabi films witnessed a major growth in 2017 and saw a number of successful films. This year films on diverse topics and a wide variety of genres were produced. Amrinder Gill's *Sarvann* was an action-packed thriller, while *Vekh Barataan Challiyan* was a typical comedy.

The biggest hit of 2017 was Gippy Grewal's '*Manje Bistre'*. The film collected Rs 15 crore net at the box office in India. Its worldwide earning went up to Rs 45 crore and so. This is a huge figure for Punjabi films to cross as it is difficult for most of them to cross Rs 10 crore.

Vekh Barataan was another box office hit in 2017. It managed to mint Rs 1 crore in the domestic market and around Rs 24 crore overseas.

In 2016 too, Punjabi movies performed well at the box office. Larger number of movies gained recognition even outside the core market of Punjabi-speaking audience. The year saw as many as 12 big releases and many of them were made under the budget of Rs 2-3 crore.

Earlier, Punjabi films were written for the big screens, but the tables have turned now. New projects are carving a niche in the hearts of the audiences, both at home and abroad.

The Punjabi film industry has grown at a CAGR of 50% between 2010 and 2015, according to a report titled 'Film Industry in North India: Reaching New Heights'. 'Chaar Sahibzaade', a 3D animation historical drama with VFX and computer-generated Imagery, grossed more than Rs 70 crore in 2014.

The industry has grown on a low turnover basis of Rs 21 crore to reach upto Rs 172 crore between 2010 and 2015. However, a larger number of releases and blockbusters with individual collections of more than Rs 10 crore and increasing interest from national and international production houses will stimulate the growth of the Punjab film industry, the report added.

The Punjabi film industry has also witnessed an increase in the number of films crossing Rs 10 crore in box office collections during this period.

While Punjabi films have started receiving recognition in India, they are a rage in the Australian market. The 2016 release 'Love Punjab' minted Rs 2.95 crore ($406,601) at the Australian box office. The film broke box office records of its predecessors. Love Punjab also outshined the opening week collections of big-banner Bollywood movies 'Airlift' and 'Bajirao Mastani'.

One major factor that works in favour of Punjabi films in Australia is growing Punjabi migrant community in the country. Big production houses are in the race to produce and distribute Punjabi films.

Findings and Results

- 100% youth respondents and 100% adult respondents knows about Pollywood and have watched Punjabi Movies.
- 40% youth watch Punjabi movies on T.V. 30% Youth prefer watching movies on the Internet and 30% Youth specially goes to Cinema halls to watch Punjabi Movies. Whereas 75%

adults watch Punjabi movies on T.V. 2% adults prefer watching movies on the Internet and 23% adults specially goes to Cinema halls to watch Punjabi Movies.

- 60% youth prefers watching Bollywood movies, 28% youth prefers watching Pollywood movies and 12% youth prefers watching Hollywood movies. Whereas, 55% adults prefer watching Bollywood movies, 43% adults prefer watching Pollywood movies and 2% adults prefer watching Hollywood movies.
- 80% youth watch Punjabi movies for entertainment purpose, 13% youth watch Punjabi movies to be related to Punjabi culture and 7% youth watch Punjabi movies for gaining education and information. Whereas, 54% adults watch Punjabi movies for entertainment purpose, 32% adults watch Punjabi movies to be related to Punjabi culture and 14% adults watch Punjabi movies for gaining education and information.
- 78% youth watch Punjabi movies because of there favourite singers or actors are part of it, 12% youth watch Punjabi movies because of their concept and 10% youth watch Punjabi movies after keeping in mind the reviews of others. Whereas, 58% adults watch Punjabi movies because of there favourite singers or actors are part of it, 40% adults watch Punjabi movies because of their concept and 2% adults watch Punjabi movies after keeping in mind the reviews of others.
- 82% youth prefer Romantic-Comedy genre of Punjabi movies, 8% Youth prefer action packed Punjabi movies and 10% youth prefer inspirational movies. 42% adults prefer Romantic-Comedy genre of Punjabi movies, 4% adults prefer action packed Punjabi movies and 54% adults prefer inspirational movies.
- 63% youth agreed that Punjabi movies have left an impact in their lives and mind, 37% youth thinks that they watch movies for entertainment and it doesn't leaves an impact on their lives. Whereas, 56% adults agreed that Punjabi movies have left an impact in their lives and mind, 44% adults think that they

watch movies for entertainment and it doesn't leaves an impact on their lives.

- 38% youth said they watch Punjabi movie because they like its music, 47% youth watch movie judging the content or storyline of the movie from a trailer and 15% youth watch a particular movie because of its actors. Whereas, 19% adults said they watch Punjabi movie because they like its music, 63% adults watch movie judging the content or storyline of the movie from a trailer and 18% adults watch a particular movie because of its actors.

Conclusion

Punjabi film industry is no new; it has its roots since the inception of cinema and even before the partition of the country. It did undergo lot of ups and downs but it overcame all and today is enjoying a status among the country not only at regional level but worldwide. Lately, Punjabi movies have started minting more money than some Bollywood movies and are giving Bollywood a tough competition. A lot of Bollywood directors, producers and most importantly actors are shifting to Pollywood seeing the growth of it. From sound to talkies to pre-post partition to starting from scratch to diaspora related movies to entertainment centric to rom-com to singers turning actors to Punjabi movies being made overseas to animated movies, the Punjabi film industry has outgrown enormously and marked a niche worldwide. Today people wait for Punjabi movies and not only Punjabis but also people who are not related to the culture follow Pollywood same as Bollywood and Hollywood.

REFERENCES

- CINEMA, A. (2018). AUDIENCE PERSPECTIVE ON PUNJABI CINEMA. Retrieved from http://myambages.blogspot.com/2017/07/audience-perspective-on-punjabi-cinema.html
- Essay on Punjabi Cinema (730 Words). (2018). Retrieved from http://www.yourarticlelibrary.com/essay/essay-on-punjabi-cinema-730-words/24366

- Movies Of Modern Punjabi Cinema (From Great to Good to Average). (2018). Retrieved from https://www.imdb.com/list/ls064541390/
- Punjabi cinema. (2018). Retrieved from https://en.wikipedia.org/wiki/Punjabi_cinema
- Punjabi films carve a niche both in India and abroad, new offering Qismat shines at box office. (2018). Retrieved from https://www.moneycontrol.com/news/trends/entertainment/punjabi-films-carve-a-niche-both-in-india-and-abroad-new-offering-qismat-shines-at-box-office-2988671.html
- Service, T. (2018). Independent films are changing the image of Punjabi cinema. Retrieved from https://www.tribuneindia.com/news/amritsar/independent-films-are-changing-the-image-of-punjabi-cinema/179928.html

7

Changing Trends of Indian Cinema Music: A Study of Remix Songs

Samiksha Sharma

History of Indian Cinema Music

If we consider Indian Music then the history has no point to be said at the start of the Musical era in this country. Mythological books say that the Gods and Goddesses were used to sing songs and dance to portray different styles and aspects of life. Then there is Classical music which is also decades old.But when we talk about the Indian Cinema Music it is said to be started by the 1st sound motion picture named as "Alam Ara". The movie came in the year 1931 from which the musical era of Indian films took place.

In the early years, the industry grew immensely. Between 1931 and 1940 India produced approximately 931 Hindi feature films with an average of 10 songs per films. This period is notable for a number of major artists. It is interesting to note that this early period did not favored "playback" singers. Many of the original actors and actresses sang their own songs. Many times, actors were chosen specifically for their singing abilities. In the late 1940s the concept of playback singers came up and became the trend in the

Indian films. Singers like Lata Mangeshkar, Mohammed Rafi, Geeta Dutt, Asha Bhosle and many more gave the industry uncountable hits which are remembered even today.

The films songs in India were accepted by the Indian audience with enthusiasm and those songs gave the playback singers unconditional love and respect from the audience.First of all, in the years of 1940s India was not an independent country, So there were many restrictions on the type of movie and songs that were been made at that time. After India got independent in the year 1947, the industry worked openly and independently but the situation of poverty do not let people to have televisions or radio in every house. So at that time the audience was not concerned about the quality of the content but they were more concerned about to atleat watch hear the content/songs.

Now, if we talk about today's Indian audience, still the audience love Bollywood songs and is a major part of everyone's day to day lives. Indian people are musical people and do not wish to watch a movie without any song in it. Songs are somehow the main source of entertainment for Indian audience.

New Bollywood Music/Remake Era

While there are lyricists and singers winning the hearts of the people by the new compositions and heartwarming lyrics, storytelling is also done through the songs of the films. In this new Bollywood era of songs the trend of remake songs has going viral. Today we see every Bollywood movie consist of atleast one remake song of the old Bollywood songs. For ex. Remake item songs like Laila Main Laila, Dilbar Dilbar, Aateiaate, Pal pal dil ke paas, chalte chalte, Hamma Hamma, Tamma Tamma and many more.

The Objective of this study is to identify the difference between old and remake versions of Bollywood songs. The researcher will also try to identify difference between the storyline/concept of the video of both the versions of the same song and and to find the acceptance of the remake versions of the old songs by Indian audience.

The hypothesis of the study is

- People like old version more than the new/remake versions of the bollywood songs.
- The lyrics of the old versions are more realistic and nice to listen according to the people.
- The new versions of the songs are ruined by adding raps in them.

Significance of the Study

- There need to be some significance or importance of the study for which the study has been conducted Otherwise it is of no use. It should help in gaining knowledge and to enhance the understanding about the particular topic on which the study has been done.
- This study can help in analyzing the scenario of the audience towards the Bollywood remake songs. This study is going to help in understanding the audience preferences towards the old and new versions of Bollywood songs as well as it will help in understanding the loop holes in both the old and new versions songs which the audience do not like.
- This study will clarify the differences in the old and remake versions of Bollywood songs on the basis of lyrics, Listening capacity, video and music composition. This will lead to give a clear picture to differentiate the old and remake version Bollywood songs accurately.

Review of Literature

Jones, JB (2009) in the research paper titled "Evergreen to remixes: Hindi Film songs and India's popular music heritage" stated that new bollywood songs which are based on the old songs sometimes create magic and people just fall in love with those songs as they touch the soul of people. Songs of the movie Veer-Zaara are based on the old tunes of the unheard melodies of the late music director Madan Mohan. The songs of that movie were liked by the audience so much. The tune, composition and the lyrics were heart touching which definitely impacted the audience in a good manner.

Jacob, L (2002) in the research paper titled "Freedom Songs" stated so many movies like Mother India, Dil se, Dil to pagal hai, Khuda Gawah, Dil Chahta hai say in that these movies and there songs have created a landmark impact on the Indian as well as Outside India audience that the movies and songs are evergreen and hard to forget. He quoted "Golden age titles now readily available disclose a cinema of astonishing depth, variety and maturity."

Basu, P (2011) in the book titled "Traversing Tradition: Celebrating Dance in India" stated that remake of songs which are used as item numbers came up as big hits. Songs like Yeh mera dil used in movie Don 2, Mehbooba Mehbooba used in movie Ram Gopal Verma ki aag were liked by many people and not lot of changes had been done in those song's lyrics, video compositions and storylines. She quoted "songs which the audience would like visit and revisit again and again."

Behl, A. Chaudhary, M (2011) in the research paper titled "A Corpus Linguistic Study of Bollywood Song Lyrics in the Framework of Complex Network Theory" stated that bollywood is an industry were song lyrics are mainly in Hindi language but is not restricted to that only but covers languages like Urdu, Devnagarietc also. Rjasthani, Maithili and Punjabi songs have always been a part and parcel of Bollywood lyrics. They quoted "Bollywood songs are generally composed in Hindi, though often the vocabulary and language usage deviate from that of standard Hindi. Extensive use of Urdu and Persian words, compositions in various dialects of Hindi been a part and parcel of Bollywood lyrics."

Gehlawat, A in the book titled "Music in Contemporary Indian Film: Memory, Voice, Identity." chapter 3. Stated that remix has became a main item in contemporary bollywood. Sometimes the lyrics are taken witha full flashed new tunes, sometimes same tune is taken with some changes in the lyrics and sometime the video composition is totally different. But the trend of using old songs to remake or remix them and use in a film is constant. In this chapter the author mainly focused on the song 'Hungama ho gaya' which is been remarked in the movie 'Queen' (2014).

He quoted "item songs are essentially detachable elements of the film that has no necessary bearing onthe larger film narrative and often feature equally detachable item girl whose appearance in the film may very well be limited to such numbers."

Results and Discussions

Song 1: Chalte Chalte (Pakeezah 1972 – Mitron 2018)

Old Version

Movie: Pakeezah (1972)

Star Cast: Meena Kumari, Kamal Kapoor

Music: Ghulam Mohammed

Lyrics: Kaifi Azmi

Singer: Lata Mangeshkar

Music: Sa Re Ga Ma

Remake Version

Movie: Mitron (2018)

Star Cast: Jackky Bhagnani, Kritika Kamra

Music: Tanishk Bagchi

Lyrics:Tanishk Bagchi

Singer: Atif Aslam

Music: Sa Re Ga Ma

Difference on the Basis of Video

- The old version of the song visualized Meena Kumari as a Kathak dancer who is performing in front of Kamal Kapoor who has came to watch her dance. He had acted as the admirer of her beauty and her dance who is watching her patiently without even distracting for a second.

- In the remake version the concept of the storyline is totally different from the old one. In new video a love angle is been shown between the main actor and actress where the Jaccky is admiring Kritika and fallin in love with her.
- In the old one proper form of Kathak dance in shown by Meena Kumari and the costumes is designed in a very traditional manner but the costumes are very casual in the remake version as daily life has been shown in the video. Scenes like roadtrips and beaches are shown in a very casual manner.

Song 2: Dilbar Dilbar (Sirf Tum 1999 – Satyamev Jayate 2018)

Difference of Lyrics

Old Version

Movie: Sirf Tum (1999)

Star Cast: Sanjay Kapoor, Sushmita Sen

Music: Nadeem-Shravan

Lyrics: Sameer

Singer: AlkaYagnik

Music Label: T-Series

Remake Version

Movie: Satyamev Jayate (2018)

Star Cast: John Abrahim, Nora Fatehi

Music: Tanishk Bagchi

Lyrics: Shabbir Ahmed, Ikka

Singer: Neha Kakkar, Dhvani Bhanushali, Ikka

Music Label: T-Series

Difference on the Basis of Video

- In the old version of the song we can see that Sushmita Sen is sitting near a pool side and the whole video is imaginary in her context then. In the remake version, the song starts with some bold dance moves of Nora.
- In the video whole video she tries to please and attract the hero towards her. The concept of the remake version is quite similar as in this also the actress is trying to attract the attention of people and mainly the hero towards her by great dance moves.
- Mainly outdoor places are being used in the old version whereas a close and dark place is used in the remake similar to any dance club/bar.
- Both the videos are mainly focusing on the actresses and their dance moves rather then the actors who are there to compliment the actress.
- Water themed backgrounds are shown in the old version whereas Arabic culture and dance is shown in the remake one.

From the survey itself, the study reveals the acceptance of remix songs we high. With changing trends, choices are also getting variations and listeners are accepting changes with open minds. Analysis also shows that audience thinks that remake version of Bollywood songsare degrading the quality of old songs as well. Hence from the study, we can see listeners have different opinions for different songs. Respondents also feel that remix songs have also negative impact on the minds of people because it vanishes the beauty of original versions.

REFERENCES

Basu, P. (2011). Traversing Tradition: Celebrating Dance in India. Connaught Place: Routledge

Behl, A. Chaudhary, M. A Corpus Linguistic Study of Bollywood Song Lyrics in the Framework of Complex Network Theory. Macmillan Publishers.

(ICON-2011) retrivedfrom https://researchweb.iiit.ac.in/~aseem.behl/aseem_monojit_ICON2011.pdf

Chaltechalte new version http://www.lyricsmint.com/2018/08/chalte-chalte-mitron.html

Chaltechalte old version Dilbar old version https://www.lyricsbogie.com/movies/chalte-chalte-1976/chalte-chalte-4.html

Dilbar old version http://www.bollymeaning.com/2018/07/dilbar-dilbar-old-original-version-lyrics.html

Dilbar new version http://www.lyricsbell.com/dilbar-lyrics-satyamev-jayate/

Gehlawat, A. (2016). Music in Contemporary Indian Film: Memory, Voice, Identity. Routledge

Jones, JB.(2009). Ethnomusicology. Evergreens to remix, 53(3), retrived from https://www.jstor.org/stable/25653086?seq=1#page_scan_tab_ contents

Jacob, L.(2002). Film Comment. Freedom songs, 38(3), retrived from https://search.proquest.com/openview/ab2cf0be8b0a9f9af77d7 b027967f7de/1?pq-origsite=gscholar&cbl=24820

https://www.ncbi.nlm.nih.gov/pmc/articles/PMC4601897/October 28, 2018

https://research-methodology.net/research-methods/survey-method/October 28, 2018

8

The Utilisation of Indian Folk Dance Forms in Bollywood – Hybridisation or Exploitation?

Dr. Vikrant Kishore

The song and dance sequences in Bollywood cinema have been predominantly used to provide spectacle and entertainment. As a result of this, the spectacle and entertainment oriented song and dance sequences in Bollywood films have developed as a hybrid form, borrowing heavily from Indian folk and classic traditions and various other song and dance cultures from all over the world, significantly Western (specifically American) popular song and dance culture. For example, the song and dance sequence, *Jaan-e-Wafa/Sweetheart*, from the 1962 film *Dil Tera Diwana/The Heart's Crazy Over You* (Hussain, 1962) was divided into three different segments that utilised flamenco dance, folk dance from Uzbekistan, and a mix of Indian classical dance forms such as Bharatanatyam and Kathak. Whereas, the song and dance *Bade Hai Dil Ke Kaale/The One with the Black Heart* from *Dil Deke Dekho/Try Falling in Love* (Panthulu, 1959) utilised folk and tribal dances from the Indian state of West Bengal and Nagaland, as well as Western dance forms like rock 'n' roll and swing.

As one of the most important aesthetic elements shaping Bollywood song and dance, folk dance traditions have been subjected to varying degrees of hybridisation and appropriated to different ends over the years. On the hybrid legacy of Hindi film song and dance, Roy (2010, p. 36) comments:

> While Bollywood music is usually regarded as an independent category of Indian music that has formed the emotional imaginary of the nation, it does not belong to any particular region. 'National popular music' is produced through Bollywood music directors' cannibalization of national classical and popular region folk music and dance over the years. 'Bambaiya' folk traditions, deterritorialised and decontextualised, have always been made to perform rustic exotica for the imagined urban viewer of Hindi cinema.

The relationship of folk forms to Bollywood song and dance is a much-neglected area of study that has not been pursued in detail by Bollywood experts or ethnomusicologists studying indigenous Indian dance traditions. Throughout this article, I will draw insights from some of the existing scholarly work alongside first-hand interviews I have conducted with a few Bollywood film directors and choreographers.

Firstly, in order to understand the role of song and dance in Bollywood cinema, I will touch upon such fundamental issues relating to Bollywood song and dance cultures as: the typical format of the Bollywood film (with its multiple song and dance sequences), how Bollywood films compare with the genre of the Hollywood musical; the relationship of song and dance to the narrative of Bollywood films, and the choreographic and musical elements which characterise Bollywood song and dance. Secondly, I will briefly trace the history of song and dance in Bollywood films in order to show that filmmakers from the 1970s onwards resorted to prolific hybridisation of indigenous Indian and global dance elements. Having established this historical context, I will argue that as a result of these experiments in hybridisation, and through the spectacularisation of song and dance sequences, folk dance forms used in Bollywood song and dance also became increasingly detached from their traditional contexts and norms of performance. Thus, I will highlight the need to investigate the subject of representation of folk dance forms in Hindi films from the 1970s onwards in order to trace those changes and understand how folk dance forms are appropriated and recreated within the creation of hybrid Bollywood song and dance sequences.

Defining Bollywood Song and Dance Sequences

The choreographic design of song-dance sequences in Bollywood films draw from various sources, like the folk, traditional, and classical dances of India, American popular dance forms, and various other world dance forms (for example the African folk dances, Russian ballet, or the Arabic dance *Raqs Sharqi*); the highlight of the construction of these song and dance sequences are the interplay of local culture with that of global. Gokulsing and Dissanayake (2004, p. 19) argue that classical Sanskrit theatre "highly spectacular dance-dramas", significantly influenced Indian classical and folk theatre, and subsequently Indian films. Barma (2004, p. 259), while looking at the historical context of the use of folk songs in folk drama, finds that rural festivals were instrumental in giving rise to the integration of song, dance and music into the storytelling mode:

> To present various dialogues through song, dance and theatre, it was naturally necessary to compose folk music and suitable dance movements to complement the music. It was to meet this necessity that the tradition of folk songs began. The introduction of dance movements and simplistic acting followed it.

The traditional folk theatres of India like *Ram Lila, Tamasha* and *Jatra* have a long history of utilising song, music and dance in various ways; sometimes as an interruption to the story to highlight a specific act. For example, in *Ram Lila*, song and dance sequences in praise of the virtuous Lord Rama are employed between the narrative sequences. Song and dance are also utilised in folk theatre to move the narrative forward. For example, in the *Jatra* performance of *Mahisasur-Mardini/The Slaying of Mahisasur*, song and dance is used to depict the story of the demon king Mahisasur's misdeeds and the power and strength of the goddess Durga.

Gokulsing and Dissanayake (2004, p. 19) agree that folk forms have immensely influenced Hindi cinema, they observe, "in the use of song and dance, humour, the structure of narrative, the informing melodramatic imagination, these folk plays had far reaching impact on the sensibility of Indian popular filmmakers." In addition, various scholars like Mishra (2002), Dwyer (2002) and Gopal and Moorti (eds. 2008) point out that Parsi theatre played an important role in influencing Indian cinema, particularly for the manner in which it employed song and dance sequences. As Gokulsing and Dissanayake (2004, p. 19) argue, "the Parsi theatre, with its lilting songs, bawdy humour, *bon mots,* sensationalism and dazzling stagecraft was designed to appeal to the broad mass of people." While, Harvie (2005, p. 161) finds that the Parsi theatre was also very much influenced by British theatre and therefore, more open to the use of Western elements; no wonder the elements of the east and west fusion in Parsi theatre facilitated Hindi films to easily borrow this fusion style much to its advantage.

With the coming of cinema to India, most of the people engaged in the production of Parsi theatre moved on to film production (such as J.F. Madan of the New Theatre, Ardheshir M. Irani, owner of the Imperial Company and producer of the first Indian talkie*Alam Ara/ The Ornament of the World*(Irani, 1931), B. Wadia and Homi Wadia of Wadia Movietone, and the renowned actor Sohrab Modi. These filmmakers brought many Parsi and Western theatrical elements into Hindi films; for example, the first Indian sound film – *Alam Ara/The Ornament of the World* was inspired by Rodgers and Hammerstein's 1929 Hollywood musical film *Show Boat* directed by Jerome Kern (Gulzar, Nihalani and Chatterjee 2003, p. 44). *Alam Ara* had seven song and dance sequences and pioneered the use of music, song and dance in Indian Cinema.

Though Hindi films utilized song and dance sequences in a different fashion to Hollywood musical, they were nevertheless, significantly influenced by Hollywood musical. Many Indian filmmakers employed song and dance sequences that were inspired by Hollywood musical, and at times imitated and indigenised/ Indianised these Hollywood sources (eds. Gopal and Moorti 2008). Bollywood filmmakers – Onir and Saurabh Narang (pers. comm., July 12, 2008) point out that many of the Hindi films since 1940s have been inspired by Hollywood musical, such as *My Fair Lady* (Cukor, 1964) was the inspiration behind the 1980 Hindi film *Man Pasand/Favourite* directed by Basu Chatterji. Whereas, *The Sound of Music* (Wise, 1965) inspired Hindi filmmaker Gulzar to make *Parichay/Introduction* (1972) in an Indianised manner. Certainly, Hollywood musical played an important part in providing Hindi filmmakers with a significant way of approaching the construction of song and dance sequences. But was this utilization of song and dance sequences in Hindi films, making Hindi films fall into the musical category?

Bollywood Film and the Musical

Almost 85 per cent of the films released in India between 1926 and 1927 were foreign films, most of which were produced in Hollywood. The dominance of American cinema during this time was more due to their technological superiority and the introduction of sound in films in 1927. India had to wait till 1931 for its first sound film – *Alam Ara*. With the introduction of talkies in India, Producers began to rise to the need and demand for Hindi language films with themes relevant to Indian life (Barnouw and Krishnaswamy, 1980). Growing opportunities in the Hindi film industry also attracted many Indian filmmakers working in the United States and the United Kingdom, who moved to Bombay, the hub of Hindi film industry (Raheja and Kothari, 2004).

The early Hollywood musicals, such as *The Jazz Singer* (1927), *Lights of New York* (1928), *The Broadway Melody* (1929) and *The Desert Song* (1929) ignited the imagination of Indian filmmakers during these formative years of the Indian talkies (Thoraval, 2000). Apart from *Alam Ara*, other pioneering films like *Maya Macchindra* (1932), *Sairandhri* (1933), *Dharmatma/ Conscientious* (1935), *Amar Jyoti/Eternal Light* (1936) and *Duniya*

Na Mane/The Unexpected (1937) also incorporated elements from Hollywood musicals (Barnouw and Krishnaswamy 1980, p. 54; Rajadhyaksha and Willeman 1994, p. 22).

From these earlier years of the Hindi talkies, song and dance sequences have been essential elements of Hindi films. One of the prime reasons for the usage of song and dance sequences in Hindi films, no matter the genre the film belonged to, was the packaging of most of Hindi films as a complete entertainment form, which providing drama, action, romance, suspense and song and dance. As Dudrah (2006, p. 25) states, "early scholarly studies in India [...] considered it [Hindi Cinema] to be an escapist fantasy for a mass audience." Though Dudrah moves on to suggest that Bollywood films, especially after the 1950s, have moved from simply being escapist fantasies to address many social issues and concerns. Nevertheless, the 1930s and 1940s escapist cinema was instrumental in not only popularising song and dance sequences, but also cementing their role as an indispensable aspect of Hindi films. These songs also flourished as independent commercial products that brought additional revenue. Therefore, many film producers utilised song and dance sequences (especially songs) as a guarantee of attaining additional revenue (Ganti 2004, p. 177; Morcom 2007, p. 208).

Given the origins of Hindi talkies, there has been much debate about whether mainstream Hindi films, with their multiple song and dance sequences, should all be categorised as musicals; and if not, in what ways they differ from Hollywood musicals. In order to examine this issue, it is important to understand how song and dance sequences operate in Hindi films.

In contrast to Hollywood films, where musicals constitute a distinct genre among many others, there is a trans-generic use of song and dance across the spectrum of mainstream Hindi films, whatever their narrative orientation. Unlike Hollywood musicals where actors either use their own voices, or songs are just played in the background, actors in Hindi films lip-synch to songs that have been pre-recorded with the voice of playback singers (this occurs much less in Hollywood films). As Morcom (2007, p. 2) notes, "songs must be 'sung' diegetically by the characters in Hindi films rather than played in the background score, which is the norm for Hollywood films since the 1960s."

According to Gokulsing and Dissanayake (2004, pp. 20-28), the fundamental distinction between Hindi films with their typical song and dance routines and the genre of Hollywood musicals, is that song and dance in Hindi films is not introduced as a separate element in the overall narrative of the film, but is a continuation of the enactment of the story by the actors: "The plot was not used to heal the split between narrative and spectacle. Instead, song and dance sequences were and are used as natural expressions of emotions and situations emerging from everyday life" (Gokulsing and Dissanayake 2004, p. 23). The introduction of a song and dance sequence at any point in the narrative is not seen as an event separate from the story, but very much a part of the storytelling process.

This insight raises the question about why such importance is accorded to song and dance in the storytelling process of Hindi films. Langford (2005, p. 100) has claimed that this may perhaps be explained by the fundamental differences in conceptions of realism and dramatic convention between Hollywood and Hindi films:

The conventions of musical integration in Hindi cinema are fundamentally different, operating not at the sub-generic level (i.e. the distinction between the [Busby] Berkeley and [Arthur] Freed musical) but in a trans-generic manner: musical performance is an accepted dramatic convention in a Discourse which operates according to different regimes of verisimilitude and concepts of realism than the Hollywood or European model.

This is perhaps the fundamental distinction between Hindi films and Hollywood musicals, and helps explain the obvious differences between the two, like the ubiquity of song and dance sequences across all genres of mainstream Hindi films with characters enacting pre-recorded musical routines. In Bollywood films, song and dance is used as a legitimate and indispensable dramatic convention in storytelling, as important as speaking or acting.

While most Hindi films use song and dance as an indispensable dramatic convention in the storytelling process, there have also been many Hindi films, like YRF's *Dil To Pagal Hai* (Chopra, 1997), *Jhoom Barabar Jhoom* (Sehgal, 2007) and *Aaja Nachle* (Mehta, 2007), that adopt what could be called a Hollywood-style musical form, with song and dance placed within the narrative as a separate staged performance. In addition, Western popular music, and dance culture, especially Rap, Hip-Hop, Pop, Rock and Jazz inspired a many Bollywood films to borrow, indigenise, and at times blatantly copy song and dance sequence from Hollywood films. A few of the contemporary Hollywood dance films that have inspired various Bollywood film spinoffs, and song and dance sequence inspiration, indigenisation, and copying are: *Saturday Night Fever* (1977), *Grease* (1978), *Beat Street* (1984), *Dirty Dancing* (1987), *Chicago* (2002) and *Take the Lead* (2006).

While the conceptualisation of song and dance as a legitimate and dominant dramatic convention in the storytelling process can help explain the ubiquitous use of song and dance in Bollywood cinema, Dudrah (2006, p. 48) puts forth another perspective which provides a different but complementary perspective on the issue:

> Indian popular films are not seen as musicals, they are not genre films at all in the Western sense of the word. Hindi cinema cannot be forced into Western filmmaking categories. In one Bollywood film it is possible to include all the Western film genres – musical, romantic, comedy, action, thriller, tragedy, and melodrama. These disparate modes of storytelling are bound together into a coherent whole by songs.

Though, to some extent, Dudrah's assertion is right that Hindi/ Bollywood films cannot be categorised as musicals, because even while using song and dance, Hindi/Bollywood films work within various other generic conventions. For example, *Company* (2002) a crime/gangster film, has four song and dance sequences; *Bhoot*

(2003) a horror film, has six song and dance sequences; *Kal Ho Na Ho* (2002) a romantic drama, featured five song and dance sequences. But I do not ascribe to Dudrah's view that songs are always the binding factor of a film's narrative. There are many Bollywood films that utilise song and dance sequences as an interruption and an escape from the narrative of the film. Post 1990s the utilisation of song and dance sequences in films are also being dictated by the commercial angle of popular FM radios and Music TV channels; especially filmmakers have realised that Hindi song and dance sequences have become quite popular on the music television channel playlists, thus providing opportunities to promote films before its release and also add to the film revenue through royalty fees. Therefore, specific song and dance sequences are designed to promote films on these TV channels; most of the times these particular song and dance sequences have no direct connection to the narrative of the film as such and operates simply for promotion purpose and generally feature during the opening titles or the credit rolls.

Onir (personal interview, 2008), an established Bollywood film director, on the question about the Bollywood films being film musicals or not, states, "I would not really call it as musical films. I would call Bollywood films, as films, which uses music and dance. Generally, films where music plays an integral part are musical, but I will not say Bollywood equals musical as there are many other elements that structures the films narrative and not just the song and dance alone (*sic*)."

Rick Altman's erudite work on Hollywood musical can further help elaborate Bollywood cinema's use of song and dance. Altman (1989, p.19) observes, "The American film musical has a dual focus, built around parallel stars of opposite sex and radically divergent values. This dual focus structure requires the viewers to be sensitive not so much to chronology and progression – for the outcome of the male/female match is entirely conventional and thus quite predictable – but to simultaneity and comparison." This 'dual focus narrative' is quite common in Bollywood films, especially in the first half of the films, where the romance between the lead pair is set up. Yash Raj Films' over the years have made romantic films with a preponderance of song-dance sequences; few of these movies like *Dil To Pagal Hai/Heart is Crazy* (Chopra, 1997), and *Aaja Nachle/Lets Dance* (Chopra, 2007) were out rightly termed as musical films. The construct of these YRF romantic films with eight to ten song-dance sequences is quite akin to the American musicals. They follow the 'Dual Focus Narrative' style, where individual attention is given to the male and female actors, and the ground is made to show the difference between their social or economic background, and circumstances are built for their clash, and eventual falling in love.

Altman further elaborates that there are three key sub-genres in the Hollywood musical – the Fairy Tale Musical, the Show Musical and the Folk Musical – each of which use song and dance in a fashion that aligns the film with a specific genre of storytelling. Altman (1987, p. 131) contends:

> Fairy Tale musical on film is a part of a tradition, which begins long before cinema. Whereas the show musical takes advantage of the invention of a new medium – sound cinema – to create new structures and new meanings, while film and theatre together give birth to the folk musical, the film Fairy Tale simply takes up where the stage operetta (all but) left off.

The Fairy Tale musical takes place in a fantastical world of unearthly characters and dreams, and draws from the older tradition of the stage opera; show musicals are modern showbiz-based musicals in which song and dance performances are presented as staged spectacles; finally, Folk musicals are nostalgic stories that draw from myths and legends.

Fairy Tale subgenre incessantly draws its attraction primarily on the need of the audience for quasi-sexual satisfaction, and therefore focuses more on the issues of sexual desire. Altman (1989, pp.141-99) provides three approaches to sexuality that the Fairy Tale musicals employ, namely - 1.Sex as sex (plot is driven by over sexual desire), 2. Sex as battle (sexual energy is projected onto bickering, fighting, or competition between potential partners), 3. Sex as adventure (one partner's apparent fear of sexuality is compensated for by the other's lawless, uncontrolled drives). These approaches towards the sexual desire runs quite strongly in Bollywood films. If *Dil to Pagal Hai/Heart is Crazy* (Chopra, 1997) employs the approach of sex as sex, and sex as battle, then *Jhoom Barabar Jhoom/Sway* (Sahgal, 2007) employs all three approaches.

Though Show musicals do not figure that prominently in Bollywood films, it was to an extent quite popular during the 1940-60s, an era when the Hindi films were quite inspired by the Hollywood musical. While, Folk Musical format seems to be the inspiration of many a Bollywood films, especially the one's that concentrates on the narrative of the Indian diaspora. Altman (1989, p.272-73) emphasizes:

> It is in the folk musical that the genre film's general tendency to glorify the past reaches its highest point. Yet memory can also produce the past faithfully, recall hardship, filth and defeat, or bring back experiences best forgotten. Suspended between observation and dream vision, memory is the perfect – if unstable – mediatory factor for a subgenre simultaneously grounded in the American heritage and the American myth.

The Indian diasporas relation with their homeland – India is frequently utilized in the Bollywood song and dance sequences. Films like *Dilwale Dulhania Le Jayenge/The Brave Heart Will Take the Bride (DDLJ)*, (Chopra, 1995), *Pardes/Foreign Land* (Ghai, 1997), *Kabhi Khushi Kabhi Gham/Sometimes Happiness, Sometimes Sadness* (Johar, 2001), *Kal Ho Na Ho/There May Or May Not Be A Tomorrow* (Advani, 2003) employ the folk musical technique to appeal to what Jameson (2007) propounds as "nostalgia for the present." This nostalgia factor is used both in terms of symbolism, as well, as a plot to return to the homeland, to their roots. *Aa Ab Laut Chalen/Come, Lets go Back* (Kapoor, 1999), works on this similar plot, and actually borrows its title from a yesteryear-popular Hindi film song, as well. The song is a call to the Indian diasporic community to come back home, and be with their loved ones; similarly, the song-dance sequence *Ghar Aaja Pardesi/Come Home, O' Foreigner* from *DDLJ,* weaves the fantasy, and the nostalgia factors to call their loved ones back to their homeland; the imagery that is created here is of the homeland (India) that is self-sufficient, where people are loving, and are waiting with open arms for their loved ones, the festivities, and communal gatherings are all about joy, love, and brotherhood.

Altman's classificatory system for different sub-genres of Hollywood musicals may not apply directly to Hindi films with their multi-generic mixture. However, the basic idea of the link of a specific musical sub-genre with a specific cultural ethos may be extended to explain how a generic form of song and dance may be used to build upon the narrative and mood at a particular moment in the film. In my opinion, the Fairy Tale subgenre with its incessant focus on desire and fantasy can be seen in the fantasy-based romance duets common in Bollywood song and dance sequences. The ethos of the Show musical subgenre can be seen in staged spectacular performances like dance club numbers. Finally, the Folk musical subgenre that plays on nostalgic sentiments can be seen in most of the folk-derived Bollywood routines.

With its multi-generic narrative form, mainstream Hindi films cannot be easily categorised into distinct genres like Hollywood films or the musical sub-genre that Altman propounds. So, a film may begin with the folkloric fantasy of the hero's idyllic childhood, then switch into a romantic mode when the hero woos the heroine, and finally end up as an action thriller as the hero encounters the villain. Instead of the common uniformity or verisimilitude of the overall narrative tone, and the rationalised presence of song and dance within a story (as in many Hollywood films), song and dance sequences often emerge abruptly to take the film into a different generic mode altogether. As Langford (2005, p. 100) finds:

> One obvious and major difference is that the great majority of Hindi films feature musical (vocal and dance) performances, and to a viewer accustomed to the integrated musical, in particular, the transitions from serious dramatic content to

> upbeat and diegetically heterogeneous musical number is bound to seem jarring.

In such a schema, the song and dance sequences act as a link that helps these different narrative modes to somehow cohere as one film. Dudrah finds that Bollywood while trying to imitate/copy/mimic Hollywood, creates its own distinct style and caters to a specific audience that is oblivious of the constructs of Hollywood.

Though I agree with Dudrah, as well as other notable scholars that Bollywood films are not musicals, but I feel that even in the guise of using five or six odd song-dance sequence either as a break in films' narrative, or as a part of narrative, or simply as a spectacular item number, Bollywood is to quite an extent impacted by the techniques of the Hollywood musicals, its structure, narrative, as well as the stylistic conventions. Even if they indigenise the Hollywood conventions, and use it according to their own interpretation, nevertheless, the influence of Hollywood can't be negated on Bollywood films.

Bollywood Song and Dance: Continuation of a Larger Indigenous Tradition

The enthusiastic co-option of music and dance in Hindi films, which has continued unabated to the present day, can also be attributed to the longstanding traditions of Sanskrit drama, folk music-dance forms and the folk theatre in India. Gopal and Moorti (eds. 2008, p. 17-8) note:

> Song and dance have been tied to Indian cinema from its very start. Although a history of the media world in which Indian film arose is still an ongoing project, there is some consensus that the centrality of music, song, and dance in pre-existing popular and folk traditions in India must partly account for the persistence of song and dance in Hindi film.

Indeed, apart from the multi-generic form of Bollywood films necessitating the ubiquitous use of song and dance, we must also look towards the historical legacy of performance traditions in India to explain why such an environment, so conducive to song and dance in films, existed in the first place. In this section, I will discuss how indigenous influences shaped the form of Hindi films and resulted in its receptivity to this musical form of filmmaking.

The impact of Sanskrit dramas on Hindu performing arts is omnipresent; therefore, Indian cinema, which took its inspiration from these performance traditions, also reflected the influence of the great Sanskritic dramas (Ganti 2004, Pauwels 2007, Trivedi 2008). Sanskrit theatre is supposed to have been at the zenith of its aesthetic form between the 2nd and 7th centuries B.C., when Sage Bharata Muni's treatise *Natya Shastra* (literally "Scripture of Dance", though it is sometimes translated as "Science of Theatre") provided the foundation for the Hindu performing arts (Srinivasan, 2007). According to Ram Gopal (in Ambrose, 1983, p. 33):

> *Natya Shastra* is a monumental work, which deals, amongst other things, with the art of drama and the dance. Bharata describes 15 types of drama ranging from one to ten acts. In addition, Bharata lays down principles for stage design, makeup, costume, dance (various movements and gestures), theory of aesthetics of emotions (*rasas* and *bhavas*), acting, directing and music.

Bharata set out a detailed theory of drama comparable to Aristotle's *Poetics*. He conceptualised an elementary theory of theatre and drama built on *rasas* (aesthetics). He defined eight principal *rasas* – love, pity, anger, disgust, heroism, awe, terror and comedy, and argued that drama should mix different *rasas* but must choose one as the dominant narrative tone. All the *rasas* of elementary dramatic emotions conceptualised by Bharata can be seen in varying proportions in Bollywood films.[1] Apart from the influence of the Sanskritic drama tradition, which melded song, dance and acting, noted Indian film critic Gupta (2008) and Haase (ed. 2008, p. 348) also assert that the importance of song and dance in Hindi cinema comes from the Hindu mythologies of *Ramayana*[2] and *Mahabharata*[3] that were written in verse form and performed through devotional singing. These longstanding ritualistic traditions of performance have also resulted in the extensive use of song and dance as part of the process of storytelling in Bollywood films.

According to Roy (2010, p. 36), folk theatre has also played an important role in shaping Bollywood cinema:

> Following indigenous performance traditions such as *Ramlila*, *Nautanki*, *Tamasha*, and Parsi theatre that combined several aesthetic modes, the Bollywood song and dance routine is seen as performing a wide range of functions including heightening a situation, accentuating a mood, commenting on theme and action, providing relief and serving as interior monologue.

Indigenous performance traditions in the Indian cultural landscape – from the classical mythological repertoire to folk traditions – have also shaped Bollywood cinema's use of song and dance as part of the storytelling function. Thus, Bollywood song and dance can be seen as a continuation of this larger tradition.

The Role of Folk Dance in Bollywood Cinema – A History of Hybridisation

In this section, I will attempt to trace a brief history of the trend towards hybridisation and experimentation in song and dance sequences, a development that gathered momentum from the 1970s onwards. I will argue that this trend had the most significant impact on the representation of folk dance forms as they were subjected to an extreme fusion that separated them from their traditional norms of performance.

If song and dance sequences in the 1930s and 1940s were predominantly influenced by Indian folk and classical dance forms, then the films of the 1950s and 1960s witnessed the increasing popularity in India of Western dance forms like the Twist, Rock 'n' Roll and American and French cabaret. Yet, in the films of those earlier decades, distinctions between different dances, especially between Western and Indian dance forms were maintained with diligence. A film would only have the twist performed in a nightclub sequence, while a folk-derived dance would be used for a rural celebration. Hindi films of the late 1960s were also considerably influenced by the Elvis Presley musicals; Shammi Kapoor, one of the biggest stars of Hindi films during this period, achieved phenomenal success when his persona was remodeled along the lines of Elvis Presley. His Elvis style dance movements and mannerisms made him popularly known as the "Indian Elvis" (Dwyer 2000a, p. 182).

From the 1970s onwards, films were being reconceptualised into big-budget spectacles with lavish sets. Song and dance sequences, in particular, were being created as centrepieces for such spectacles. Filmmakers like Manmohan Desai (*Saccha Jhootha/Honest and Liar* 1970, *Amar Akbar Anthony 1977*), Raj Kapoor (*Bobby* 1973, *Ram Teri Ganga Maili/Ram, your Ganges is Polluted* 1985), Manoj Kumar (*Purab aur Paschim/East and West* 1970, *Roti Kapda aur Makaan/Food, Clothing and Shelter* 1974), Prakash Mehra (*Zanjeer/Bracelet* 1973, *Laawaris/Orphan* 1981) Ramesh Sippy (*Sholay/Embers* 1975, *Shaan/Pride* 1980), Nasir Hussain (*Yaadon Ki Baraat/Procession of Memories* 1973, *Hum Kisi Se Kum Nahin/We are not Less than Anyone* 1977) and Subhash Ghai (*Karz/In-debt* 1980, *Hero* 1981) were making films on a lavish scale that featured multiple stars, opulent sets and song and dance sequences shot in exotic locations.With this broader move to create song and dance spectacles, filmmakers also embarked on a process of unprecedented experimentation to create novel dance routines. The distinctions between various dance forms – Western and Indian, or different regional dance styles, such as Punjabi and Gujarati – that were maintained in the films of earlier decades, were being blurred.

This era of experimentation saw the emergence of Hindi film song and dance as a distinct genre of *Hindi filmi naatch* (literally Hindi film dance). *Hindi filmi naatch* is designed as a lavish spectacle with elements of glamour, exoticism and sensuality. It uses hybridised dance routines based on a fusion of Indian folk and classical dances, with influences taken from countries and regions across the globe including America, Russia, the Middle-East and Latin America. Another key contribution of *Hindi filmi naatch* was the promotion of a particular dance step as the "signature style"[4] of a sequence, aiding the retentive potential of the sequence amongst audiences. The signature steps could be easily recognised, imitated and appropriated by audiences. In my view, it is the 1970s, with its experimentation with the unprecedented fusion of dance forms, that has had the most significant impact on folk dance forms in contemporary Hindi film song and dance. As I noted earlier, films in earlier decades would maintain the demarcation between different dance forms. From the late 1970s onwards, one witnessed the fusion of Indian folk and classical dance with Western and other foreign dance forms.

This era of hybridisation was taken further in the 1980s, as the genre of Disco made its large-scale entry into Hindi films. During the 1980s, films built explicitly around dance were becoming popular. There were two main varieties of these dance-based films. The first of these were Hindi films produced by the South Indian filmmakers K. Bapaiyah, K. Ragavendra Rao and T. Ramarao, which utilised a mix of Indian classical and folk dance forms, featuring colossal sets or exotic locations and large contingents of chorus line dancers. These films were mostly remakes of South Indian family dramas and invariably had Jeetendra, the dancing star of the time, as their lead actor (in films like *Himmatwala/The Courageous* 1983, *Tohfa/The Gift* 1984, *Dosti Dushmani/Friendship and Enmity* 1986).

The second variety of these dance films were the Disco-based films of B. Subhash and Shibu Mitra, starring Mithun Chakraborty (*Disco Dancer* 1982, *Kasam Paida Karne Wale Ki/I Swear on my Mother* 1984, *Dance Dance* 1987) and Govinda (*Ilzaam/Blame* 1986, *Khudgarz/Selfish* 1987, *Hatya/Murder* 1987). It was this second variety of films that left an indelible mark on the Hindi film song and dance, infiltrating the whole genre. Mithun Chakraborty became a dancing sensation with his film *Disco Dancer* that was inspired by the Hollywood film *Saturday Night Fever* (1977), and the Hindi fusion Disco routines it contained gained phenomenal success in India as well as the Soviet Union and the Middle East (Rajagopalan 2008, p. 93). Disco was also a part of the sub-culture of urban Indian youth in the 1980s; and Bollywood films were attempting to draw on its popularity to attract those audiences. The inroads made by Disco took Hindi film music into the age of upbeat, glamorous and spectacular club numbers. As Richard Dyer (1979, online) contends:

> Disco is more than just a form of music, although certainly the music is at the heart of it. Disco is also kinds of dancing, club, fashion, film etc., in a word, a certain sensibility manifest in music clubs, etc., historically and culturally specific, economically, technologically, ideologically and aesthetically determined - and worth thinking about.

An important example of this shift towards Disco was the film *Qurbani/Sacrifice* (1980) – a glamorous film about a love triangle between three urban characters – that had a completely*Disco*-based musical score composed by the British-Indian composer Biddu[5]. It is still considered a landmark of Bollywood cinema's update of westernised music.

The influence of Disco resulted in a significant shift in Hindi film song and dance, as these sequences became increasingly eroticised, glamourised spectacles. According to Dyer (1979, online), "Disco is not just a dance genre but a cultural form that imbibes a sense of uninhibited sexuality, eroticisation and physical proximity in commercialised settings." Hindi film song and dance, derived from Indian folk or classical dance genres, was generally devoid of physical contact. It was Western dance forms that brought the element of physical contact into Hindi film song and dance.

But while Western forms like ballroom dance and the twist, used in the Hindi films of the 1940s, 1950s and 1960s, enabled some physical proximity between the lead pairs, cabaret dance was utilised in many of the Hindi films of the 1960s to provide eroticised song and dance sequences. But these cabaret song and dance sequences, because of the form's association with eroticism and vulgarity, primarily featured the "Hindi film vamp" and rarely involved the lead actors.

It was Disco song and dance that helped Hindi filmmakers to introduce elements of overt sensuality and eroticisation into their films. For example, the song and dance sequence "Hari Om Hari" from *Pyara Dushman/Sweet Enemy* (1980) depicted a scantily clad "hippy" siren sensuously dancing with beer bottles in a Disco style as the men around her gaze at her gyrating body voyeuristically. Disco-derived Bollywood sequences also employed lyrics laced with overt sexual content. The First Step Do Ajnabi/First Step of Two Strangers from *Hawalaat/Prison* (1987) depicts a dance at a nightclub where the bar dancer (Anita Raj) sings "step by step we fall in love, step by step we make love", and the chorus line dancers enact the love making scene.

This particular erotic and physical aspect of Western dance forms, especially Disco, has created religious and political consternation in India. The website allaboutsikhs.com dedicated to the Sikh religion (the Sikhism followers are mainly based in the north Indian state of Punjab) outlines the reasons for the rejection of dance forms like Disco by the Sikh community:

> Disco is a blend of physical movements related to loud pop music. The lights in the hall or the room are deliberately kept dim to enable the partners to get closer and make love easier. As Disco is likely to arouse sexual feelings, it is not permitted to the Sikhs. Dances purely for the promotion of physical health or fitness are not taboo. Similarly dating or mixing of boys with girls alone for the purpose of illicit love or petting or flirting is forbidden in Sikhism. (www.allaboutsikhs.com 2010)

However, Disco was not only utilised to exploit sexuality, it was also part of the sub-culture of urban Indian youth of the 1980s that broke from the conservatism of traditional cultural dance forms.

India witnessed a major change in the 1990s when the trend towards fusion music came to dominate Hindi film song and dance.

Folk dance forms began to take on a completely new shape with the impact of popular culture brought about by globalised music channels like MTV and Channel [V]. With India's newfound place in the global market place and the proliferation of mass media-based popular culture, the *Hindi film naatch* mutated into the genre of "Bollywood dance". This genre or form of "Bollywood dance" was being recognised and promoted in various film magazines (such as *Stardust, Filmfare* and *Cine Blitz*). It began to move into more and more territories in the field of hybridisation and showed little compunction about maintaining distinctions between the lineages of the different dance forms being mixed.

Describing the "fusion form" of this revitalised genre of global "Bollywood dance", Sresthova (2008, p.12) observes that, "what has been now termed as "Bollywood Dance" is the result of the fusion of these disparate dance forms, showing "the manifested interplay between uprooted, globally accessible film content and geographically rooted live performance." "Bollywood dance" of the 1990s utilised wide-ranging styles from rap, hip-hop, techno and jazz, but these Western dance and music forms have largely been subsumed under the broader banner of Disco in India. This subsumption of various Western electronic music-based song and dance forms under the broad label of Disco is the outcome of a lack of a deeper understanding of Western popular music among Indian audiences and the majority of Indian film and music journalists.

The Bollywood choreographer Shiamak Davar is known for the experimental choreography that introduced Western jazz into the Bollywood film *Dil To Pagal Hai/Heart is Crazy* (1997), and that gave an international look and flavour to "Bollywood dance" ('Shiamak' 2010). This inspired other Bollywood choreographers to draw upon eclectic sources of musical dance from around the globe. As Shresthova (2008, p. 91) states:

> Davar applies two overlapping labels to his Hindi film choreography: Bollywood Jazz and Indo-Jazz. Indo-Jazz is the label he applies to his non-film-based movement. Both styles draw on the studio jazz dance movement and incorporate

> Indian dance elements including gesture, rhythm, and expression as they strive towards a more contemporary kind of dance content that reflects a "globally savvy," in India at home and abroad.

The consolidation of "Bollywood dance" as a genre occurred in the late 1990s and early 2000s, as it unyoked itself from the singular influence of Disco and people began to appreciate the plethora of global dance forms incorporated within it.

Noting the rise of the genre of "Bollywood dance" in recent decades, Shresthova (2008, p. 3) states that, "Bollywood dance is a term used by film professionals, amateur performers, and audiences to describe dances choreographed to Hindi film songs." Many Bollywood choreographers established their own dance schools – Shiamak Davar founded the Shiamak Davar Institute for the Performing Arts (SDIPA) in 1992, and Ashley Lobo founded Danceworx Academy in 1998. "Bollywood dance" was now being taught in these schools as an established genre of dancing equivalent to samba or the foxtrot. Such studios have now found significant patronage outside India as well. In a way "Bollywood dance" can be seen as the culmination of this process of hybridisation that gained momentum from the 1970s onwards. When asked about this meteoric rise of "Bollywood dance", choreographer and dancer Remo D'Souza (pers. comm., 5 July 2009) said:

> Bollywood song and dance, especially after the 1980s was quite inspired by popular dance forms that are seen in American dance films, and by the 1990s, with the coming of the satellite channels, music videos from MTV and Channel [V]. Music videos of pop stars like Beyonce, Jennifer Lopez, Shakira, Michael Jackson, the Backstreet Boys, Christina Aguilera and Britney Spears have influenced the work of choreographers. But let me clarify that American influence is only one of the ingredients in "Bollywood dance". Indian folk dance and classical dance movements also form an integral part in the construction of "Bollywood dance"; and then there

are many other dance forms from around the world, which are utilised by various choreographers according to the needs of the sequence and the film (*sic*).

According to my own observations and discussions with different Bollywood choreographers such as Longinus Fernandes[6] and Remo D'Souza[7], some of the distinguishing characteristics of "Bollywood dance" are:

- One male and one female lead dancer (a heterosexual pairing), backed by a chorus line.
- The dance mixes different styles from across the globe (depending on the choreographer's choice, the film's narrative requirements, as well as input from the others involved in the film's production). The base of "Bollywood dance" is Indian folk and classical dance styles, to which Western dance forms (Disco, hip hop, breakdance, jazz, ballet etc.), and at times dances from Latin America, Africa, the Middle-East, Russia and Far-East Asia are added.
- The lead dancers are given a signature style unique to the song and dance sequence.
- The sets are built and designed on a lavish scale.
- The use of exotic locations (especially those in Western countries like Switzerland, France, the United States and the United Kingdom).
- There can be innumerable costume changes, the use of multiples sets and locations during individual song and dance sequences.

The Appropriation of Folk Dance Forms in the Hybridisation Process

With such dramatic transformations through the decades – from the nascent fusion *Hindi film naatch-gana* of the 1970s to contemporary "Bollywood dance" – much attention has focussed on this new phenomenon called "Bollywood dance" (Shreshthova 2008, eds. Gopal and Moorti 2008). But there has hardly been any sustained analysis of how the folk dance forms used in Bollywood song and dance have borne those changes over the decades. Folk dance forms are also one of the founding influences on Bollywood song and dance. Elements of different folk dance forms can be seen explicitly in most Bollywood routines.

Amitava Roy's (in Lal and Dasgupta 1995b, pp. 9-12) touches upon the problems of utilising folk forms in the context of a theatrical performance meant for an urban middle-class or elite audience. He draws a parallel between these urban theatre performances to Hindi films, commenting on how folk dance forms are utilised at will by Bollywood cinema. These forms are incautiously reinterpreted to conform to the notion of image of "rustic exotica".

While Bollywood music is usually regarded as an independent category of Indian music that informs the emotional imaginary of the nation, it does not belong to any particular region. A "national popular music" is produced through Bollywood music directors' cannibalization of national classical and popular regional folk music and dance. "Bambaiya" folk traditions, deterritorialised and decontextualised, have always been made to perform the role of "rustic exotica" for the imagined urban viewer of Hindi cinema.

There have been a handful of films, mostly belonging to the alternative art-house strain of Indian cinema (such as *Bhavni Bhavai* 1980, *Mrigayaa* 1976), which have depicted folk forms beyond the conventions of spectacular Bollywood song and dance. These films have attempted to incorporate the socio-religious-ritualistic contexts and traditional norms of folk-dance performance with a degree of sensitivity. But in Bollywood films, which form the bulwark of Indian popular culture, such caution in relation to tradition is negligible. I wish to draw further on Roy's cursory comment cited above to examine how Bollywood appropriate these dance forms. In my opinion, Bollywood films tend to alter the choreography, costumes, accessories, staging, musical instrumentation and context of the performance of folk dance forms when appropriating them for their song and dance sequences. The processes of hybridisation unduly affecting these folk dance forms to the extent that they lose their authenticity is real and something very concerning.Thus, the larger question to safeguard the intangible cultural heritage also comes into play and requires further interrogation.

(Note: This article was first published as a part of the book – From Reel to Real: Folk Dances of India in Bollywood Cinema, 2014 published by UNESCO-Apnieve)

BIBLIOGRAPHY

Allaboutsikh.Com, 2010. *What is the Sikh Attitude to Dancing* [online]. All About Sikhs (www.allaboutsikhs.com). <http://www.allaboutsikhs.com/sikhism-faqs/sikhism-faqswhat-is-the-sikh-attitude-to-dancing.html>[Access Date: 21 March 2010].

Altman, R., 1987. *The American Film Musical* Bloomington: Indiana University Press.

Ambrose, K., 1983. *Classical Dances and Costumes of India,* second ed. London: A&C Black (Publishers) Ltd.

Barma, S., 2004. *Bhâwâiyâ: Ethnomusicological Study,* Global Vision Publishing House: New Delhi.

Barnouw, E. & Krishnaswamy, S., 1980. *Indian Film,* Second ed. New York: Oxford University Press.

Dudrah, R.K., 2006. *Bollywood: Sociology Goes to the Movies,* New Delhi: SAGE Publications.

Dwyer, R., 1998. The Hindi Romantic Cinema: Yash Chopra's Kabhi Kabhie and Silsila. *South Asia: Journal of South Asian Studies,* 21, 181 — 212.

Dwyer, R., 2000a. Bombay Ishtyle. *In* P.C.G. Stella Bruzzi (ed.) *Fashion Cultures: Theories, Explorations and Analysis.* Oxon: Routledge, 416.

Dwyer, R., 2000b. The Erotics of the Wet Sari in Hindi Films. *Journal of South Asian Studies,* 23, 143-160.

Dwyer, R., 2000c. *All You Want is Money, All You Need is Love: Sexuality and Romance in Modern India* London: Casell.

Dwyer, R., 2002. *Yash Chopra* London British Film Institute.

Dwyer, R., 2004. Yeh Shaadi Nahin Ho Sakti ("This Wedding Cannot Happen!): Romance and Marriage in Contemporary Hindi Cinema. *In* G.W. Jones & K. Ramdas (eds.) *(Un)tying the Knot: ideal and Reality in Asian Marriage.* Asian Research Institute, National University of Singapore.

Dyer, R. (1979). In Defence of Disco Retrieved from http://history-is-made-at-night.blogspot.com/2008/05/in-defence-of-disco-richard-dyer.html

Ganti, T., 2004. *Bollywood: A Guidebook to Popular Hindi Cinema,* New York, London: Routledge.

Gokulsing & Dissanayake, 2004. *Indian Popular Cinema: A Narrative of Cultural Change,* Second ed. Staffordshire: Trentham Books.

Gokulsing, K.M. & Dissanayake, W., 2008. *Popular Culture in a Globalised India.* Routledge: Taylor & Francis Group.

Gopal, S. & Moorti, S. (eds.) (2008) *Global Bollywood: Travels of Hindi Song and Dance,* Minneapolis, London: University of Minnesota Press.

Gulzar, 2003. A Song Travels... *In* Gulzar, G. Nihalani & S. Chatterjee (eds.) *Encyclopaedia of Hindi Cinema.* New Delhi: Popular Prakashan.

Gulzar, Joshi, L.M. & Malcolm, D. (eds.) (2002) *Bollywood: Popular Indian Cinema,* London: Dakini Books.

Gulzar, Nihalani, G. & Chatterjee, S. (eds.) (2003) *Encyclopaedia of Hindi Cinema,* New Delhi: Popular Prakashan.

Gupta, C.D., 2008. *Seeing is Believing: Selected Writings on Cinema,* New Delhi: Penguin Group.

Haase, D. (ed.) (2008) *The Greenwood Encyclopedia of Folk Tales and Fairy Tales,* Westport: Greenwood Press.

Harvie, J., 2005. *Staging the UK,* Manchester: Manchester University Press.

Lal, A. & Dasgupta, C. (eds.) (1995b) *RASA: The Indian Performing arts in the Last Twenty-five Years,* Vol. II. Kolkata: Anamika Kala Sangam Research and Publications.

Langford, B., 2005. *Film Genre: Hollywood and Beyond,* Edinburgh: Edinburgh University Press.

Morcom, A., 2007. *Hindi Film Songs and the Cinema,* Hampshire: Ashgate Publishing, Ltd.

Morcom, A., 2008. Tapping the Mass Market: The Commercial Life of Hindi Film Songs. *In* S. Gopal & S. Moorti (eds.) *Global Bollywood: Travels of Hindi Song and Dance.* Minneapolis, London: University of Minnesota Press.

Pauwels, H.R.M., 2008. *The Goddess as Role Model: Sîtâ and Râdhâ in Scripture and on Screen*: Oxford University Press.

Raheja, D. & Kothari, D., 2004. *Indian Cinema: The Bollywood Saga,* New Delhi: Roli Books.

Rajadhyaksha, A., 2003. The 'Bollywoodization' of the Indian Cinema: Cultural Nationalism in a Global Arena. *Inter-Asia Cultural Studies.* Oxon, New York: Routledge.

Rajadhyaksha, A., 2008. The 'Bollywoodization' of the Indian cinema: Cultural Nationalism in a Global Arena. *In* A.P. Kavoori & A. Punathambekar (eds.) *Global Bollywood.* New York: New York University Press.

Rajadhyaksha, A. & Willeman, P. (eds.) (1994) *Encyclopaedia of Indian Cinema,* London: British Film Institute and Oxford University Press.

Rajagopalan, S., 2008. *Leave Disco Dancer Alone! Indian Cinema and Soviet Movie-Going after Stalin,* New Delhi: Yoda Press.

Roy, A.G., 2010. Is Everybody Saying 'Shava Shava' to Bollywood Bhangra? *In* R.B. Mehta & R. Pandharipande (eds.) *Bollywood and Globalization: Indian Popular Cinema, Nation, and Diaspora.* London: Anthem Press.

Roy, A.G. & Bhatia, N. (eds.) (2008) *Partitioned Lives: Narratives of Home, Displacement, and Resettlement,* Delhi: Dorling Kindersley (India) Pvt. Ltd.

Roy, R., 2003. Jatra/Yatra. *In* P.J. Claus, S. Diamond & M.A. Mills (eds.) *South Asian Folklore: An Encyclopedia— Afghanistan, Bangladesh, India, Nepal, Pakistan, Sri Lanka.* New York: Routledge.

Thoraval, Y., 2000. *The Cinemas of India (1896-2000),* Delhi: Macmillan India Ltd.

Shresthova, S., 2008. Dancing to an Indian Beat: "Dola" Goes my Diasporic Heart. *In* S. Gopal & S. Moorti (eds.) *Global Bollywood: Travels of Hindi Song and Dance.* Minneapolis, London: University of Minnesota Press.

'Shiamak', 2010. *About Shiamak* [online]. <http://www.shiamak.com> [Access Date: 4 June 2010].

Shresthova, S., 2003. Strictly Bollywood? Story, Camera and Movement in Hindi Film Dance. Massachusetts Institute of Technology.

Shresthova, S., 2008. Between Cinema and Performance: Globalizing Bollywood Dance. Doctorate Thesis. University of California, Los Angeles.

Trivedi, H., 2008. From Bollywood to Hollywood: The Globalisation of Hindi Cinema. *In* R. Krishnaswamy & J.C. Hawley (eds.) *The Postcolonial and the Global.* Minneapolis: University of Minnesota Press.

FOOTNOTES

1. Many Indian film scholars have discussed the influence of Natya Shastra on Indian films. See Dwyer 2002, Mishra 1998, Srinivasan 2007.

2. *Ramayana* is an ancient Sanskrit epic and a part of the Hindu canon (smriti). Written by Valmiki, *Ramayana* has been translated and interpreted by many poets and writers over the centuries. The story of *Ramayana* revolves around the Suryavansh dynasty, headed by king Dashratha and his four princes Rama, Lakhsmana, Bharata and Shatrughana. It celebrates the

virtuous life of Prince Rama–an incarnation of lord Vishnu. See Buck (1981).

3. *Mahabharata* is an ancient Hindu Sanskrit epic, written between the second century B.C. and second century A.D. Vyasa Muni has been traditionally ascribed as the narrator/storyteller of *Mahabharata*; but the epic has been reinterpreted and rewritten by many other writers over the ages. Nooten (in Buck, 1981) says, "*Mahabharata* is the story of a dynastic struggle culminating in an awesome battle between two branches of a single Indian ruling family. The account of the fight between the Kurus and the Pandavas for the fertile and wealthy land at the confluence of the Yamuna and Ganges riversin Delhi is enhanced by peripheral stories that provide a social, moral, and cosmological background to the climactic battle."

4. Bollywood choreographers pay a lot of attention to constructing a dance step with a "signature style". Amitabh Bachchan's comedic dance in the song and dance "My Name is Anthony Gonsalves" (*Amar Akbar Anthony* 1977), Jeetendra's exuberant dance in "Mast Baharon Ka Main Aashiq" (*Farz* 1961) for which he was given the title of "Jumping Jack", Shammi Kapoor's steps modelled on Elvis Presley in "O Haseena Julfon Waali" (*Teesri Manzil* 1966), and Rajesh Khanna's typical head movements in the song and dance "Jai Jai Shiv Shankar" (*Aap Ki Kasam* 1974), are examples of signature dance styles remembered and emulated by film audiences over the years.

5. Biddu continued his collaboration with Nazia Hassan, through suchsuccessful pop music albums as "Disco Deewane", "Boom Boom" and "Hotline" in the 1980s. These albums made Nazia Hassan one of the most popular Disco singing stars of the Indian subcontinent.

6. Personal interview with Dance Director Longinus Fernandes (Choreographer–*Slumdog Millionaire*, 2008), 3rd July 2009.

7. Personal interview with Dance Director Remo D'Souza (Choreographer–*Kal Ho Na Ho*, 2004), 5th July 2009.

PART 3

Biopics and Period Drama in Indian Cinema

9

Biopics as Source of Motivation amongst Youth: A Study in Noida amongst Students at UG Level

Mohd. Kamil

Introduction

Biopic Films are a sub-class of the bigger dramatization and epic film classifications (Gupta, 2016). In spite of the fact that they achieved a pinnacle of fame during the 1930s, they are as yet noticeable right up 'til today. 'Biopics' is a term derived from the combination of the words "biography" and "pictures." These movies delineate and sensationalize the life of an imperative verifiable personage (or gathering) from the past or present time. Here and there, verifiable biopics extend reality and recount a biography with differing degrees of precision.

Big screen biopics cross numerous genre types, since these movies may exhibit a western outlaw, a criminal, a melodic author, a religious figure or pioneer of a development, a performer; a craftsman, a designer, researcher, or specialist, a government official or President, a games legend or superstar, or an explorer.

According to Filmsite.org:

Much of the time, these movies put an accentuation on the bigger occasions (wartime, political or social conditions) encompassing the individual's whole life as they ascend to notoriety and brilliance. Some start with the individual's youth, however others focus on grown-up accomplishments. Biopics have existed since the most punctual long periods of quiet film in movies, for example, French producer Georges Melies' full length epic Jeanne D'Arc (1899) (and Cecil B. DeMille's Joan the Woman (1916) with musical drama star Geraldine Farrar), D.W. Griffith's religious epic Judith of Bethulia (1914), Abel Gance's imaginative six-hour-long epic Napoleon (1927), and executive Lloyd Ingraham's Jesse James (1927) with Fred Thomson as the western outlaw.

Introduction of Biopics in India

Indian Film experts have considered 'Raja Harishchandra' as the first biopic in Indian cinema. Raja Harishchandra which was made in 1913, is a silent film, directed and produced by Dadasaheb Phalke, and it is also the first full-length Indian feature film.

The film was based on the legend of Raja Harishchandra, recounted in the Ramayana and Mahabharata. Although a silent film with inter-titles in Marathi, English and Hindi, its cast and staff were Marathi people and it is therefore regarded as the first Marathi film. The film marked a historic benchmark in the film industry in India. Only one print of the film was made and shown at the Coronation Cinematograph. It was a commercial success and paved the way for more such films.

Impact of Biopics on Audience

We can see the impact of biopics on Indian film industry and also on audience. Sometimes biopics put emphasis on the larger events (War, Politics, Society, Games etc.) and surround the person's entire life as they rise to fame and story. Some biopics begin with childhood and some of the adult achievements.

Biopics are generally more influential because it reveals the facts about which we have read the book or heard by someone. Although fiction movies are also related to our life and social events these are imaginary in general. On the other hand, biopic movies are dramatized on the real life of a non-fictional or historically based person or people. The central character's real name is also used in the biopic. It touches our internal feelings deeply.

In India, hundreds of biopics have been made in Indian Film Industry. But the audience was not ready to like and appreciate biopics in the past. After the success of 'Bhaag Milkha Bhaag', it seems Biopic has become the favorite genre of Bollywood. Many biopics are being announced with top actors and actresses in lead. We can see the impact of biopics on Indian film industry as so many movies on real-life heroes are releasing these days.

Some famous biopics of Bollywood are as follows – Marry Kom (2014), Bhaag Milkha Bhaag (2013), Shahid (2013), Pan Singh Tomar (2013), The Dirty Picture (2011), Rang Rasia (2008), Jodha Akbar (2008), Guru (2007), The Rising: Ballad of Mangal Pandey (2005), The Legend of Bhagat Singh (2002).

Recently M.S. Dhoni: The Untold Story (2016) biopic based on the life of famous Indian cricketer Mahendra Singh Dhoni is released. It is becoming the most successful biopic in the Bollywood history after it crossed the 100 crore mark in nine days. Now audience wants to see the reality which is on the framework of a personality, his ups, and downs, from the struggle for success. Fictions may be a close to reality but imaginary in general. Biopics also have a great impact and impression on the younger generation. We can see the impact of biopics on youth.

Review of Literature

The biographical film or biopic is a staple of film production in all major film industries and yet, within film studies, its generic, aesthetic, and cultural significance has remained underexplored. The Biopic in Contemporary Film Culture fills this gap, conceptualizing the biopic with a particular eye toward the life of the genre internationally. New theoretical approaches combine with specially commissioned chapters on contemporary biographical film production in India, Italy, South Korea, France, Russia, Great Britain, and the US, in order to present a selective but well-rounded portrait of the biopic's place in film culture. (In Brown, T., & In Vidal, B. (2014))

In Cheshire, E. (2015), '*Bio-pics: A Life in Pictures*' offers a series of case studies which throw light on this most unique of genres. Is the bio-pic a genre in its own right? Or are such films merely footnotes in other more traditional genres such as the western or costume drama, depending on the historical figure under scrutiny. Unlike other genre forms bio-pics seemingly share no familiar iconography, codes or conventions. They can be set anywhere and at any time. What links them is quite simply that the films depict the life of an important person. Through a carefully selected range of thematically linked (English-language) bio-pics released since 1990 this book explores key issues surrounding their resurgence, narrative structure, production, subject representation or misrepresentation, and critical response. The films under discussion are grouped around a profession (writers, singers, politicians, sportsmen, criminals, artists) allowing for comparisons to be drawn in approaches to similar subject matter.

Significance of the Study

There has been a drastic change in the society from the time when people used to listen to the courageous deeds of their heroes, admiring them and incorporating their qualities in bringing about a change in the society to the current scenario when they witness such deeds on the big screen and receive a big impact directly from them. The study helped us in understanding the current trend of biopic watching pattern amongst the youth and what significance this genre of movies holds in their life.

Research Objectives

- To examine the current trends in Indian cinema in regards with biopics

- To study the impact of biopics on Youth
- To find out the watching habits of biopics of Youth

Research Methodology

To collect the relevant data, survey method was used. As survey method studies the sampling of individual units from a population, questionnaires were sent to the respondents to collect the primary data. The number of respondents taken for the survey was '50'.

Analysis and Interpretation

From the study it was analysed that young generation, especially students' like to watch biopics which revolves around a character having multiple shades in his/her life. They like biopics which have a strong story and good mix of Bollywood drama and music.

From the date it was retrieved that among the recently released biopics, around 42% of the respondents like Sanju. A film that follows the life of Bollywood actor Sanjay Dutt, his addiction with drugs, arrest for alleged association with the 1993 Bombay bombings, relationship with his father, comeback in the industry and the eventual drop of charges from Bombay blasts, and release after completing his jail term.

It was then followed by 'M.S Dhoni: An Untold Story' a biopic on the struggle story of one the finest cricket captains of Indian team, Mahendra Pal Singh Dhoni. It was liked by around 20% of the respondents.

On the other hand, Biopics like 'Sachin: A billion dreams' failed to impress the young audience as only one out of 50 respondents liked this movie.

As far as influence of biopics on respondents is concerned, 43.8% respondents believed that movies of this genre have a strong influence. While a good 45.8% respondents found partial influence of biopics on them. Also, 10.4% of the respondents though biopics have no influence on them.

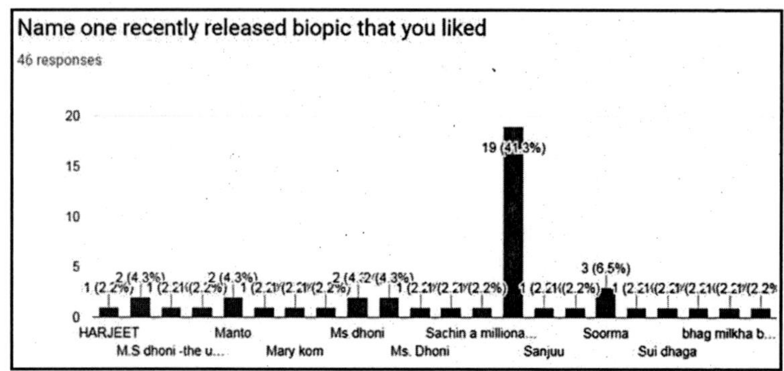

Figure: 1

Another interesting data fetched from the respondents was while 47.9% of the students preferred watching a biopic on the social appeal, a whopping 33.3% of the respondents went for the biopics just after watching a trailer. Surprisingly a meager 4.2% of the respondent preferred watching biopic based on the life story of the person. Another factor which pulled the audience in watching a biopic was direction. Around 8.3% respondents went to watch a biopic if a well-known director is associated with the movie.

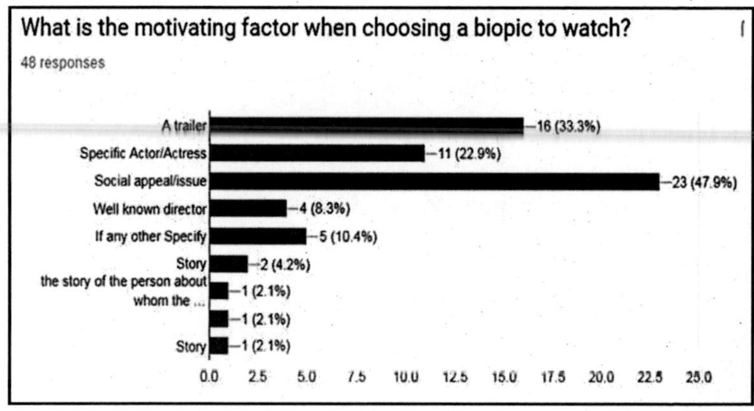

Figure: 2

As far as checking facts of biopics are concerned, 34.7% respondents would check facts after watching a biopic, while 18.4% would check facts before watching it. But the highest percentage of respondents, i.e. 38.8% was those who would check facts before and after watching a biopic.

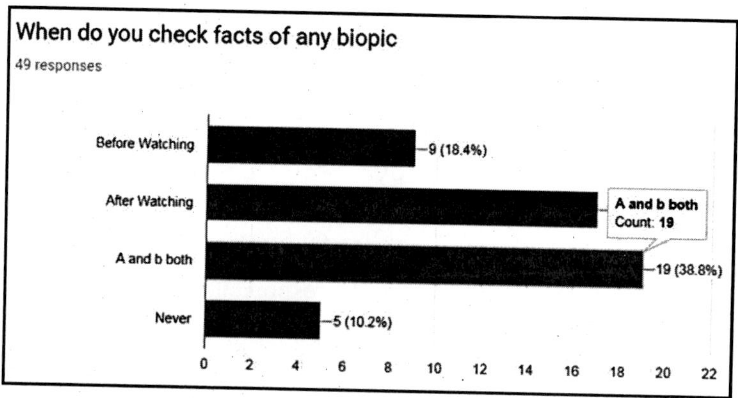

Figure: 3

While answering the question, do biopics influence the respondents, 43.8% said that they have strong influence of biopics on them while 45.8% came under partial influence category.

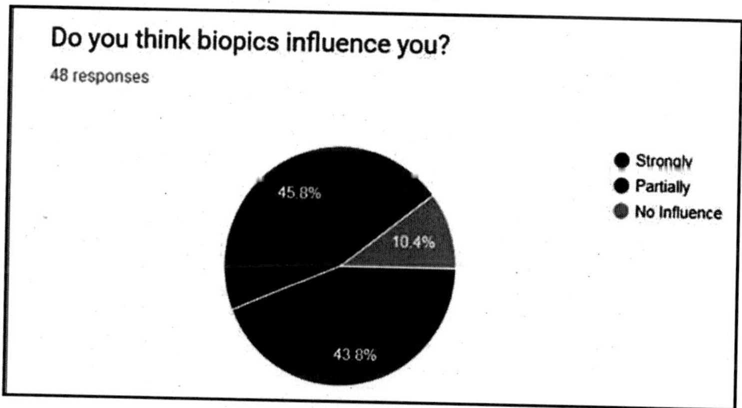

Figure: 4

As far as kind of changes are concerned, 28.6% incorporated change in the mindset regarding highlighted issues. Also, 16.3% brought change in their personality after watching biopics.

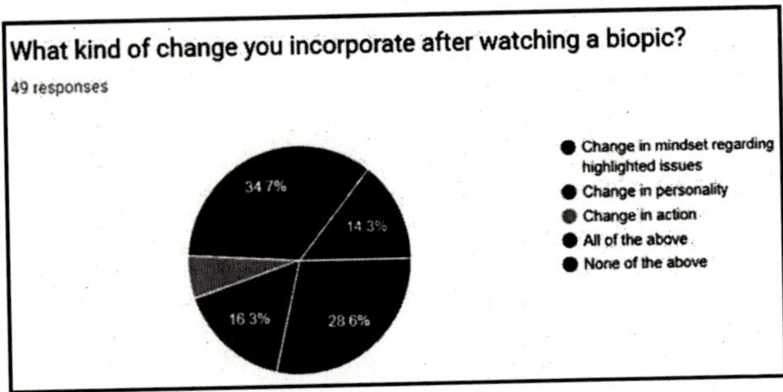

Figure: 5

Through these changes 55.1% respondents felt encourage to come up with new and better ideas to change society after watching biopics.

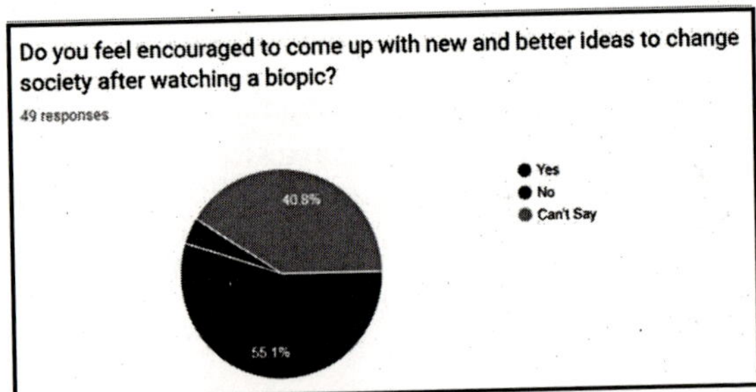

Figure: 6

Also 70.8% students respondod that they preach these changes in the society also.

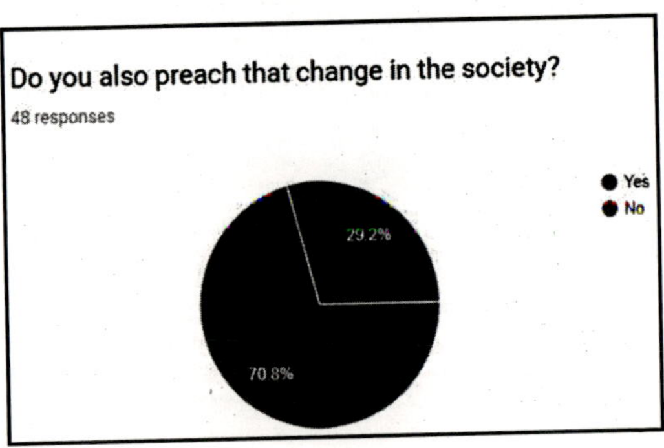

Figure: 7

Out of 50 respondents 28 were males and 22 were females. 90% the respondents were between 18-21 years of age.

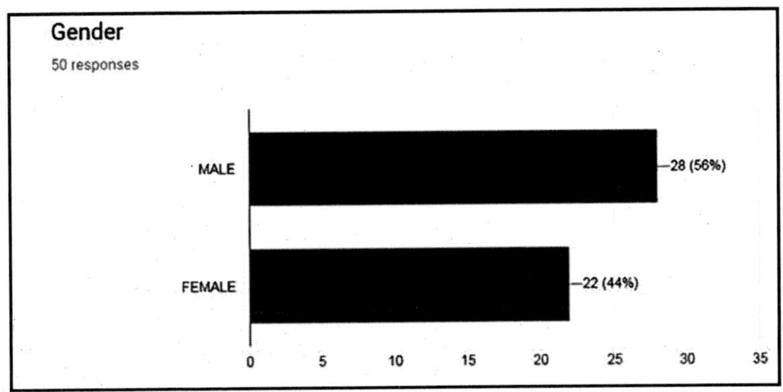

Figure: 8

Conclusion

As far as objectives to study biopics as source of motivation amongst the youth and to analyse the current patterns in Indian cinema in respects with biopics, the result of the study is that biopics motivates young generation to vast degree. From the data, it was retrieved that 43.8% respondents have strong influence of biopics on them while 45.8% said they have partial influence of biopics on them. As 55.1% respondents felt encourage to come up with new and better ideas to change society after watching biopics, it can be concluded that biopics even encourage them to bring about changes in the society which they see on the big screen. Respondents get inspiration from the reel heroes and they even endeavor to execute messages they get from biopics.

Moving on the second objective that is to study the impact of biopics on Youth, it was concluded that there was a high impact of biopics on youth. A whopping 70.8% of the students responded that they preach changes in the society which they learn through biopics and get motivation to do better things for the society.

To the extent watching propensities for biopics of youths are concerned they get a kick out of the chance to watch biopics which rotate around a central character having numerous good and bad times of his/her life. They generally incline toward taking biopics having a motivational interest dependent on the life of any common man so they could correspond with the main protagonist. They like biopics which have a solid story and great blend of Bollywood dramatization and music.

REFERENCES

Keval J. Kumar (2011). Mass Communication in India, Jaico publishing house, 166-170. ISBN: 10:81-7224-373-1.

Dr. Govind Swaroop Gupta. (2017, December 5). The Impact of Biopics on Film Indutries. Retrieved from http://www.thepov.in/the-impact-of-biopics-on-film-industries/

The Biopic in Contemporary Film Culture (AFI Film Readers) 1st Edition

Cheshire, E. (2015). *Bio-pics: A Life in Pictures*. London: Columbia University Press.

In Brown, T., & In Vidal, B. (2014). *The Biopic in contemporary film culture*. New York: Routledge.

http://www.filmsite.org/biopics.html

http://www.thepov.in/the-impact-of-biopics-on-film-industries/

10

Role of Biopic Films in Promoting Sportsmen and Sports in India

Annu Sangwan and Dr. Manasvi Maheshwari

Introduction

Indian cinema is one of the oldest (more than 100 years) and the largest multi-lingual cinema in the world in terms of film production. According to a study, many scholars have found, as many as 1,600 films produced in various languages every year with over 3.5 billion tickets were sold. Bollywood which is based in Mumbai, began in 1913, representing 43% of net box office revenue, while Tamil cinema, and Telugu cinema representing 36%, and rest of the regional cinema represent 21% as of 2014, Indian films are also popular in countries that have large India or Pakistani communities, such as the United Kingdom. In India only about 4% (estimated 1.2 billion) people actually go to the movies on a regular basis.

Indian cinema has recently witnessed the drastic change and unprecedented growth to the production of Biopics films. "The Term Biopic is derived from the combination of the words "biography" and "pictures." These films depict and dramatize the life of an important historical personage (or group) from the past or present era." (Filmsite) Most of the time, Biopic put emphasis only on the one Important big event related to somebody and sometimes emphasis on its entire life to show its journey and struggle. To count a few like Sanju on Sanjay dutt, Raazi, Parmanu they all based on a specific event. In 2018, people has seen few films that either whole life based and true event based. Biopics have various and unlimited categories which are projected on the day to day basis worldwide. Some of the categories are: Music, Crime, Entertainment based or Military person, Scientist, Celebrity, Sports personality based and so on.

Biopics have existed since the days of silent films. The films like Bhakta Raidas (1943), Bhakta Surdas (1942), Dr. Kotnis Ki Amar Kahani (1946), Narsi Bhagat (1940), Sant Dnyaneshwar (1940), Tansen (1943), and Vikramaditya (1945) are some of the biopics early Indian cinema days. Biopics is a different genre and box office show that audience is excited to see biopics. Biopics have made actors popular at times. Sports Biopics in one such type of films which has given identity to the actor/actress for example Priyanka Chopra in and as Mary Kom, Sushant Singh Rajput as Dhoni, Farhan Akhtar as Milkha Singh and list goes on. In a country like India wherein sports have always been overrated in terms of nationalism and pride, many famous directors and experts admit that biopic films are Inspirational, Motivational and easily connect with viewers.

There is no doubt that Bollywood has influenced Indian society and culture for a long time and it is the most vibrant medium for telling the stories. So the stories of success, struggle, sacrifice, nationalism, and pride are taken the form of films to spread, to influence, to encourage and to promote the good will among the audience.

Review of Literature

"Many Scholars and Researchers have done studies on Biopic Films. Even the film critic and experts have highlighted the importance of biopics. The studies conclude that "Biopics offer viewers a chance to delve deep into a personality, also piquing their curiosity to go beyond aspects presented on screen. One can't expect movies to go full throttle with the detailing and explore different dimensions, given the three-hour span that limits the filmmaker. However, the positives are significant. The fascination for biopics means that it has become a starting point for many to dig into books to understand the individual on a holistic level before/after the movie release " (Srivathsan Nadadhur, 2018MAY 24, 2018 MAY 24, 2018)

"Another reason for the directors to prefer young champions over those who are faded and fabled and forgotten is viewers' growing interest in real-life heroes who continue to impact popular culture into which the movies about them submerge. Since the fans are happy to get every update on their stars; through social media, it is a logical step for the filmmakers to delve deeper into their lives via biopics". (Divya Pal, News 18, July 19, 2018)

"Sports biopics are big. Not only do they captivate audience's imaginations with strong, inspirational stories, but they also set cash registers ringing. Starting with 'Chak De India,' which was a true story inspired by the life of Mir Ranjan Negi, the coach of Indian women's hockey team, who led a team of girls from the hinterlands to soaring heights. It was critically acclaimed and did decent business, paving the way for films in the genre. " (India Times, Jan 28, 2017)

"Life picturing" has been seen as driven by the generic plot of 'national identity'. This is decidedly true in the case of India's sports biopics in which the lives of its sporting heroes—Tendulkar, Dhoni, Azhar—are very clearly cast as national lives, their work (and play) as embodying the nation's interests. The biopics focus on the affect generated when the cricketer on screen scores or is out: the nation mourns or celebrates accordingly. A Billion Dreams in the Tendulkar biopic's title is precisely that: he embodies the dreams of the entire Indian population of one billion. The biopic constructs the sporting figure as a key "national symbolic" (Berlant 155) around whom." (Pramod K. Nayar, 2017)

"Rachel Dwyer (2012) in her work traces the growth of the genre in the Indian context and mentions that the biopic genre has

been relatively unproductive in India despite the massive international critical and commercial success of the 1982 Indo-British biopic Gandhi by Richard Attenborough. In India, biopic has been a rarely used term and is not widely known, and it is usually being classed as "Historicals". She observes that, since biopic is a hybrid genre, "the biography does have some problems with fitting in the Hindi film form, which must have a hero, melodrama, spectacle, music, and also a star. The director of Paan Singh Tomar (2010) Tigmanshu Dhulia points out, that the audiences would classify a biopic without stars among documentaries; and a certain resistance to the documentary in India can be seen as this form has never been commercially successful".

"Biopics, especially sports biopics, have become immensely popular. Sports personalities have become a huge source of inspiration for filmmakers keen to make films based on them. Apart from this, there is a sudden surge of biopics about common people in Bollywood. These films are quite different from the usual biopics as the focus has shifted from only celebrating the life stories of the famous. These biopics create drama out of the stories of ordinary people who face extraordinary circumstances and still emerge as successful in their endeavours. Films like Manjhi. Manjunath, Sarabjit, etc. are quite successful examples of such biopics. Reality (in terms of biopics) as a formula is gaining prominence in Bollywood, with even fictional scripts creating thrust on authentic characters and situations". (India Times, Jan 28, 2017)

Research Design

The objective of this research paper is to study the role of biopic films in creating awareness about the sports/sportsmen, also to know perception of viewers towards sports biopic films and to analyze the content and presentation of the sports biopic films on the pre-determined parameters.

Survey

A survey has been conducted using questionnaire to know viewers perception about the biopic films. The sample size for survey was

203. The data has been collected from respondents of 15 years and above. The reason for choosing this age group was because this is the time when children are planning for their career options and start exploring various career opportunities. At this age when they are aspiring for new opportunities a movie can bring in difference in their opinion and choices. The study has been conducted in Delhi NCR. It was ensured that respondents have seen atleast one sports biopic.

Content Analysis

There are eight sports biopics movies made in Hindi film industry from year 2013 to 2018. For the purpose of the study researcher has done content analysis of all the eight films mentioned below:

1. Bhaag Milkha Bhaag
2. Mary Kom
3. Azhar
4. Budhiasingh-Born to run
5. M.S. Dhoni: the untold story
6. Dangal
7. Soorma
8. Gold: dream that united our nation

Data Analysis

Survey

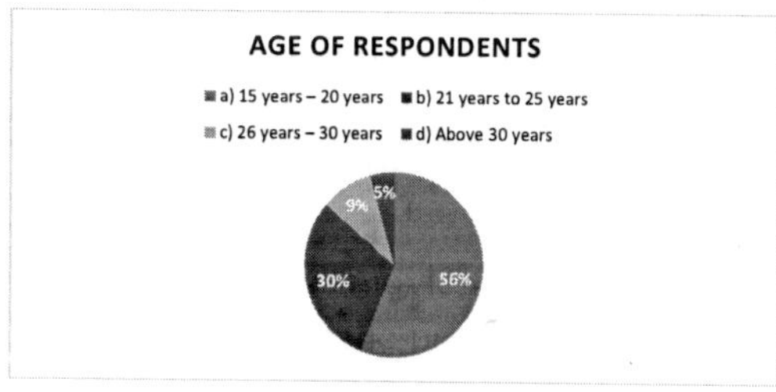

Fig. 1: Age of the Respondents

56% of respondents were in the age group of 15-20 years, 30% respondents were between the age group of 21-25 years.

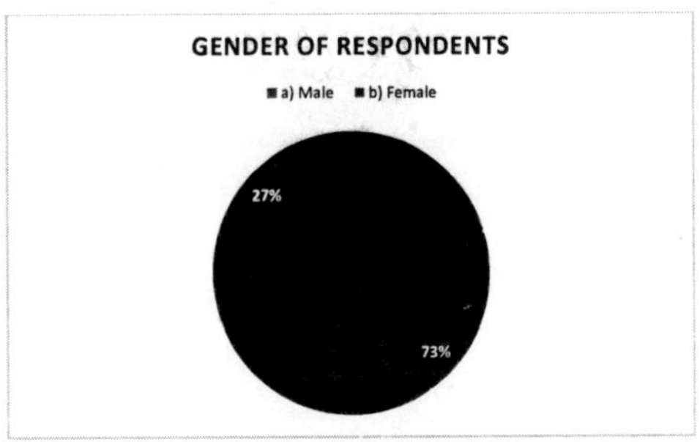

Fig. 2: Gender of the Respondents

73% respondents were male and 27% were female.

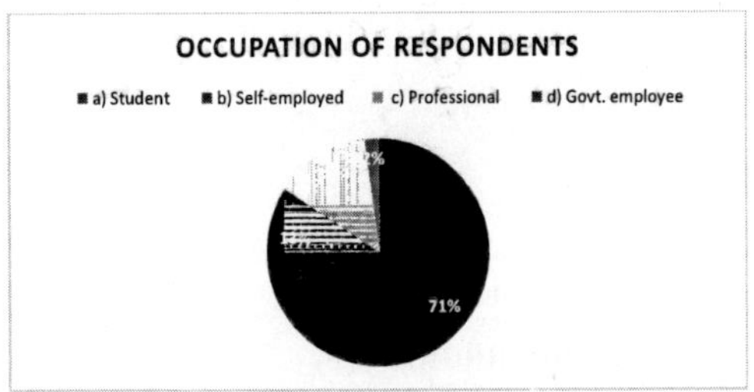

Fig. 3: Occupation of the Respondents

The respondents were from all walks of life majority were student 71%, 14% professionals, 13% self-employed and 2% government employees.

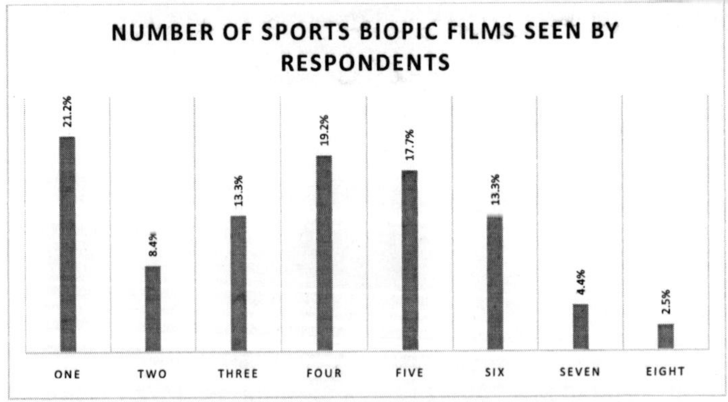

Fig. 4: Number of Sports Biopics Seen

21.2% of respondents have seen one Sports Biopic out of Eight. Only 2.5% have watched all the eight sports biopics. Majority have seen 4-5 films.

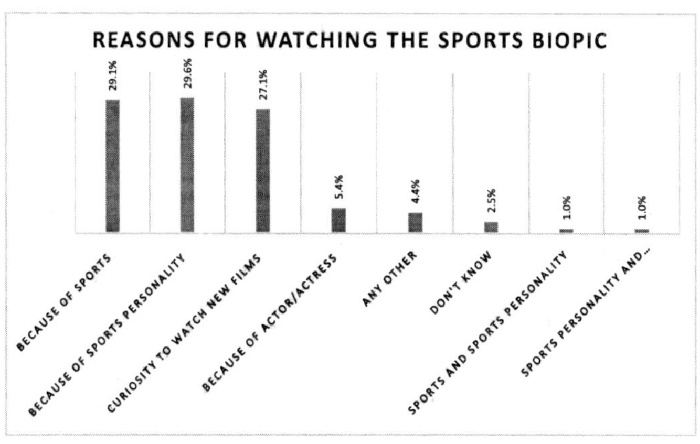

Fig. 5: Reason for watching the Sports Biopics

The majority of respondents (29.6% and 29.1%) have watched the sports biopic because of sports personality and sports respectively. 27.1% respondents watched the film because of curiosity to watch the new film. 4.4% of respondents cited various reasons for watching the film such as to know about the struggle and success, to know about the struggle of player,storyline and script, to get knowledge about sports and learn some new techniques, and inspiration and motivation these films carry.

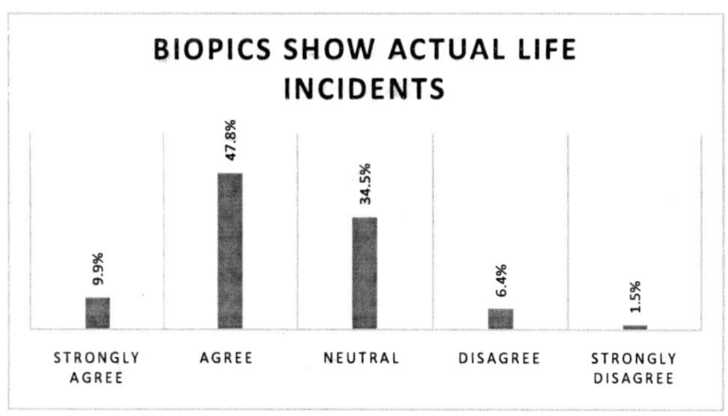

Fig. 6: Biopics show actual life incidents

47.8% of respondents agree and 9.9% strongly agree that biopics are based on actual life incidents while 34.5% respondents were not sure about the fact.

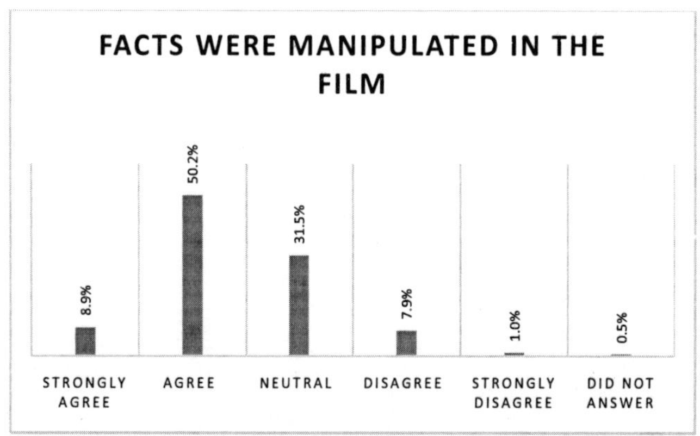

Fig. 7: Facts were manipulated in the films

50.2% of respondents agree and 8.9% strongly agree that facts were manipulated in sports biopics.

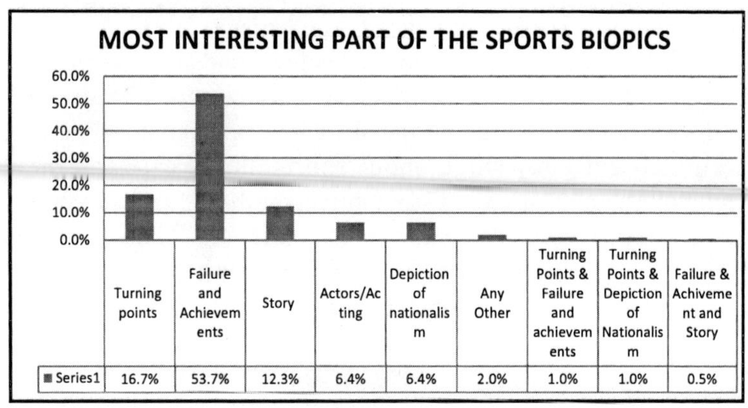

	Turning points	Failure and Achievements	Story	Actors/Acting	Depiction of nationalism	Any Other	Turning Points & Failure and achievements	Turning Points & Depiction of Nationalism	Failure & Achivement and Story
Series1	16.7%	53.7%	12.3%	6.4%	6.4%	2.0%	1.0%	1.0%	0.5%

Fig. 8: Most interesting part of the Sports Biopics

53.7% of respondents stated that failure and achievements is the most interesting part of any sports biopic. 16.7% respondents consider turning points in the film are the most interesting part of sports biopics.

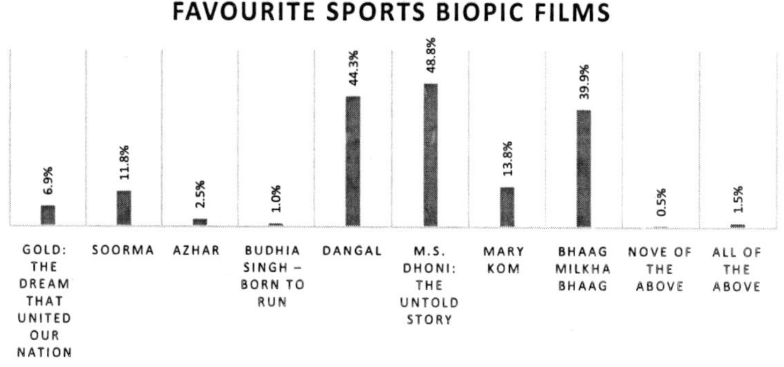

Fig. 9: Favourite Sports Biopic film

The respondents were asked to mark their favourite sports biopic our of eight choices given to them. Majority of the respondents i.e. 48.8% marked M.S. Dhoni: The untold story as their favourite sports biopic. Keeping in the order of ranking Dangal was second most liked sports biopic followed by Bhaag Milkha Bhaag.

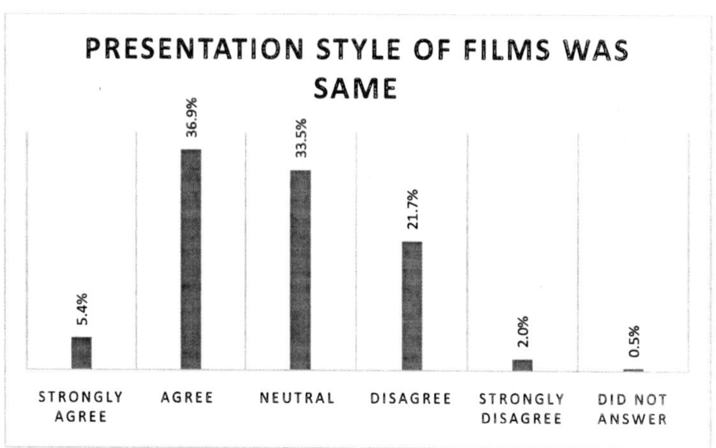

Fig. 10: Presentation style of films was same

36.9% of respondents agree and 5.4% respondents strongly agree to that the presentation style of sports biopics was same.

33.5% respondents were not sure while 21.7% and 2% did not agree that presentation style was same of all the films.

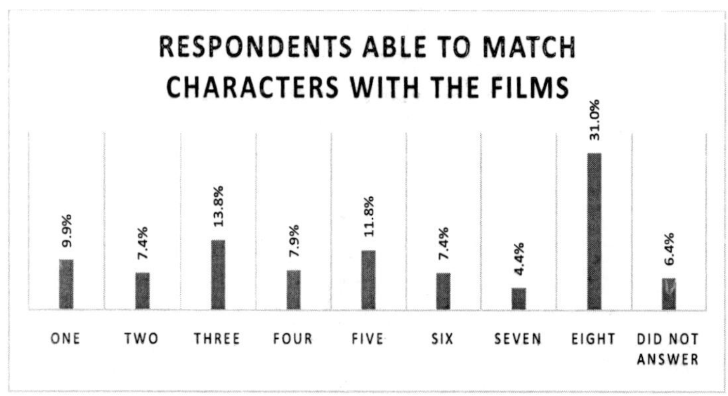

Fig. 11: Match characters with the film

In one question respondents were asked to match characters with the film name. 31% of the respondents were able to match all the eight sports biopics with the real characters. 6.4% respondents did not answer the question.

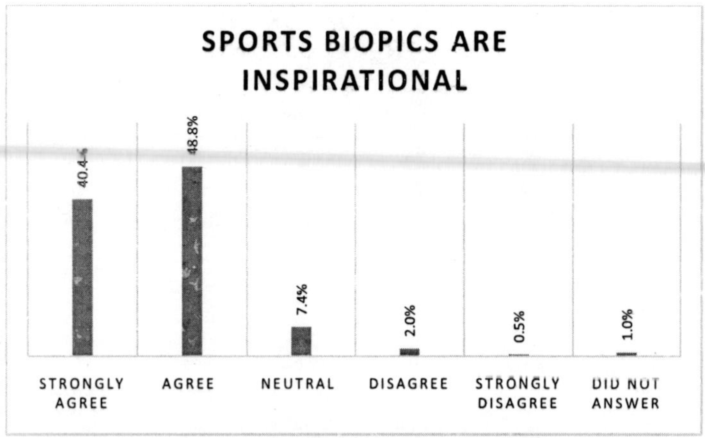

Fig. 12: Sports Biopics are inspirational

48.8% of respondents agree and 40% strongly agree that sports biopics are inspirational for the viewers.

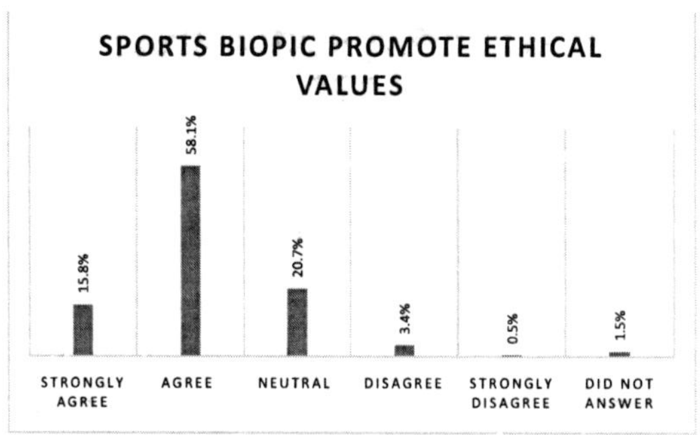

Fig. 13: Sports Biopics promote ethical values

58.1% of respondents agree and 15.8% strongly agree that the sports biopics promote ethical values.

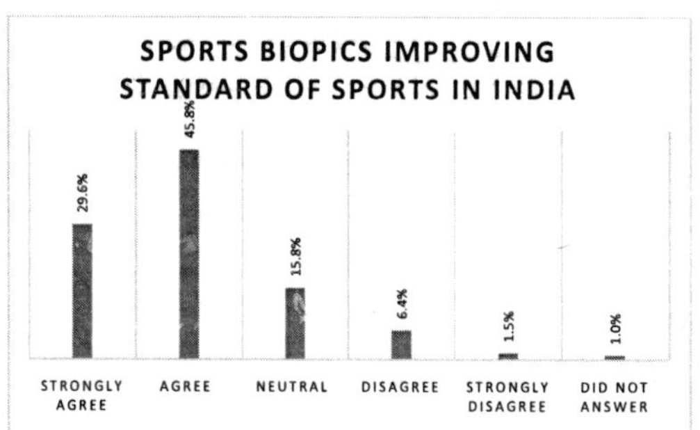

Fig. 14: Sports Biopics improving standard of sports in India

45.8% of respondents agree and 29.6% strongly agree that sports biopics are improving the standard of sports in India.

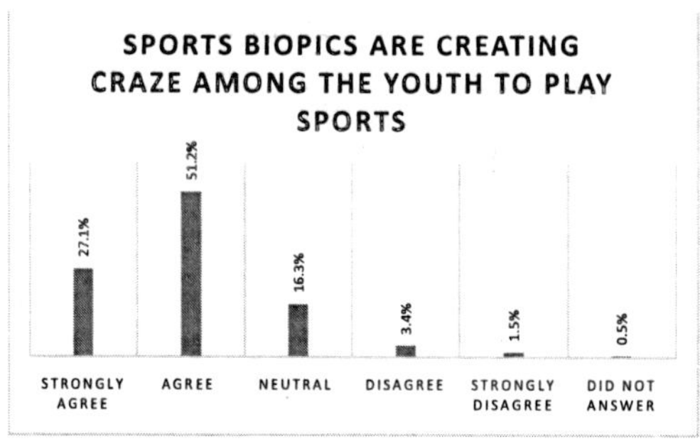

Fig. 15: Sports Biopics are creating craze among the youth to play sports

51.2% of respondents agree and 27.1% strongly agree that sports biopics are creating craze among the youth to play sports.

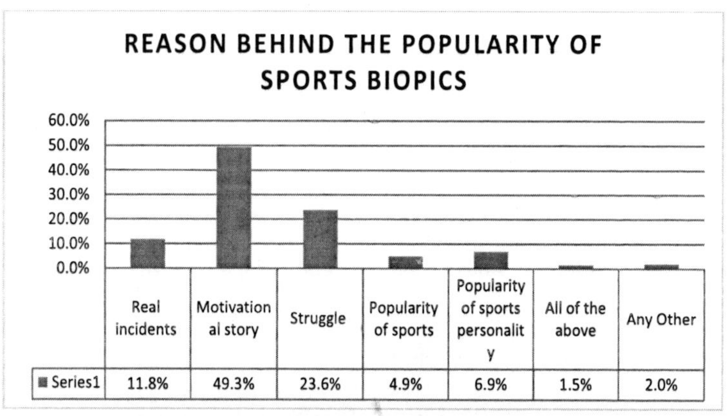

Fig. 16: Reason behind the popularity of Sports Biopics

49.3% of respondents stated that motivational stories of the sports person are the reason behind the popularity of sports biopics. 23.6% respondents agreed that struggle of sports person contribute in increasing popularity of the films while real incidents of the film make it popular. One of the respondentstated that eagerness to know about other's life is the reason why sports biopics are popular nowadays.

Content Analysis

Table 1: Synopsis of the films

Bhaag Milkha Bhaag – 2013 Director: Rakeysh Omprakash Mehra Actor: Farhaan Akhtar played the role of Milkha Singh	The film was based on Milkha Singh, an Indian athlete, world champion, Olympian. He was titles as 'The Flying Sikh'. The story is about Milkha's childhood days, sufferings, struggle and what he and his family went through during partition. The story of his survival for living in refugee camps, his love life and finally landing in army. The movie shows why and how he got into racing, role of various important people in his life, how he gets distracted but makes a comeback and finally how he becomes world famous. His commitment and hard work to achieve name and fame pays him for his life.

(Contd...)

Mary Kom – 2014 Director: Actress: Priyanka Chopra played the role of Mary Kom	The film is about Mangte Chungneijang Kom (Mary Kom) famous Indian Boxer. The story is about her interest in boxing and how she convinces Narjit Singh (Sunil Thapa) to be her boxing coach. She challenges a local wrestler for money to earn bread and butter for family where she mets footballer OnlerKom. She also faces reluctance from her father who later accepts her passion for sports. She marries Onler who encourages her to restart her career after having twins and she makes a comeback in National Xing Championship. She is focused, motivated and passionate player titled 'Magnificent Mary'.
Azhar – 2016 Actor: Emraan Hashmi played Azhar	Azharis based on the life of the former Indian International cricketer Mohammad Azharuddin. The movie is about match fixing allegations he faced in 2000 and gets a life ban. He challenges the court decision. The movie dated back to 1963 and gives an account of Azhar's family, dreams and struggle he went through to be selected in Indian cricket team. The film gives account of the criticism he faces for being Muslim. Azharis famous for his expensive lifestyle as a result he comes into the eyes of match-fixers. The film is more about his struggle to prove himself innocent.
Budhia Singh – 2016 Actor: Manoj Bajpayee played Brianchi Das coach of Budhia	'Budhia Singh - Born to Run' is made on world's youngest marathon runner. The National award winning film is based on the controversial true story of Odisha's wonder boy Budhia Singh (played by Mayur Mahendra Patole) and his mentor Biranchi Das (Manoj Bajpayee), who faces opposition from various quarters for seeing an Olympic dream for the world's youngest marathon runner.Riddled with extreme poverty, a four-year-old Budhia was sold to a peddler by his mother for Rs 800. Biranchi, a local judo coach, takes the spunky boy under his wing. However, the coach faced backlash on ethical grounds for imposing vigorous training practices on the child. The government inquiry, public scrutiny and media circus that followed, clipped the boy's wings and banned him from running long-distances.This incredible film must be lauded for presenting a debatable topic in the most balanced fashion. It doesn't take sides; however, it questions the society at large for making a joke out of a boy who deserved to dream big.

(Contd...)

MS Dhoni: The Untold Story – 2016 Director: Neeraj Pandey Actor: Sushant Rajput as Mahindra Singh Dhoni	The film is about MS Dhoni, Indian Cricket team captain. It is a journey of a small town player to make it large. His school cricket coach asks him to join cricket after watching him play as goalkeeper in school football team. He plays for state, joins Indian Railways as TC and plays cricket for the railways after long wait of 4 years he gets selected in Indian Cricket team and turns to be one of the best cricketing captains in history of Indian Cricket. He faces tough time with selectors time and again.
Dangal- 2016 Director- Nitesh Tiwari Actor-Aamir Khan played Mahavir Singh phogat	Dangal is a story of female wrestler Phogat Sisters and their father Mahavir Singh phogat efforts for making them world level wrestlers. He has a dream to win gold in Olympics for India. Mahavir is a caring father as well as a strict coach at a time. After training under Mahavir, Geeta needs to go national sports academy. She got distracted from her goals and loses the 4 major tournaments. Then her father and sister help her to fulfil her father's dream of winning gold and become the first girl as professional wrestler.
Soorma- 2018 Director-Shaad Ali Actor- Diljit dosanjh as Sandeep Singh	The film is about the story of a hockey player Sandeep Singh. He started playing hockey when his elder brother (Bikram) finds that how effortlessly and smoothly he pulls off the hardest drag flick shot of hockey. At the peak of his career, He got paralysed when accidentally a gunshot hits him in train. He decides to overcome his disabilities and make a comeback to play hockey again and to lead Indian hockey team to victory.
Gold- 2018 Director- Reema Kagti Actor- Akshay Kumar played Tapan Das	Gold is about the manager of Indian hockey team Tapan Das. Post-independence story of struggles, political obstacles in the way to play in Olympics. Das prepare his team for game in the hope of getting first gold medal for Independent India. Tapan Das is the calm and ambitious in nature which help him to win the first Olympic gold and bring the glory and pride for nation.

Result and Discussions

Biopics are undoubtedly the most popular and liked genre of Hindi film industry. Audience are always willing and keen to see the background, struggle, problem and insights of popular personalities. Sports being priority of majority of Indian audience specifically the teenagers and youth always enjoys upper hand even in cinema. Sports promote nationalism, integrity and unity. Biopics based on sports/sportsmen have enjoyed positive feedback at box office and even by film critics. Many experienced and veteran directors have explored sports biopics and have left an impact on the viewers with their inspirational stories. The majority of respondents in survey agreed that they watched sports biopics because of sports or sports personality. Majority of respondents also believed that the movie was based on actual and true facts. The Indian audience love to watch failure and achievement stories and turning points of a sports biopic. The respondents also agreed that sports biopics are inspirational, promote ethical values, improving standard of sports in India and increasing craze amongst youth to play sports or take keen interest in sports.

The content analyses also revealed that all the eight sports biopics showed struggle of an individual, their failures, their passion, hard work, commitment, fighting spirit, inspiring coaches. According to survey majority of respondents feel that the actual and true facts were manipulated. It is a known fact that the biopic is based on true and actual incident but directors manipulate some of the facts and make it more compelling to watch its means an interesting treatment to actual story. The films are motivational in presentation and have capacity to incite feeling of nationalism amongst the viewers. The sports biopics also highlights the turning points of an individual lives and how they cope up with the adverse circumstances. Although all the 8 biopic films were directed by different directors but style of presenting the film was almost similar.

REFERENCES

Chaiyapinunt, U. (n.d.). The Success Of Biopics Explained. Retrieved from http://www.neontommy.com/news/2015/03/why-biopics-are-dominating-oscars.html

Dwyer, R. (2012). The Biopic in Hindi Cinema. In R. A. Rosenstone and C. Parvulescu (Ed.) A Companion to the Historical Film (pp. 219-232). WileyBlackwell.

Edgington, K., Erskine, T., & Welsh, J. M. (2010). *Encyclopedia of Sports Films*. Scarecrow Press.

Janardhan, A. (2016, May 1). Why sports biopics are the flavour of the season. Retrieved from https://www.livemint.com/Sundayapp/pD5GaPBvprD2n42l6XxFAJ/Why-sports-biopics-are-the-flavour-of-the-season.html

Nayar, P. K. (2017). Biopics: The Year in India. *Biography*, *40*(4), 604-610.

Nadadhur, S. (2018, May 24). Books or biopics: For a complete picture. Retrieved from https://www.thehindu.com/books/books-or-biopics-for-a-complete-picture/article23977058.ece

Neerja, V. (2017). Narrative Form of Selected Hindi Biopics An Empirical Study of Style and Structure.

Pal, D. (2018, July 19). Why is Bollywood Focusing on Biopics About People Still Alive? Retrieved from https://www.news18.com/news/movies/why-is-bollywood-focusing-on-biopics-about-people-still-alive-1813455.html

Why sports biopics are gaining momentum in Bollywood? - Times of India. (2017, January 28). Retrieved fromhttps://timesofindia.indiatimes.com/entertainment/hindi/bollywood/news/Why-sports-biopics-are-gaining-momentum-in-Bollywood/articleshow/51240421.cms

7 biopics based on sports. (2018, October 6). Retrieved from https://www.filmfare.com/features/7-biopics-based-on-sports-28396.html

11

Distortion of History in Bollywood Period Drama (Films)

Kritika Sati

Introduction

Seeing is believing. Several research have suggested or indicated that visual cues are more helpful in retrieving and remembering information. In fact, research also suggest that words are abstract and rather difficult for the brain to retain, whereas visuals are concrete and, as such, more easily remembered. (Haig Kouyoumdjian, 2012)

Talking about cinema; it is basically a glorious presentation of visuals. Therefore, there is a very high possibility that what people see in movies, tends to remain in their memory much more strongly than what they read. Therefore, films leave a tremendous and everlasting impact on the minds of the viewers and due to this reason, cinema is considered to be one of the most potent and powerful means of mass communication which can transform peoples' perceptions.

This power of cinema can definitely be useful in highlighting the problems of the society and urging required changes. Also, there's no harm in recalling a comedy scene from an entertainment movie or remembering romantic sequences. However, when it comes to the genre of period films, things become slightly complicated.

What are Period Drama/Films?

Period drama or film is that genre which deals with movies set in a particular era and involve certain historic characters. Such films often tell the tale of a famous personality from the past who still inspires the masses or of a long lost hero whose story calls for a revival. Similarly, a period film can either be a narrative of a real character from the history or can be a fictionalised plot inspired from some incident. In any case, such movies usually involves special costumes, props, sets and overall make-over to re-create the era and take the audience back in time.

According to Oxford dictionary, period drama refers to 'a television or film production set in a particular historical period and characterized by the use of costumes, sets, and props that are typical or evocative of the era.' Collin's dictionary defines period drama as 'a drama set in a particular historical period.'

Bollywood, one of the largest film producers of the world, is full of such movies. Mughal-E-Azam (1960), Lagaan (2001), Asoka (2001), The Legend of Bhagat Singh (2002), Mangal Pandey: The Rising (2005), Jodhaa Akbar (2008), Bajirao Mastani (2015) and Padmaavat (2018); all are examples of period dramas/ films which transported the audience to a bygone era through their grandeur and larger than life production.

Origin of Indian Cinema and Period Dramas/Films

Cinema came to India with Lumiere brothers who screened the first few films for Indian audiences on July 7, 1896 at Watson Hotel, laying the foundation for Indian film industry. They were the inventors of the 'Cinematographe', a compact and portable machine that with a few adjustments could be used as a camera or projector or printing machine. (Kumar, 2010, p. 168)

Soon, Indian pioneers like Harischandra S. Bhatwadekar (alias Save Dada), R.G. Torney and Dhandiraj Govindraj Phalke (alias Dadasaheb Phalke) started trying their hands at film making.

It is interesting to note that even the first feature film of India, Raja Harishchandra, directed by Dadasaheb Phalke in 1913 is indeed a period drama. Interspersed with text in English and Hindi, the film is a story of righteous king Harischandra who sacrifices his kingdom and family to keep the honour his words given to sage Vishwamitra, and goes into exile. Though it is a silent film, it is certainly an example of period drama.

In fact, a large number of initial films were drawn from epics like Ramayana and Mahabharata or folklores like Mohini Bhasmasur, Lanka Dahan, Keechaka Vadham, which was South India's first film directed by R. Nataraja Mudaliar, and so on.

Though in subsequent decades, many different genre of movies emerged, it seems that period dramas have not really lost their charm. The only difference is in the magnanimity of the production of such movies. Majestic sets, fancy ornament, heavy costumes, latest technologies–these are regular feature of today's grand movies.

Problem with Period Drama/Films

When a movie is simply a work of fiction, it is more or less harmless; of course there can be exceptions in case of controversial themes. But when history and facts are involved, complications increase and as a result, majority of such movies are met with sharp criticism and outrage by certain groups on the grounds of distortion of history. Some popular movies that faced such controversies are Sanjay Leela Bhansali's Padmaavat and Bajirao Mastani, Ashutosh Gowariker's Jodhaa Akbar, Santosh Sivan's Asoka and so on.

Though movie directors often resort to 'artistic liberties' and 'disclaimers' to quench the fire but the greater concern remains that due to a general unawareness about historical facts among masses, especially youngsters, any distortion or retouching of facts is likely to change the way we know the history forever.

Objective and Methodology

The objective of this study is to analyse how much distortion of history possibly occurs in period movies, leading to controversies, and how it can impact peoples' understanding of history. For this, case study will be done, taking the cases of Padmaavat, Bajirao Mastani and Jodhaa Akbar.

Literature Review

Bollywood's love for period films is pretty evident, given the sheer number of such historical movies, and has been a subject of research for many scholars. While doing an analysis of Bajirao Mastani, which is based on N.S. Inamdar's Marathi novel 'Rau' (1974); Ajaonkar & Talule (2017) in their research titled 'Transformation of the Book into Cinema: A Critical Perspective on a Bollywood Movie Bajirao-Mastani' said:

> Dwelling upon the unrealistic aspects of movie is a tough task as well. The scenes where Kashibai and Mastani meet become dramatic and unreal. So is the case with the dance and music. Bajirao Peshwa is shown dancing after one of his battles, which is unimaginable through the contemporary social standards and also by the standards of royal stature. (Ajaonkar & Talule, 2017, p. 120)

They further stated, "Some of the critics and veteran film actors like Nana Patekar have scathingly ironized meeting, and dancing of Kashibai and Mastani warning Bhansali about the Cheapness." (p. 120)

If we talk about Sanjay Leela Bhansali's Padmaavat, which is based on the epic poem by the same name written by Sufi poet Malik Muhammad Jayasi in 1540, again many anomalies can be found. In a study titled 'Padmavati, the Legendary Woman, From Real to Reel Life (A Historic-Analytical Perspective)' Rachna Mehta, while analyzing Jayasi's poem, also talks about different versions of the story stating, "Many other written and oral tradition versions of her life exist in Hindu and Jain traditions. These versions differ from the Sufi poet Jayasi's version." (Mehta, 2018,

p. 58) Criticizing the changes or alterations that occur in the chronicles through stage, films or printed literature, she further says, "It is required that nobody should change the chronicles and historical facts for the sake of providing entertainment to the people. History is not meant for any change. Once something becomes history, it is unaltered history forever." (p. 61)

Discussion and Analysis

There's a general trend of Bollywood movies becoming part of popular culture. This holds true for the historical period movies as well. Be it the terrifying character of Sultan Khilji dancing to Khalibali or the victorious and spirited Peshwa Bajirao shaking a leg on Malhari or the elegant queen Padmavati performing a graceful Ghoomar; all these acts and performances become a part of popular culture and are remembered by people for a very long time. Therefore, it becomes extremely important how these historic personalities are portrayed on screen.

In 'Figuring the Past- Period Film and the Mannerist Aesthetic' Belen Vidal explains period films as:

> Films, in which, the 'the Past' (as original myth or foundational moment) resonates in the present through the visual (and aural) spectacle of pastness, and its intricate signs. The period films stages a return to a place and time whose codes may seem strange and, more often than not, irrelevant. However, period objects and rituals are a source of continuing fascination, which accounts for the genre's enduring popularity. (Vidal, 2012, p. 9)

Indeed period films do fascinate the audiences with their extravagance as well as the fact that they are based on the real lives of the historic figures who not only are big names from the past but are also an innate part of the country's folklores. Thus, watching those characters, about whom people have just heard or read about, coming to life on screen is actually enchanting.

But unfortunately, there is a severe lack of awareness about these historic figures and their real tales. Also, it is indeed hard to confirm the accurate facts as there are different sources of information with varied versions of the same story and very few people actually take the pain of going through the historic texts before or after watching a movie and thus rely mainly on the film as the source of information. Thus, the cinema takes place of history instructor for a large number of people. But when Bollywood distorts or alters the history for a better or more entertaining narrative; wrong and misleading messages are sent to the audience, who in turn may believe in that message and perceive the history as shown in the movie. This is a matter of serious concern, especially for the younger audience which rely on movies and television for information and has little knowledge about facts, as such distortion can change their perception of history forever.

Though, it is true that film-makers do give a disclaimer at the beginning to inform people, but the fact remains that the impact of cinema is so strong that it getsinto people's imagination, play with their emotions and ultimately influences them into believing it.

Here, this study will elaborate about the issue of distortion of history in period films by taking certain cases and talking about the various conflicting versions of the story and the version presented in the movie.

Jodhaa-Akbar (2008)

Jodhaa Akbar is a historical period movie, set in 16th century co-written, produced and directed by Ashutosh Gowariker. The film revolves around the love story of the Rajput princess Jodha Bai who is forced to marry Mughal Emperor Akbar for a political alliance. In fact, the love story of Jodha and Akbar has served as a base plot for several movies and television series. However, many historians claim that the character of Jodha did not even exist!

According to a report of Times of India, renowned historian and former chairman of Indian Council of Historical Research, Prof. Irfan Habib asserts, "There was not any historical character called Jodha Bai. It's true that Akbar married Amber ruler Raja

Bharmal's eldest daughter but her name is not mentioned anywhere. And she was certainly not Jahangir's mother. Even Jahangir in his memoirs (Tuzuk-i-Jahangiri) does not mention anything about his mother's side." (Sharma, 2006) The report further quoted former president of Indian History Congress and chairman of history department, Aligarh University, Prof. Iqtedar Alam Khan saying that, "It is only a Punjab historian Sujan Rai Bhandari, who in his book Khulasat-ut-Tawarikh mentions for the first time that the Amber princess whom Akbar married was Jahangir's mother. But even Rai does not refer to her as Jodha Bai." In fact, even the biography of Akbar, Akbarnama, does not mention that Akbar had any Hindu Rajput wife by the name Jodha Bai. (IMDb, 2008)

This is not all. There is another twist to this tale. When the movie was set to release, it was met with strong backlash from some Rajput groups who accused that the movie has distorted the history. According to them, Jodhaa was the daughter of Udai Singh of Marwar and was married to Salim, Akbar's son. (Sharma, 2006)

The question then arises is that if there are doubts regarding the very existence of Jodha Bai, how can a film-maker serve a mere folklore as a slice of history. In such confusing situation, one cannot be sure if there was any relationship between Jodha and Akbar and there is definitely a possibility that this entire concept of love story between these two can be simply a fantasy or cooked up story. But if we see from layman's point of view, we realise that Jodha and Akbar have now become a part of popular culture and everyone associate them as lovers and married couple. This concept has travelled from the silver screen to small screen as well with numerous shows presenting the story of Jodha Akbar with their own twist and turns.

Bajirao Mastani (2015)

Bajirao Mastani, directed by Sanjay Leela Bhansali, starring Ranveer Singh, Deepika Padukone and Priyanka Chopra as Peshwa Bajirao, Mastani and Kashibai, also landed into controversy as soon as its trailers and songs came out. The movie was based on

N.S. Inamdar's Marathi novel 'Rau'. As soon as the song 'Pinga' was released, the descendents of the historic figures shown in the movie started accusing Bhansali for misinterpreting the history. The song even invited a petition as it was considered offensive to Marathi culture. A descendent of queen Kashibai, who wished not to be named, claimed that Kashibai suffered from an arthritis-like ailment at a very young age and was bed-ridden for most of her life. (Indian Express, 2015) She further added that Kashibai also suffered from asthma, and hence it was highly impossible that she danced with Mastani as shown in Pinga.

Similarly revolting groups reportedly also claimed that Kashibai and Mastani met only once, that too formally. However, in the movie, they share a number of scenes together and are shown dancing together as well.

Apart from that, there was much disapproval about the costumes of Deepika and Priyanka in the song 'Pinga'.

Protesters who opposed the release of Bhansali's magnum opus also issued a release stating that "The trailers and promotional videos of the movie prove that it is an attempt to distort the historical figures of Maharashtra and Bundelkhand, requesting the concerned people to remove these trailers and the objectionable content from the movie, which does not comply with the actual history." (TNN, 2015)

The protesters also gave a brief account of the history and said that, "When Bundelkhand was attacked by Muhammad Shah Bangash, Chhatrasal Bundela asked Bajirao Peshwa to intervene. Bajirao defeated Bangash and was offered Mastani's hand by Bundela, her father. She came in Bajirao's life in 1722 and died in 1740." (TNN, 2015)

Now, the movie claims to be an adaption of the novel 'Rau'. However, the film's narrative deviates from the novel's storyline too. For instance, in the book 'Rau', Mastani was not a princess, but simply a dancer who fell in love with Peshwa and he too fell for her and their love bloomed. In the paper titled 'Transformation of the Book into Cinema: A Critical Perspective on a Bollywood Movie Bajirao-Mastani', Ajaonkar & Talule (2017) mentioned, "Mastani of Rau is an ordinary dancer with a common background and of Muslim religion but Mastani of Bhansali is a half Muslim princess of Bundelkhand, the daughter of King Chhatrasal by his Muslim wife." (p. 121) They further stated, "The novel doesn't portray what happens to Mastani later on, while taking cinematic description, the movie shows both of their deaths." (p. 121)

Yet again, the story of the movie doesn't match either with the accounts of the people who claim to be the descendents of the historic figures nor truly to the novel of which it is an adaptation. But ultimately, people who got effected due to such distortion or misinterpretation of history were the common movie goers who watched the film with great enthusiasm and appreciation and came back convinced with the true love of Bajirao and Mastani. But the question remains whether it is even a true account or are people again made to believe a newly framed history.

Padmaavat (2018)

Sanjay Leela Bhansali found himself yet again face to face with protestants who demonstrated sharply again his dream project based on the life and Jauhar of queen Padmavati or Padmini. The film starred Deepika Padukone as the legendary queen Padmavati, Shahid Kapoor as her husband Rawal Ratan Singh and Ranveer Singh as Delhi Sultanate ruler Alauddin Khilji.

The controversy sparked massively with the rumor of a dream sequence between Khilji and Padmavati. However, Bhansali cleared the air that there was no such dream sequence between the two, the protestors still accused Bhansali of manipulating with the historical facts.

The first thing to notice is the origin of the famous queen Padmaavat. According to the epic poem by Sufi poet Malik Muhammad Jayasi, she was the daughter of the king of Singhal kingdom, former Sri Lanka and got married to Rawal Ratan Singh and thus came to Chittor with him. (TNN, 2017)

However, there's another version (James Tod's version) which is quite different from the other versions. It mentions Padmini as the daughter of Hamir Sank, Chauhan ruler of Ceylon, while, Chittor was ruled by Lachhman Singh. Padmini married Bhim Singh and Alauddin besieged Chittor because he had heard many of her beauty. (TNN, 2017)

Though the ultimate result of both the stories is same that Alauddin Khilji besieges Chittor and queen Padmavati commits the brave act of Jauhar along with 16000 Rajput women to protect their honour from the intruding enemy.

But the most controversial thing is that many historian even question the existence of queen Padmavati as the first mention of her name is in Jayasi's poem by the name Padmavat, which was written 2 centuries after the depicted incidence.

Yet another twist in the story is that as per the report of India Today, another historian Aziz Ahmed, claims that it was Ghiyasuddin of Malwa and not Khilji who was obsessed with Rani Padmini. (Palat, 2017) According to the same report, this theory is also supported by the inscription in Udaipur, which said that Ghiyasuddin had faced a crushing defeat at the hands of a Rajput chieftain, Badal and Gora, in 1488, which also happened to be the name of the twins who helped Ratan Singh escape the fort, as mentioned by Jayasi in his Padmavat.

Similarly, there's a point of conflict about the death of Rawal Ratan Singh too. According to the epic poem by Jayasi, the Rajput king died in a duel with Devpal, the king of Kumbhalner. After which, the queen and other women committed Jauhar to save their dignity from Khilji who had already attacked Chittor. However, in the movie, Singh fights the duel with Khilji and dies.

Another gnawing fact is the representation of Sultan Khilji–a rough man with kohl rimmed eyes, scarred face, unruly hair and a man who eats flesh from bones like a savage. Such a representation of the Sultan also did not go well down some people who claim that Khilji was anything but a savage. According to a report of Hindustan Times, historian Rana Safvi claimed, "It was under his rule the Delhi Sultanate heavily drew from Persia, one of the oldest and most sophisticated civilisations of all time." (Hindustan Times, 2018) She further added that "The rulers followed the exact code of conduct and etiquette as in Persia. It would have been very formal — the eating, dining and sartorial choices."

No doubt, the movie did portrayed the queen as a head-strong and brave woman who braced death over humiliation at the hands of the enemy and saved her honour. But again, if there's some misinterpretation of history in any way, it will surely leave the audience with a wrong perception of history at the end.

Conclusion

Thus, from the cases considered and the secondary material studied for the research, it is evident that distortion and misinterpretation of history does occur in Bollywood to a great extend. Such distortion has the power to completely change the history and image of historic figures for people, specially youngster who watch the movies and get misguided by whatever is portrayed onscreen.

It can further be studied in subsequent researches that to what extend does such period dramas effect the youth and what is their level of knowledge and awareness regarding the actual historical facts.

REFERENCES

Kouyoumdjian, H. (2012, July 12). Learning Through Visuals. Retrieved from https://www.psychologytoday.com/us/blog/get-psyched/201207/learning-through-visuals

Kumar, K. J. (2010). *Mass Communication in India*.

Ajaonkar, S. R., & Talule, D. C. (2017). *Transformation of the Book into Cinema: A Critical Perspective on a Bollywood Movie Bajirao-Mastani.*

Mehta, R. (2018, February). Padmavati, the Legendary Woman, From Real to Reel Life (A Historic-Analytical Perspective).

Vidal, B. (2012). *'Figuring the Past- Period Film and the Mannerist Aesthetic.*

Sharma, R. (2006, September 16). *Did a JodhaBai ever exist, ask historians - Times of India.* Retrieved from https://timesofindia.indiatimes.com/india/Did-a-Jodha-Bai-ever-exist-ask-historians/articleshow/1996384.cms

IMDb. (2008). *Jodhaa Akbar (2008).* Retrieved from https://www.imdb.com/title/tt0449994/goofs

Express Web Desk. (2015, December 16). *Major controversies that have hit 'BajiraoMastani'.* Retrieved from https://indianexpress.com/article/entertainment/bollywood/major-controversies-that-have-hit-deepika-padukone-ranveer-singhs-bajirao-mastani/

TNN. (2015, December 15). BajiraoMastani controversy: Bhansali's effigy burnt in Pune! - Times of India ?. Retrieved from https://timesofindia.indiatimes.com/entertainment/hindi/bollywood/news/Bajirao-Mastani-controversy-Bhansalis-effigy-burnt-in-Pune/articleshow/50182583.cms

TNN. (2017, November 17). Rani Padmavati history: Know the complete story of Rani Padmavati - Times of India. Retrieved from https://timesofindia.indiatimes.com/life-style/spotlight/rani-padmavati-history-know-the-complete-story-of-rani-padmavati/articleshow/61685630.cms

Hindustan Times. (2018, January 25). Whose history is it anyway: Padmaavat taints AlauddinKhilji, not Padmavati. Retrieved from https://www.hindustantimes.com/bollywood/whose-history-is-it-anyway-padmaavat-taints-alauddin-khilji-not-padmavati/story-MvpB4OREqm4auO0nVHKt5K.html

Palat, L. N. (2017, November 22). Padmavati row: Who was Rani Padmavati's husband MaharawalRatan Singh?. Retrieved from https://www.indiatoday.in/movies/bollywood/story/padmavati-who-was-rani-padmini-husband-maharawal-ratan-singh-1091009-2017-11-21

12

Studying Approach of Indian Community towards Indian Cinema of Different Periods

Nidhi Suryavanshi

Introduction

In this paper I want to give a glimpse towards the growth of Indian cinema with the different time periods. Cinema continues to be one of the most prolific cinemas in the world; critical texts examining this cinema are on the rise. While Indian cinema's influence increases globally, however, a persistent streak remains in its study, namely, an adherence to the concept of the nation-state, whose underpinnings are used to frame the subsequent discussion of Indian cinema. This tendency ensues despite an acknowledgement of Indian cinema's increasingly global span as well as its increasingly transnational composition.

If we see the complete history of Indian cinema then it all can be fit into two boxes as pure commercial and other side also subjective films. But there is included as in which manner Indian cinema been degraded with time, as films are mainly become a source of earning money and includes more violence, abusive language, sex, and vulgarity.

And primarily the focus area of this research includes is how 1950s and 1960s are considered to be the golden era of Indian cinema

And 1970s is identified as pioneer of masala movies.

1990s introduces technology to elevate and upgrade Indian cinema.

21st century cinema is completely changed with new concepts and elements.

Methodology

For the study an online survey was conducted on twitter and accordingly the data was collected.

- 100% people voted Acting as the main element been changed in 21st century cinema.
- 75% people like old film 90s to 20s.
- 25% people like new film of 21st century.
- 50% people think originality and depth in making film has disappeared in 21st century.
- 60% people think 'More sexual content' is the most interesting part and 20% voted for acting and 20% for storyline of 21st century's cinema.
- 100% think originality is the most interesting part of old films.

Literature Review

Indian cinema is 'unquestionably nationally dominance' as blending theatrical and cinematic element. Plus an assortment of western and indigenous genres such as musical, dance, drama and melodrama; such a blending also referred to as masala (a spicy mix), pioneer movies.

Satyajit Ray, for instance, called the bollywood film 'a well-mixed potpourri of popular entertainment.'

He directly linked this composition to an audience comprised of 'tired untutored minds with undeveloped tastes'.

Kazmi 1999 identified Indian cinema as a commercial or conventional.

Just as the Indian cinema rather than neatly fitting into any one category, defines itself through its parody and transgression of each, such a critical intervention will be achieved through a combination of fields and approaches, including the filmic, theatrical, ethnographic, and postcolonial.

Kakar, for instance, likens the Indian film to 'daydream' and claims that the reason for its resounding success in India is due to the Indian psyche's ability to 'regress temporarily to childhood modes'. This is because 'in India the child's world of magic is not as far removed from adult consciousness as it may be in some other cultures' (Kakar 1989)

It might be true because from beginning 'cinema' word is completely attached with the word of 'entertainment' that today's audience could not imagine any seriousness from this, they knows that the life of stage is not the truth of life, even they cries with it and they laughs with it. They believe to watch this world of dream is only an entertainment, but in mean while they forget that dream is also an expression of their inner world, their inner consciousness. That is why the life of cinema cannot be differentiated from the audiences' life.

Main Body of Paper/Argument

The paper shows how at the beginning Indian cinema been born and how it grows from different time periods it didn't become static instead a dynamic slide. A flowing river that continually changes, and adapted good things and also few negative things. As society, economy, culture and the changing mindset influence cinema. India's 100-year film history spans colonialism, independence, partition, and globalization.

Where at the one side Indian cinema from beginning struggled with social customs at the next side also has made films on romance and family oriented. As few films make save and nourish the social values at next few also do work of breaking them. Indian cinema has played double role in making and breaking the basic and well-arranged system of society.

In 1950s and 1960s when most of the Classics were Made

K. Asif's Mughal-e-Azam, Guru Dutt's Pyaasa, Kagaz ke Phool, Raj Kapoor's Awara, and Shree 420, Mehboob Khan's Mother India kind of extraordinary films came and made it golden era of Indian cinema in the manner of everything as legendary actors as Nargis, Meena Kumari, Madhubala, Nutan, Waheeda Rehman, and Sadhna. And male actors as considered incomparable from today as exceptional Raj Kapoor, Dilip Kumar, Guru Dutt and ultimate trend setting superstar Dev Anand. And all the directors, storyline base on social themes such as challenges of working class and chaotic lifestyle of urban situated people. The depth of acting, music, the originality and the authenticity including all the era gave Indian cinema a lot more than any other period in the cinema's existence.

These classics inspired and influenced both Indian cinemas for decades to amplify and to follow. This era started after independence that given the birth of the modern Indian and Indian-western touch in cinema.

1970s the Pioneer of Masala Movies

Masala films are the holy grail of mainstream Hindi films in terms of genre; it is like the king of all genres,

Masala films – to meant the continental spice mix, as multi-star flicks that contained a little each of all genres, comedy, drama, musical and romance and it becomes major crowd-volition.

Sholay – action, adventure, and comedy

Deewaar – action, crime, drama

Anand – drama

Gol Maal – comedy, drama, romance,

Aakrosh – drama, mystery, thriller

Pakeezah – musical, romance, drama

Trishul – multi-starrer, action, drama, musical

Don – Action, crime, thriller

Nagin – Fantasy, thriller, action

1990s changes the complete scenario as we used to watch films

A complete new batch of actor entered in cinema and new technologies introduces that make an exceptional change in Indian cinema. As we were introduced to colour TV, DD Metro, cable channels, and watched everything from Hollywood 'Titanic' to bollywood 'Andaz Apna Apna.'

Films of different kind as family centric– Hum Aapke Hain Koun...', Hum Hain Rahi Pyar Ke, Naam, Kroadh, Hero No. 1 and film like 'Rangeela' (1995) a decade defining film also came in 90s as not for entertainment or a sensorial piece instead as a very example of beauty and art.

2000 to 21st century films make a big diverse shift in Indian cinema.

In this era advanced technology was introduced in the country. This phase introduced a lot of technical advancements in the ways movies are made. From Koi Mil Gaya (2003) till Ra One (2011), movies put a greater emphasis on the visual effects rather than the story. The content, storyline and the music everything changes because the cinema and audiences both are reciprocal as the society changes cinema will definitely change.

Where expression of love changes it includes fear, anger, euphoria and all emotions, action films changed with special effects and trained stunt men. Comedy film changes, traveling based films came and the biggest shift is towards women-centric films those completely turned the route of Indian cinema such as Highway,

Queen, Piku, Kahani, Tanu weds Manu, Mardani and so more; as before Indian cinema been suffused by the mindset of man-prominence. There wasn't any independent character, not any strong existence and any heroic portray.

'Chokher Bali' 2003 film seems as a silent painting of unsuccessful love story, some films made as to fill the passion of doing anything for nation such as 'Chak De India', 'Rang De Basanti', and then 'Halla Bol' and films like 'A Wednesday' attract much praises.

'Three Idiots' 2010 of Rajkumar Hirani become a mile-stone in Indian cinema and as given the sublime message 'knowledge is much necessary then information in education'.

Conclusion

Indian cinema has prided itself on being a sole distraction and recess industry for nearly a century. Indian cinema used to take the content and ingredients from society and literature both since beginning of its development. The casual link between cinema and society is such that society is the cause and the cinematic content is the effect. Nationalism, religion, history, politics, crime, violence, corruption and more are its favorite subjects. One thing is very clear that the growth of Indian cinema includes consistency and magnitude but also it falls in some manner. As violence, abusive content, nudity, sex and poor acting get add but in mean-while number of films been possible to imprint its mark on society and also in business.

Indian cinema is a 'commercial' aesthetic, and as comprising many number of song and dance numbers endorses consumerism. Today Indian cinema reconciles global consumer lifestyle with traditional 'Indian values'.

REFERENCE

Book– Theories of Popular Hindi Cinema by

PART 4
Regulation and Antagonism in Indian Cinema

13

Freedom of Speech and Expression of Filmmakers/ Artists and Censorship

Kush Kalra

Introduction

"I may not agree with what you say, but will defend to the death, your right to say it", said the author Voltaire (Attributed to Voltaire by S.G. Tallentyre in "The Friends of Voltaire", 1907).

India has the benefit of one of the most modern and liberal Constitutions. It is reflective of its rich and diverse heritage, yet enunciating the modern principles of democracy, as distinguished from a feudal society. One of the most cherished rights under our Constitution is to speak one's mind and write what one thinks. No doubt, this is subject to reasonable restrictions, but then the ambit of what one can do is wide.

Whether the society is ready to read a particular book and absorb what it says without being offended, is a debate which has been raging for years together. Times have changed. What was not acceptable earlier became acceptable later. "Lady Chatterley's Lover" is a classical example of it. The choice to read is always with the reader. If you do not like a book, throw it away. There is no compulsion to read a book. Literary tastes may vary – what is right and acceptable to one may not be so to others. Yet, the right to write is unhindered[1]. If the contents seek to challenge or go against the very Constitutional values, raise racial issues, denigrate[2] castes, contain blasphemous[3] dialogues, carry unacceptable sexual contents or start a war against the very existence of our country, the State would, no doubt, step in.

The very heart of democracy is the freedom to think and act differently. Implicit therein is a freedom to react and respond to same situations differently and distinctly. The very charm of democracy is that there are multiple views, thoughts and expressions. One cannot expect everybody to express themselves in the same manner. There is fresh blood injected in the film industry. This fresh blood is definitely enthusiastic and wants to set its foot in the industry. Such fresh blood has been welcomed by the film industry and the viewing public. Their works have been accepted, applauded[4] and even rewarded by the State. These works are based on a certain thinking and which is of their own. They hold independent views and thoughts not only on how the film industry must function, but the medium as a whole should be handled. They feel that film is a powerful and strong medium and its potential has remained unutilized or under-utilized.

The film makers of today may feel that their predecessors sold dreams and seldom dared to portray reality. They created an audience loyal to them by churning out love stories or such stories which had no connection with the common man's day-to-day existence and life. The stories of Kings and Queens, the stories of those wealthy and rich who never faced the pangs of hunger nor suffered because of unemployment and poverty, therefore, occupied most of the screen time.

Thus, pure entertaining and escapist stuff was thrown at the viewing public without any variety and for years together. There were few noteworthy exceptions to this unwritten rule. The audience was cultivated and made to accept this work which in the opinion of today's film makers hardly did credit to the worth of the medium nor brought any laurels to the industry. Of course today's youth admire, appreciate and respect some of the yesterday icons and their work. They are aware that even during the times when the films were unreal, mere fantasies, there were film makers who presented the other side. All such film makers were respected and are noteworthy for they opened up our mind to "Bharat" and not concentrated only on "India". The poor, the lower middle class and the middle class found place and voice in their work.

Yet, according to the present-day film makers, earlier work was not complete and does not deserve to be carried forward in the same way. It is such ideology which has influenced today's film making. Therefore, a direct depiction[5], without fun and frolic, but brazen and bold, of the reality in the society is their focal theme. They do not wish to beat around the bush and hide problems like alcoholism, crime and terrorism prevalent in today's world. These makers are of the view that a serious, somewhat glory and detailed depiction of the vices in and threats to the society may open up the eyes of, not only the public, but public officials and the State. It is this desire as well which drives them to present their work in the manner currently presented by some of them. There is a contrary view in the society.

Men and women in administration or otherwise, teachers, professors, critics, writers, thinkers and experts in the field of science, medicine, technology, humanities etc. may feel that today's films have a temporary and short-term impact. Burning social, psychological problems and behavioral issues are not handled with enough sensitivity, maturity, compassion and conviction. At times, commerce and trade control the medium of films is the view expressed. This contrary perception of the medium must be welcomed because that is how an audience for films is developed and nurtured. Eventually, all wise men leave the fate of the film to the public.

Freedom of Speech and Expression

The State is obliged to create an atmosphere congenial for the development and promotion of art and culture consistent with the Constitutional mandate as enshrined in our Preamble[6].

The Constitution aims at securing to all its citizens liberty of thought, expression, belief, faith and worship. All its provisions are intended to uphold these fundamental values and when it secures its citizens justice, social, economic and political, equality of status and opportunity and to promote among them all fraternity[7] assuring the dignity of the individual and the unity and integrity of the Nation, then, not only the Board officials but even the film makers ought to realise that true democracy does not mean a license to dictate and foist[8] one's views and ideas on others. Equally it gives no license to nudity, vulgarity, indecency and immorality. The film makers also need to realise that a repetitive and one-sided depiction and exposure would generate nausea[9] and aversion. The audience expects a package. If it does not get it in that form and measure, it would walk out. At times it may not only like to know about the defects and infirmities in the working of the Police or State machinery, but would expect some solutions as well.

Therefore, it is for the film makers to decide and take a call on whether they need to mould themselves and their ideas in the changing times. Surely, the State and particularly the Central Board of Film Certification cannot, in the garb of alleged public interest or audience taste, try to mould, shape and control public opinion. That would be disastrous and would strike at the very root of the democracy and the fundamental freedom so dearly cherished by all. A balance and blend in right measure, of entertainment and message, may be required so that the objectives of film certificattion are achieved.

According to it (CBFC) the objectives, particularly of ensuring that the medium of film remains responsible and sensitive to the values and standards of society, the medium of films provides clean and healthy entertainment and as far as possible, the film is of aesthetic[10] value and cinematically of a good standard may enable the Board to certify films with cuts and deletions, but it must not overlook or brush aside equally important objectives of not unduly curbing artistic expression and creative freedom and its certification being responsive to social change.

Thus, the objectives of film certification cannot be applied ignoring the Constitutional guarantee or to defeat and frustrate it completely. The Board certifies films for exhibiting them to the members of public or restricted sections or classes of the same and not necessarily censors them.

If the creative freedom as guaranteed by Article 19 (1) (a) to the makers and of choosing any theme and selecting characters to indicate as to how any issue concerning the society has assumed serious proportions, then, within the four corners of the Cinematograph Act, 1952, the authorities must decide as to whether the work/film is fit to be certified not for universal public viewing but by the adults. True it is that some cuts can be made.

Judiciary and Freedom of Speech and Expression

In *S. Rangarajan v. P. Jagjivan Ram and Ors.*[11] , while interpreting Article 19 (2) High Court borrowed from the American test of clear and present danger and observed:

> *"Our commitment to freedom of expression demands that it cannot be suppressed unless the situations created by allowing the freedom are pressing and the community interest is endangered. The anticipated danger should not be remote, conjectural or far-fetched. It should have proximate and direct nexus with the expression. The expression of thought should be intrinsically dangerous to the public interest.*

Public decency and morality is outside the purview of the protection of free speech and expression, and thus a balance should be maintained between freedom of speech and expression and public decency and morality but the former must never come in the way of the latter and should not substantially transgress the latter.

Freedom of Expression and Duty of the State to Protect Rights

1. *S. Rangarajan v. P. Jagjivan Ram*[12], the case related to the revocation[13] of the 'U Certificate'[14] granted to the film

'Ore Oru Gramathile[15]', which was an anti-reservation film. There were protests against this film.

It was held therein that the effect of the so called offending words must be judged from the standards of reasonable, strong minded, firm and courageous men and not those of weak and vacillating minds. It was further held that the State cannot plead its inability to handle the problem of hostile audience. It is its obligatory duty to prevent it and protect the freedom of expression.

2. *Prakash Jha Productions v. Union of India*[16], case involved the suspension of the Hindi film 'Aarakshan' by the State of Uttar Pradesh even after the Censor Certificate was issued on grounds that it would cause a 'law and order' issue.

   The Supreme Court held that the film was to be allowed to be screened. 'Law and order' maintenance was the duty of the State. The Court held that it is the duty of the State to maintain law and order and therefore, the State shall maintain it effectively and potentially.

3. *Srishti School of Art, Design & Technology v. Chairperson, Central Board of Film Certification*[17], in this case, the makers of the documentary called 'Had Anhad' were asked to carry out cuts, which the petitioner protested against.

   It was held that the cuts proposed were violative of the petitioner's right to free speech and expression and was allowed.

   The Court observed that the Indian Constitution provides a democratic space to voice views unacceptable to others but for the reason it is unacceptable, it cannot be prevented from being expressed.

   It was thus held that a book must be read as a whole and the context must not be ignored and it is reasonable to see what would be the reaction of a common reader.

4. *LYCA Productions Pvt. Ltd. v. Government of Tamil Nadu*[18], in this case, the producers of the popular Tamil commercial feature film 'Kathi' were Sri Lankans and the film was objected to owing to the nationality of its producers. They were forced to sign an agreement to remove their names from the movie hoardings, which the police attempted to enforce against them.

   High Court held agreement not valid and cannot be enforced. It was observed that the letter of undertaking cannot be relied upon by the Police, which cannot grant a seal of approval to such letters of undertaking, as the same tantamounts to the creation of a super-censor Board. It was further observed that the police should not permit attempts of such blackmails to succeed, which if allowed, would automatically lead to extortion and the surrender of power of governance and the rule of law to a few intolerant people.

5. *Ajay Gautam v. Union of India*[19], the movie 'PK[20]' was sought to be banned on the grounds that it hurt the religious sentiments of the Hindus and violated the rights of the Hindus under Article 19(2).

   Holding that no one is captive audience and it is a conscious choice of a viewer, who is free to avoid watching the film, the case was dismissed.

6. *S. Khushboo v. Kanniammal*[21], this case pertained to the quashing of cases filed against the petitioner[22] for remarks made by her on pre-marital sex.

   High Court observed that a culture of responsible reading is to be inculcated amongst the prudent readers. Morality and criminality are far from being co-extensive. An expression of opinion in favour of non-dogmatic and non-conventional morality has to be tolerated as the same cannot be a ground to penalize the author.

7. *Sony Pictures v. State*[23], in this case, the ban imposed by the State of Tamil Nadu on the English film 'The Da Vinci Code' was challenged.

A learned single Judge of High Court observed that when the State has a duty to prevent all threats of demonstrations and processions which amount to intimidating the right of freedom of expression, it cannot plead its inability to handle breach of peace if and when it arises. The order imposing the ban on the film was thus quashed.

Conclusion

In today's world, new generation of film makers born in the 80s has entered the scene. We cannot expect that they will present current and live issues and problems in the same manner as the older or earlier generation. They want to chart a course of their own, uninfluenced by earlier works. A certain degree of freshness, a change of attitude and a different way of looking at the same medium by itself and without anything more should not result in bringing about disruptions or creating hurdles and obstacles in their way. To stop them abruptly and by extreme responses will not only discourage them but may kill creativity. If they are allowed to go ahead in their own way but with timely cautioning and warning, they may respond positively and take the same in proper spirit.

However, to interfere with their work again and again, mindlessly will only invite extreme reactions. That would not be conducive to the growth of the medium. Eventually, it must march with the times and compete with the best of the works made locally and globally. That apart, the appeal of the social media, the advent of television which operates on a multi channel basis 24X7 resulting in large scale production and distribution of teleserials, teledramas, telefilms presents a enormous challenge and is virtually threatening the existence or efficacy of a celluloid[24] film. A full length feature film needs to hold the audience to the seat for certain hours. Its story line, theme, script and the overall content should have that capacity and potency. Else, the audience interest will wane and vanish. Hence, filmmakers, producers, directors of today have changed their strategies.

The filmmakers of today are direct, forthright, attacking, aggressive and even brutal in their presentation. It is not only in the technical departments but in the story telling as well they have set their own standards. There is a marked deviation from the earlier genre[25] and an attempt to create a unique style on par with film making and presentation internationally. Just because they are not soft, subtle in their approach, one cannot be unduly strict and harsh. Holding up the certificates or suggesting cuts and excisions in virtually every alternate scene would not be counterproductive.

Suggestions

(*i*) There is bound to be a presumption in favour of free speech and expression as envisaged under Article 19 (1) (a) of the Constitution of India unless a court of law finds it otherwise as falling within the domain of a reasonable restriction under Article 19 (2) of the Constitution of India. This presumption must be kept in mind if there are complaints against publications, art, drama, film, song, poem, cartoons or any other creative expressions.

(*ii*) The State's responsibility to maintain law and order would not permit any compulsion on the artistes concerned to withdraw from his/her stand and non-State players cannot be allowed to determine what is permissible and what is not.

(*iii*) It is high time the Government constitutes an expert body to deal with situations arising from such conflicts of views, such expert body to consist of qualified persons in the branch of creative literature and art so that an independent opinion is forthcoming, keeping in mind the law evolved by the judiciary. In such matters of art and culture, the issue cannot be left to the police authorities or the local administration alone, especially when there is a spurt in such conflicts.

(*iv*) The State has to ensure proper police protection where such authors and artistes come under attack from a section of the society.

(*v*) Regular programmes need to be conducted for sensitizing officials over matters dealing with such conflicts of artistic and literary appreciation.

REFERENCES

1. **Meaning of unhindered:** Not slowed or blocked or interfered with
2. **Meaning of denigrate:**
   1. To attack the character or reputation of; speak ill of; defame
   2. To disparage; belittle
3. **Meaning of blasphemy:** The crime committed if a person insults, offends, or vilifies the deity
4. **Meaning of applaud:** To express approval, especially by clapping the hands.
5. **Meaning of depict:**
   1. To represent in a picture or sculpture
   2. To represent in words; describe
6. **Meaning of preamble:**
   1. A preliminary statement, especially:
      a. The introduction to a formal document that explains its purpose.
      b. A statement accompanying a law or regulation specifying its purpose or reason for enactment.
   2. An introductory occurrence or fact; a preliminary.
7. **Meaning of fraternity:**
   1. A body of people associated for a common purpose or interest, such as a guild.
   2. A group of people joined by similar backgrounds, occupations, interests, or tastes
8. **Meaning of foist:**
   1. To pass off as genuine, valuable, or worthy
   2. To impose (something or someone unwanted) upon another by coercion or trickery

9. **Meaning of nausea:**

   1. A feeling of sickness in the stomach characterized by an urge to vomit.

   2. Strong aversion; disgust.

10. **Meaning of aesthetic:**

    1. Relating to the philosophy or theories of aesthetics.

    2.

    a. Of or concerning the appreciation of beauty or good taste

    b. Attractive or appealing

11. (1989) 2 SCC 574

12. (1989) 2 S.C.C. 574

13. **Meaning of revocation:** The act or an instance of revoking.

14. **U** (Unrestricted Public Exhibition): Films with the U certification are fit for public exhibition, and are often family friendly. These films can contain universal themes like education, family, drama, romance, sci - fi, and action etc. Now, these films can also contain some mild violence, but it should not be prolonged. It may also contain very mild sexual scenes (without any traces of nudity or sexual detail).

15. ***Ore Oru Gramathile*** is a 1989 Tamil Indian feature film directed by K. Jyothi Pandian. The film stars Lakshmi and Nizhalgal Ravi in the lead roles. The film was banned for criticizing caste based reservations. The Supreme Court of India later allowed its release.

16. (2011) 8 S.C.C 372

17. 2011 (123) D.R.J.

18. 2014 S.C.C. Online Mad. 1448

19. 2015 S.C.C. Online Del 6479

20. ***PK*** is a 2014 Indian satirical science fiction comedy film. The film was directed by Rajkumar Hirani, produced by Hirani and Vidhu Vinod Chopra, and written by Hirani and Abhijat Joshi. The film stars Aamir Khan in the title role with Anushka Sharma, Sushant Singh Rajput, Boman Irani, Saurabh Shukla, and Sanjay Dutt in supporting roles. It tells the story of an alien who comes to Earth on a research mission. He befriends a television journalist and questions religious dogmas and superstitions.

21. 2010 (5) S.C.C. 600

22. **Meaning of petitioner:** A person who presents a petition

23. 2006 3 L.W. 728

24. **Meaning of celluloid:**

    1. A colorless flammable material made from nitrocellulose and camphor and used to make photographic film.

    2. **a.** Motion-picture film

       b. The cinema; motion pictures

25. **Meaning of genre:**

    a. A category of artistic composition, as in music or literature, marked by a distinctive style, form, or content

    b. A realistic style of painting that depicts scenes from everyday life.

14

Indian Cinema: Role of Censorship in Indian Society

Dr. Radhika Mehta and Divya Khera

Introduction

Censorship is the censoring of books, plays, films, or reports, especially by government officials because they are considered immoral or secret in some way.

"*Censorship is when a work of art expressing an idea which does not fall under current convention is seized, cut up, withdrawn, impounded, ignored, maligned, or otherwise made inaccessible to its audience.*"

— Ritu Menon, for Women's World Organisation for Rights, Literature, and Development

The term 'censorship' comes from the Latin Word 'censere' meaning to give one's opinion, or to assess. In ancient Rome the censors, two Roman magistrates, conducted the census and regulated the manners and morals of the citizens.

Censorship's may be applied to both written and oral communications. Its span encompasses books, magazines, newspapers, radio, TV, movies, dramas, paintings, plays, speeches, dance, music, art, literature, photographs, mails, emails, websites etc. deemed to be offensive, indecent, obscene and sexually explicit.

Methods

Censorship methodologies include suppression, prohibition, formal book banning, pressure not to acquire works, proscription, removal, suspension of publication, and restriction of access to electronic materials. The use of legislation, law suits, licensing, registration requirements, filtering software, or codes of behavior may all constitute methods of censorship.

What is Cinema?

Cinema is an artistic expression of ideas, stories and often opinions sometimes inspired by reality occasionally set to music, designed to mesmerize and enchant or simply to entertain. There are hardly any other mediums of expression that can actually change our perception about any issue prevailing in the society. A film motivates thought & action and assures a high degree of attention & retention as compared to the printed word. The combination of act and speech, sight and sound in semi darkness of the theatre with elimination of all distracting ideas will have a strong impact on the minds of the viewers and can affect emotions. Therefore, it has as much potential for evil as it has for good and has an equal potential to instill or cultivate violent or bad behavior. It cannot be equated with other modes of communication.

So, **Film censorship** becomes necessary because censorship by prior restraint is, therefore, not only desirable but also necessary. It is a systematic ban on films and other cinematic makings. Observing audience taste for films may sometimes reflects negativity and anti-social scenes in the scripts which are constitutionally prohibited. Those scenes are clipped off from the movies this process is called film censorship.

Cinematographic films are the most attractive means of exercising the freedom of speech and expression. The films have been banned due to various issues such as, obscenity, sex, violence, maintaining public order in the society, respecting religious beliefs and sentiments and traditional values of a particular cultural group or the film may involve in criticizing against the State on certain subjects under various provisions.

What is Cinematograph Act, 1952?

The Wikipedia defines that **Central Board of Film Certification** is a statutory censorship and classification body under the Ministry of Information and Broadcasting, Government of India. It is tasked with "regulating the public exhibition of films under the provisions of the Cinematograph Act 1952". Films can be publicly exhibited in India only after they are certified by the Board, including films shown on television. CBFC India is considered to be one of the most powerful film censor boards in the world due to its strict ways of functioning.

The Central Board of Film Certification has mainly four kinds of certifications:

U – Universal – Unrestricted Public Exhibition throughout India and holds no restriction for age groups. They might contain educational, family, or social oriented themes. They may also include fantasy violence or minimal or mild bad languages.

UA – Parental guidance – This category explains that the film is suitable for all ages, however it is best if children below 12 are accompanied by parents, as the theme may be a bit inappropriate for the child. These rated films may include mature themes, mild sex scenes, sexual references, mild violence or infrequent use of crude language.

A – Adults Only – This is restricted to adults audience only, that means those above 18 years of age. Films in this category may contain adult or disturbing themes, brutal violence, strong sex scenes, or scenes of drug abuse, which is not suitable for the minors.

S – Restricted to any special class of persons – These rated films are for a special class like in the case of doctors.

Importance of Film Censorship

Official accounts claim that Indian film industry is the largest in the world producing over a thousand films in a year screened over 13,000 cinema halls in the country. Every week an audience as large as the country's entire population flocks to the cinema hall.

If we analyze the history of film censorship in India, one can state that a film is banned or censored on the following reasons: i) Sexuality, ii) Religion, iii) Communal conflict, iv) Incorrect portrayal of someone or something, v) Extreme violence, vi) Politics

(i) **Sexuality**: Indian society has been following a firm social structure. A medium whether written or audio-visual portraying sexuality which has not been accepted by Indian society openly is banned on the ground that it may degrade the morals of Indians. On this ground,***Kamasutra,*** an erotic film was banned in India because of its depiction of sexual content. ***Murder***, this super-hit movie had bold scenes between Mallika Sherawat and Emraan Hashmi which shocked the masses and stirred controversies across India. Sexuality has never been discussed openly in India. Some religions completely discourage all forms of sexuality. It is a fact in our day today life which is always kept secret. Even imparting sex education in schools has always been debatable topic but still it is not a part of the syllabi.

(ii) **Religion**: Religion as an institution does not approve any kind of disobedience towards the values it propagates. Any medium that distorts the religious characters of a religion is criticized and censored by the same. Religious sentiment does cause film censorship in India. The film ***PK*** was caught up in controversy as it was a satire on various sensitive issues like political beliefs, religion and superstitions which are so deeply rooted in the social consciousness of India. Hindutva groups took offence to certain scenes, while some others pointed out that the film "unnecessarily" mocked Hindu beliefs and rituals. There were also concerns that the film did not reach any

conclusion on the existence of religion, but simply questioned superstitions.

(iii) **Caste and Communal Conflict**: A film is also censored if it incites any kind of communal conflict under a heterogeneous nation. Heterogeneity is a feature of India as a nation. The film ***Aarakshan*** touched the sensitive nerves of some people when it portrayed the caste based reservation system in India. As a result, the movie was banned in Uttar Pradesh, Punjab and Andhra Pradesh before its release. The ban from Uttar Pradesh was later lifted by the Supreme Court. Another example is ***Parzania*** this movie around the worst communal riots of India was not shown in Gujarat which was the centre of the riots. After an initiative by ANHAD, a civil rights group, the movie was shown in some parts of Gujarat. The topic of the movie was so sensitive that it remained under controversy throughout. As well as the movie named ***MSG*** kicked off controversies even before it released. Various groups of the Sikh community demanded a ban against this movie because it 'hurt' their sentiments.

(iv) **Negative portrayal of a popular figure or an institution:** Sometime it is a popular man who objects to his own depiction in a medium and goes for censoring it. ***The Dirty Picture***, this movie based on Silk Smitha's life was received greatly by the audience but it got into a lot of controversies. The posters of the movie were the first reason. The second reason was the objection by Silk Smitha's brothers who even sent notices to the makers of the movie. Another movie named ***Haider*** faced backlash because of the negative portrayal of the Indian Army in the movie. It also received negative reviews from some chunks of the audience who called for a boycott of this movie.

(v) **Extreme Violence**: Portraying extreme violence disturbs human mind. One of the primary purposes of watching films is entertainment although violence is a fact of life.

Portraying extreme violence in films affects the people psychologically. ***Paanch,*** an Anurag Kashyap movie, faced a lot of heat from the Censor Board. Said to be based on the Joshi-Abhyankar serial murders in 1997, the movie was a thriller with high violence, insensitive language and drug abuse. No wonder, the Censor Board decided to ban the film and people awaiting the release of the movie had to make-do with the pirated version of the film. The other movie ***NH 10*** which was about honor killing created the extreme violence in the human minds.

(*vi*) **Politics**: Political forces cannot be isolated as far as the topic of censorship is concerned. Censoring a film by a political state is always supported by the parties who are with the authority directly or indirectly. A medium describing a political situation allegorically or directly, is banned by a government who is a party to it. The song ***'Sadda Haq'*** from the movie ***Rockstar*** faced the anger of censor board because it featured a flag with "Free Tibet" written over it. Eventually the flags were blurred because it sent a strong political message. Protests by Students for Free Tibet (SFT) were also staged against the Censor Board.

Conclusion

Cinema or motion picture has been defined as the art of colorful moving images. It is a medium through which a larger picture of society is depicted on the screen. So, expression of ideas and free thoughts must remain unrestricted from any kind of censorship but at the same time one must not forget the practical realities of the societiesin which such ideas are broadcasted.

Henceforth, a balance between freedom of expression and reasonable restriction should be maintained by CBFC, So that a positive impact of the films can be reflected to the society.

REFERENCES

Central Board of Film Certification, Ministry of Information and Broadcasting, Government of India, 2012

Cinematograph Act, 1952 and 1983, Government of India

Dictionary, Oxford English."Oxford English dictionary online."Oxford University Press, 2016.

Deshpande, Sudhanva. "The Children of 1984", The Frontline, Vol 22, Issue 04, February, 2005

Dictionary, Oxford English."OED online."Oxford University Press. http://www.oed. com, Accessed April 21, 2016.

Daiya, Kavita. Violent belongings: partition, gender, and national culture in postcolonial India. Temple University Press, 2011.

Fundamental Rights, Constitution of India-Part III, Article 19

Fincher, David, "The Girl with the Dragon Tattoo cancelled in India". Guardian News and Media

https://en.wikipedia.org/wiki/Central_Board_of_Film_Certification

Censorship: A Case Study by Ashodh Ganga

15

Dissecting Director G. Aravindan's Classic–Kanchana Sita (1977)

Adv. Anand Kumar. V.

Ramayana needs no introduction. The epic containing about 24000 Sanskrit verses was composed by Sage Valmiki who is considered as 'adi-kavi' or the first poet. Interesting storyline, majestic kingdoms, super-human characters, beautifully interlaced sub-plots and for the messages it conveys, Ramayana provides ample scope for research. It expands the wings of imagination of the writers, poets, painters, sculptors, singers, dancers and theatre artists giving opportunities to explore Ramayana by rereading, rewriting, or adapting the same using specific characters, plots, themes or subjects.

Since the introduction of cinema in India, a number of movies have been produced based on Ramayana in various Indian languages. One such attempt was the Malayalam classic 'Kanchana Sita' (1977), directed by Padma Sri. G. Aravindhan, one of the pioneers of parallel cinema and one of the greatest filmmakers in India. The movie was adapted from C.N. Sreekumar Nair's play of the same name, which in itself was an adoption of Uttrakanda of Valmiki's Ramayana.

Kanchana Sita is a retelling of Ramayana from Sita's perspective. Interestingly, Sita is never shown in the film, but her virtual existence as Mother Nature is enchantingly portrayed in each and every frame. This paper dives deep into this movie and divulges into the nuances of the style of story-telling and film making. An attempt has also been made to dissect the significance of the movie, the title, the plot, concept, casting, dialogues, screenplay, narrative style, portrayal of characters like Rama, Sita, Lakshamana, Bharatha, the film's reception and impact upon release among others. An effort has been made to compare and contrast with the original Ramayana wherever possible.

Ramayana

Ramayana is Aadhi-Kavya or the first poem to have been composed in the world. Any attempt made to comprehend or interpret Ramayana into words can be futile, as it is up to the reader, listener or viewer to understand, appreciate and get touched by the story, characters, morals or the devotional aspect of the epic.

Ramayana is the unison of words Rama + Ayana which means the story of Rama's Travel. Ramayana is one of the greatest epics of the world, and along with Mahabharata forms the part of Hindu itihasa (Sastri, 1994). Ramayana is considered to be the oldest literary work in the world and is credited to Sage Valmiki who composed the work in Sanskrit Language. It consists of about 24000 verses set in slokha meter and is divided into seven kanda/cantos namely Bala Kanda, Ayodhya Kanda, Aranya Kanda, Kishkintha Kanda, Sundara Kanda, Yuddha Kanda and Uttra Kanda; and about 500 sargas/chapters. Exact timeline of Ramayana has been a matter of debate; many research scholars date Ramayana 5000-6000 years back. The epic narrates the story of King Rama of Ayodhya, his life, travels, adventures, struggles, victory, coronation, reign and his exit from this world. The impact and influence of Ramayana in the Indian subcontinent is second to none.

Ramayana is often considered as a sacred text among the Hindus and is regularly read in the houses on auspicious occasions. (Sastri, 1994) Though the author Valmiki as portrayed Rama and others as human beings, the later retellings have positioned Rama as an avatar of Lord Vishnu and his wife Sita as Mahalaxmi. Almost all the Indian languages have their own Ramayana. Either they have been composed as translations of the Valmiki Ramayana, or as adaptions of the original work with few alterations according to the times or as an altogether retelling of Ramayana with the basic story drawn from the Sanskrit version. There are also Cambodian, Indonesian, Filipino, Thai, Lao, Burmese and Malaysian versions of the tale. (Wikipedia, Ramayana, 2018)

Ramayana is the repository of values, ethics, morals and messages. Over many centuries people have been worshipping Rama and Sita as Gods and composed hyms and bhajans on them. (Sastri, 1994)

It is also interesting to note that, though the title is Ramayana or Rama's travel, naming the work as Sitayana or Sita's travel would also be apt as Sita is the nucleus around which the plot revolves. Sita is present in all the 7 kandas, while there is a kanda where Rama is not present, and that Sundara Kanda, which describes the valour of Hanuman crossing the ocean and reaching Lanka to search the whereabouts of Sita. It also includes the conversation between Hanuman and Sita. Thus in all probability the title Sitayana can also be attributed to the work.

Malayalam Cinema

Malayalam cinema is one of the Indian regional film industries based out of Kerala, producing motion pictures in Malayalam language. Called by the sobriquet Mollywood, the Malayalam cinema has been blessed with best minds in the Indian film industry. Over the years people have excelled in the field of direction, cinematography, editing, art direction, music, playback singing, and acting among others. Along with Bengali movie makers, Malayalam directors have dominated the parallel cinema with compelling storyline, realism, raw music scores, aesthetic visuals, limited dialogues and different in many other ways from the main stream cinema.

Director G. Aravindhan

G. Aravindan, (1935-1991) was a multi-talented person from Kerala, who wore many hats in his successful career. He was a cartoonist, screenwriter, painter, film director, and musician. He was one of the pioneers of Parallel Cinema in Malayalam film industry and is considered as one of the greatest filmmakers in India. He along with Adoor Gopalakrishnan transformed the style of filmmaking in Mollywood. He was known for his unconventional way of filmmaking; his formula to success can be attributed to his experiments in narrating the story without regular narrative clichés. Earlier to film making, he was a well-known cartoonist. His cartoon series Cheriya Manushyarum Valya Lokavum (Small Men and the Big World) became huge hit among the readers. He also worked with documentaries and theatre. He was honored with Padma Shri in 1991 (Affiars, 2018) and won National Film Awards for Best Director thrice for Kanchana Sita (1978), Thampu (1979), Oridathu (1987).

The Director won the National Film Awards under Best Direction category for Kanchana Sita in the 25th National Film Awards, 1978 presented by Directorate of Film Festivals and the citation read as follows *"For its courageous and uncompromising exploration of an ancient epic through a pronouncedly new cinematic language, for making the camera speak more eloquently than the introspective characters of the Ramayana, for projecting the interior landscape of the protagonists against the vast backdrop of nature, for matching profound philosophical ideas with astonishing evocations of the beauties of the physical world."* (Festivals, 1978)

Prologue to the Making of Kanchana Sita

The film is an adaption of C.N. Sreekumar Nair's play Kanchana Sita which in itself is a rework of Uttara Kanda of original Ramayana. (Wikipedia, Kanchana Sita, 2018) Director G. Aravindhan tries to convey the story through Sita, who is never shown in the entire film. The story revolves around the emotional conflict in Rama after he sent his wife into jungle to appease his subjects. How does Rama overcome his inner conflict with the help of all pervasive Sita forms the crux of the story.

Plot

The film starts with the voyage of Rama and Lakshmana to execute Shambuka – the shudra who performs penance – however Shambuka's wife argues for his life, and he is saved. Rama and Lakshmana come back to Ayodhya and meet Urmila, the vivacious spouse of Lakshmana. Rama addresses her censures for deserting Sita.

The following day, Guru Vasishta lands to propose that Rama perform the Ashvamedha yaga however Rama can't imagine a sacrifice without Sita beside him and is hesitant. Bharata, returns to Ayodhya. He protests Rama from performing yaga without Sita. Their contention nearly finishes in a battle, yet Sita, in the form of nature stops them.

The yaga starts, and the horse is let loose. The horse strays into Maharishi Valmiki's ashram, where Rama's children Lava and Kusha are being raised by the Maharishi. Lava stops the horse and is not ready to let go the horse and prepares to fight with Lakshmana. At that moment, the nature once again intervenes and stops the fight. Valmiki is moved by what he witnessed, and he starts to write the Uttara Rama Charita.

The horse is brought back to Ayodhya, and the ceremony begins. Rama keeps a golden idol of Sita beside him in the sacrifice and performs the yaga. As the sacrifice nears finish, Valmiki comes with Lava and Kusha, the two sons of Rama. Rama recognizes his children, and takes them to his heart.

Cast and Crew of Kanchana Sita

K. Ravindran Nair or General Pictures Ravi, known for fostering the parallel cinema movement in Mollywood produced Kanchana Sita under his production house General Pictures. The Producer-Director duo went to make three more movies after this film, making them one of the successful pair in the art film category.

They roped in industries most acclaimed technicians of that time, making Kanchana Sita one of the technically rich and sound films. Artist Namboothri handled the art department, cinematography by Shaji N. Karun, editing by Ramesan and the soulful original score was done by noted classical musician and sarod player Rajeev Taranath. (Wikipedia, 2018)

Quite contrast to the star studded crew, the casting was completely off-beat. The ideal Rama character as seen and understood by us through pictures, paintings and also through the films as a handsome looking, charming person, personified by Telugu Super star N T Rama Rao or Ramayana television Seriesfame actor Arun Govil was completely different in this film. Rama's character was played by village chief of a tribal community, Ramadas, though his real name remains unknown. The hero though was well built, had big tummy and an expressionless face. The quest for the film's hero and other casts started in Kerala and ended in Andhra Pradesh. The film casted Adivasis/Tribal People from Andhra Pradesh called the Rama Chenchus (India, 1991), who claim that they are the descendants of the Rama's clan. The idea was not to use mainstream actors, but to find mature individuals who would fit into the role and also associate with the characters. Rama Chenchu healers play the pivotal roles of Rama, Lakshmana, Bharata, Lava, and Kusha. Shambukha's character was played by a wayside tapasvi, while a destitute woman acted in the role of his wife. (Zacharias, 2008) Though the casing created a stir, the director remained steadfast in his task and mastered in getting the best outcome possible from the actors. Although the critics termed the actors did not fit into the roles and their acting was artificial and immature, the performance was widely received well with the audience.

According to the Director's own statement in an interview, he said *"These tribals come to Trivandrum to sell herbal medicine. They are extremely intelligent. In fact, the tribals inhabiting the nine villages around the Godavari River in Andhra are supposed to have the highest I.Q. among Indian tribals. The tribe I selected is known as the Rama Chenchus. They claim to belong to the dynasty of Rama. Physically, I feel, they fit the description given by Valmiki."* (Aravindhan, 1991)

This experiment in casting resulted in several difficulties during production. A precise detailing had to be done because most of the actors could only react to demonstrated instructions. Communication with the actors was carried out with the help of Manohar Dutt, painter and lecturer at the College of Fine Arts, Hyderabad. Dutt also accompanied Aravindan and his associate, journalist and filmmaker Chintha Ravi, on a preliminary trip to Andhra Pradesh to finalise the locations.

Location

The film was completely shot at Andhra Pradesh primarily in three locations, in Vicarabad forest belt, on the banks of Godavari and a few scenes at Undavalli in Vijayawada. (Wikipedia, 2018) The locations were amidst the nature and it was the very nature that was depicted as Sita. The leaves, rivers, mountains, rocks, caves not only helped in adding aesthetics in the film, but kept reminding us that the all-pervasive nature is also a part of human life and is one of the guiding forces for the mankind.

Dialogues

One of the highlights of the film was the dialogues. They were limited and subdued but at the same time the dialogues were sharp, subtle and carried a sense of a X factor which helped to uplift the film from being an ordinary film to one of the classics. The cinematic style of delivering long, lengthy and punchy dialogues were visibly absent and all the conversations were kept to suggest the human sentiments and as far as the nature, it was left for the interpretation of the audience. The five elements of the nature (panchabhoota) namely, the rippling river, the blue sky, the blowing winds, the raging fire, and the forest land all compelling evoked the virtual presence of Sita without the need of dialogues.

Criticism and Critical Acclaim

Criticism and critical acclaim goes hand in hand for the director. The critics had gone on to become admirers and the hardcore fans became his greatest critic. The switching of loyalties among the two sections of people was no different in this film also.

Critic's Complaints and the Director's Response:

1. The casting was ordinary and the casts fail to live up to the expectations of the storyline.

   The director felt that the people who had been casted had reached a sense of awareness that the role required and the same level of awareness could not be reprised even by senior artists.

2. Scholar V. Rajakrishnan noted that Aravindan had not fully considered the implications of locating Rama's story in an Adivasi community. (Zacharias, 2008)

The director in one of his interviews in Times of India said "Unfortunately a controversy arose because I had cast tribals. They have classical features and are marvelous actors. Yet I was accused of blasphemy." (Aravindhan, 1991)

Critical Acclaim

Upon its release, the film was a huge hit among the audience. The path breaking screenplay and narration received widespread appreciation from reviewers and film critics alike. Many film reviews carried a positive feedback and appreciated the director for his out of the box making of the film. The Hindu described Kanchana Sita as one of the most poetic films in Malayalam, (Venkiteswaran, 2009) while Vidyarthy Chatterjee of The Economic Times said, "Visually stunning in many passages and using sound in such a manner as to make for heightened aesthetic pleasure, Kanchana Sita is a milestone that has unfortunately been bypassed by many who would have done better to focus on its innovative elements". (Chatterjee, 2008)Poet and scholar Ayyappa Panicker views Sita's absence as typical of Aravindan's style, in which there is a conscious, meticulous effort "not to communicate in order to communicate". (Zacharias, 2008)

Dissecting Director's Classic

The main objective of this paper is to dissect the director's movie Kanchana Sita, and discuss the finer aspects of his work, efforts are also made to bring it to the notice of the readers the insight about his classic and how different it was from the original Ramayana. While there are many aspects that can be described and elaborated, here four major points are been discussed in detail:

1. How it is different from the original Ramayana?
2. The characterization of Rama – Ethical Dilemma Personified
3. The central character Sita – Virtual Reality
4. The climax

1. How it is different from the original Ramayana?

The story of Rama and his struggle and subsequent ascend to throne of Ayodhya is known to generation of Indians and is one of the household stories with the moral "triumph of good over evil". While there have been many regional versions of Ramayana that are different from the original storyline in terms of spiritual concepts and main stream narration that includes addendums, interpolations, recensions and rerecensions, any adulteration in storyline is met with lot of criticisms from scholars and commoners alike.

While the plot remains the same, the narration or the style of retelling has evolved over the years bringing a new outlook to the story. There have been so many plays and movies that have come before and after this film, but this movie has stood the test of times in terms of nativity, narration and novelty.

(a) **Nativity:** The story of Ramayana as read and seen is often associated with grandeur. The majestic kingdoms, super-human characters, wealth in the kingdom and innumerable army possessed by the kings often add wow factor and take the imagination of the readers to a completely new horizon.

In this film, the grandeur is in its visuals and in its aesthetic appeal, while the characters are portrayed in human form without the pomp and splendor. The majestic kingdoms are replaced with jungles, the caves are their palaces. The king in his resplendent ornaments and dresses and the queen in all her charm are swapped for bark and ordinary clothes which includes leaves, straws and deer skin. The entire film is shot in and around the jungle and thus there is no scope for display of wealth in terms of gold, silver, stockpile or army. The hero and others are seen carrying bow and arrows made of wood. Kothanda – Rama's powerful bow and Rama Banas – Rama's all conquering arrows are just another ordinary bow and arrows without any superlatives.

(b) Narration: The Uttra Kanda of Ramayana is the main plot of the movie. While the usually familiar narrating style is not present in the film, the director handles the finer details of inner human conflicts, the desire for sovereignty and the desire for nirvana and how the nature comes to one's rescue. The finesse of director is found in the narration and screenplay. While he has taken all liberty to alter the settings of Ramayana, he has also tactfully yet subtly changed the way the story is unfolded. The discussion between Rama and Urmila, Rama and Bharatha, Rama and Vasishta, Rama and Lakshmana, Lakshmana and Valmiki are compelling and induces the viewers to interpret it in their own way. The striking revelations are found when Rama is in a state of confusion and not able to make decisions, Sita in the form of nature comes to his rescue.

(c) Novelty: Sita, the central character of Ramayana is never shown in the film, but her virtual existence as Mother Nature is enchantingly portrayed in each and every frame. The prakruthi-purusha relationship is shown in the movie.

Prakruthi can be attributed as Nature and Purusha can be defined as all mortal entities. While prakruthi is all pervasive and independent, purusha is dependent and dissolved in prakruthi. Prakruthi binds purusha and controls him in the spiritual sense. The actual awakening of inner self happens when purusha understands prakruthi and tries to embrace prakruthi.

Here Rama is attributed as purusha and Sita as prakruthi and Rama's mission to find his Sita and become one with her form the main part of the storyline.

2. **Characterization of Rama – Ethical Dilemma Personified**

The characterization of Rama is the most interesting. He had been the epitome of an ideal human being in every respect; yet he is one who has faced tragedy of greatest magnitude. Rama is shown as an ordinary human being. Rama is portrayed as a person who enters into a series of ethical dilemmas – the beheading of Shambuka, the arguments with Bharatha and Urmila over the significance of the ashwameda yagna, the challenge from his own sons to recognize them and to accept them as they recite songs relating his life are the most striking aspect of Rama's character is his ethical commitment.

The best dialogue in the film is spilled from the mouth of Rama when he says "*Raja simhasnam oru agni kundamanu- Sitayude Bharthavu Prajakalude oru Dasan Mathram*" (Aravindhan, Kanchana Sita, 1977) The King's throne is like that of a sacrificial fire, and that I, Sita's husband is only a servant of the people. Here the director establishes the mindset of Rama and that he is just performing his duty as a king without any prejudice or expectations. Unlike the legendary unfathomable, super human of Ramayana, Rama of Kanchana Sita is a tragic hero, who is not able to take a stand when it comes to his personal life. Rama requires constant support and guidance from Sita, and his desire to become one with Sita is shown in every scene.

Finally, Rama gathers strength and decides to merge with prakruthi. At the point, he had performed all his duties and is no longer interested to continue living in this world. He is now interested to get himself liberated and join Sita, his ultimate savior. It is also interesting that, the only time Rama is clear in his action and taken a decision without any inhibition is when he decides to leave the world, and that can be attributed to his longing for Sita and his desire to become one with her.

3. The Central Character Sita – Virtual Reality

Sita is the main character in the movie and though she is not shown, she is felt in the movie. All the five elements are Sita, the chirping birds, rising sun, falling leaves, etc all gets life energy from her. The action, reaction and the consequences of the reactions of the characters in the film are all nothing but Sita. She is the guiding force and the generator, operator and destructor of the earth. She is the Shakti and she is the prakruthi. Her physical absence liberates her from sensual, temporal limitations to permeate the narrative as an all pervasive presence of the cosmic life force.

In the later part of the film, Sita is shown as the golden idol who sits beside Rama during the ashwameda sacrifice. The golden image of Sita engulfed in flames, is unscathed by flames and appears to be fire itself shows the purity of Sita and at the same time she is the embodiment of enlightenment and soul of lives which cannot be destroyed. Time and again she has been tested and has been asked to undergo various or deals in life, which would have made any other ordinary being to quit, but for Sita, it has made her strong, resilient and as a living example for others to follow.

4. Climax:

One of the best parts of the movie was its climax. Rama after successfully performing the sacrifice and meeting his children is calm and controlled. He takes the decision to merge with Sita and get himself released from his mortal body. He decides to go through the Mahaprasthana, which is one's last journey in attaining nirvana. With a sacrificial fire in his hands, Rama goes into the river with full contentment and bliss. He is happy and attained the state of ecstasy as he is going to become one with his dear Sita, and nobody would tell them to part their ways again. He is also satisfied that as a king he has performed his duties in protecting and taking care of the wellbeing of his subjects, and as a dutiful father, he has now handed over the reins of his kingdom, to his sons. He has attained the state of liberation, free from all emotions ready to dissolve in prakruthi. *This is the essence of the nature, we are born from Prakruthi and end in unison with her and that is the moment when life comes to a full circle.*

It is also interesting to state the opening scroll, "This film is an interpretation of the Uttara Kanda of the Ramayana. Our mythologies and the epics are constantly re-created in retellings. The epic is the basis for this visual interpretation as well. This film deviates from established norms in how it visualizes the protagonists and portrays the course of events in the epic". (Aravindhan, Kanchana Sita, 1977) The scroll explains that the film will try to reflect what it calls the epic's adi-sankalpam (original conception) of the theme and the protagonists. It states that "the inner essence of the film is that woman is Prakriti. Ultimately Purusha, here conceived of as the masculine self, dissolves into Prakriti.

Conclusion

Director G. Aravindhan's Kanchana Sita is a classic that needs to be revisited. The film is both visually as well as story wise, appealing and touching. Both the critics as well as the audience received the movie positively. The different screenplay, compelling visuals and new concepts made the film a must watch for movie goers. Director Arvindhan broke many a stereotypes and opened way for other film makers to follow a nonchalant yet engaging movie that shall be appreciated by both the mainstream audience as well as the lovers of art films.

Even after 4 decades, Kanchana Sita mesmerizes people and makes them fall in love with it again. It is one of those rare combinations of story line where one can watch Ramayana and at the same time appreciate the strong story from a feminist perspective highlighting the importance of nature and women for the welfare of the mankind.

REFERENCES

Abraham, J. (2011, February 1). "Remembering One and Only G Aravindan through Kanchana Seetha". *Indian Ruminations*.

Affiars, M. o. (2018). *Padma Awards*. Retrieved October 22, 2018, from Padma Awards: https://padmaawards.gov.in/

Aravindhan, G. (Director). (1977). *Kanchana Sita* [Motion Picture].

Aravindhan, G. (1991). "Aravindhan, film maker of poetic vision, dead". (K. Mohamed, Interviewer)

Chatterjee, V. (2008). *"Silence of Frames: Re-visiting Thampu"*. ET Bureau.

Festivals, D. o. (1978). *25th National Film Awards*. Delhi: Minsitry of Information and Broadcasting, Government of India.

India, R. G. (1991). *List of Notified Scheduled Tribes*. Minsitry of Home Affiars.

Nagpal, K. (1978). *"A Film Maker Pitches His Teny"*. Times of India.

Nair, C. N. (2006). *Retelling the Ramayana: Voices from Kerala*. Oxford University Press.

Richman, P. (2008). *"Ramayana Stories in Modern South India – An Anthology"*.

Sastri, R. H. (1994). *"Lectures on Ramayana"*. Chennai: Madras Sanskrit Academy.

Venkiteswaran, C. S. (2009, June 19). The alchemist of cinema. *The Hindu*.

Wikipedia. (2018). *Kanchana Sita*. Retrieved October 14, 2018, from Wikipedia: https://en.wikipedia.org/wiki/Kanchana_Sita

Wikipedia. (2018). *Ramayana*. Retrieved October 15, 2018, from Wikipedia: https://en.wikipedia.org/wiki/Ramayana

Zacharias, U. (2008). *"Union with Nature: Prakriti and sovereignty in Aravindan's Kanchana Sita"*.

16

Antagonists the New Emerging Heroes of Bollywood

Shikha Sharma

Indian Film industry start blooming from the day after less than a year of Lumiere brothers came to project their films in India. On July 7, 1896, Lumiere Brothers (Indian Film Industry – Indian Mirror) showcased their six films at the Watson Hotel in Bombay; this day was marked as the birth of Indian Cinema. Harishchandra Sakharam Bhatavdekar well known as Save Dada was very much influenced by the Lumiere Brother's work that he ordered a camera from England. He shot his first film 'The Wrestlers' in Hanging Gardens in Mumbai. This film was just a recording of a wrestling match which was first screened in 1899 and it was considered the first motion picture of Indian Film Industry.

In 1913, Dadasahab Phalke (known as the father of Indian cinema) ("July 7th 1896 – Indian Cinema is Born," n.d.) released his first ever full-length feature film Raja Harishchandra which was 3700 feet long in size. This silent film in Marathi was a commercial success. This film inspires a lot of creative people in the field of Cinema. After that India's first talking film Alam Ara made by Ardeshir Irani came in 14th March 1931. With the advent of sound technology films in 1930's, industry saw the practice of music in Indian films like Indra Sabha and Devi Deviyani, who was known as the first song and dance films in India.

India got independence in 1947, but remorsefully got the partition also, which really affected the Indian film industry a lot. Lots of films were made after the partition that was based on this theme. From here the Golden Age of Indian cinema started where a new kind of Cinema known as Parallel cinema came into limelight. Films like 'Do Bhigha Zameen', 'Naagrik' etc. were became quite popular in their audience for there down to earth topics. Side by side commercial cinema also starts flourishing and entertaining the Indian audience. In 1947 film industry sees various changes in its topics; earlier films were depicting mythological and historical stories which shifted to films on social-reforms, such as on the dowry system, prostitution etc. in 1950s directors like Satyajit Ray focuses on the lower class as they were the most ignored subjects. 1960s saw a new kind of cinema known as New wave mainly derived by Satyajit Ray, Mrinal Sen and Ritwik Ghatak in the search of realism in the depiction of common man and its circumstances.

The 1970's Bollywood films saw the advent of Masala movies, where the audiences were enchanted by the appearance of the Bollywood actors like Dharmendra, Rajesh Khanna, and Amitabh Bachchan etc. Manmohan Desai ("History of Bollywood Cinema from 1913 to the Present," n.d.) was known as the most successful director of 1970s. He was known as the father of these Masala films, While talking about his approach towards films, he said "I want people to forget their miseries while watching my films. My films would take them into a world where there is no poverty, or scarcity, where everything sounds good, fate is in favor and the God is busy with their flocks."

If we talk about Indian Film Industry statistics, it's really an eye opener for us. The overall value of this industry is 138.2 Billion (Rupees)("Film Industry in India – Statistics & Facts | Statista," n.d.), every year this industry produces1903 films, which generate box office revenue of 111 billion. Indian film industry comprises of many significant Regional industries ("Bollywood, Pollywood, Tollywood, and More – Film Industry Nicknames Around The World – WorldAtlas.com," n.d.) for example Bollywood (Hindi movies), Tollywood (Telgu & Bengali movies), Kollywood (Tamil movies), Mollywood (Malyalam movies) etc. Bollywood is a Mumbai based film industry and produces films in Hindi language. Bollywood is an informal term which is popularly used for the Hindi language film industry placed in Mumbai, India. It's interesting to that the Oxford English Dictionary in 2007 accepted the Bollywood word in it. **Rachel Dwyer** in his book '100 Bollywood Films' talks about the noticeable features of Bollywood cinema, such as the excess of melodrama, intense emotions around the families, captivating storyline, presence of stars, glamour, heavy emotional dialogues and last but not the least songs without which we can't imagine Bollywood films.

Bollywood is the largest film revenue generating industry with 45% alone out of the total revenue generated by film industry in India. Brad Pitt highlighted in an interview with IANS (News Agency) that he "would love to work in Bollywood films as they have so much color and drama in these films." Bollywood industry caters their audience through various Genres ("(PDF) Recent Genre Based Categorized Comparisons of Bollywood Movies Through Radar Plots," n.d.) like action, comedy, horror, thriller, romance, drama, epic/historical etc. These all genres help the audience to choose their specific film to watch and enjoy it in the 70 mm screen. But the most common thing for which the Bollywood films were obsessed with was the concept of Protagonist and Antagonist and their struggle against each other. Hero is always treated with love and inspiration whereas the antagonist always faces the hatred of the audience.

According to **Tim Stout** ("Eight Character Roles," 2011) (Writer & Editor) in a story there are mainly eight characters which creates an interesting plot for the viewers and Protagonist and the Antagonist are main in them. But with the changing scenario the discrimination between the villain and the hero is blurring. Now the heroes have the traits of antagonist and the villain portrays the role of protagonist in Bollywood. This formula was first portrayed by Amitabh Bachchan in his film Parwana ("When Lead Actor Played Antagonist's Role too in a Bollywood Film," 2018), where he was the protagonist and as the story develops his character becomes negative and he killed the father of the heroine. This was the first experiment conducted in Bollywood but after this formula become so popular that every superstar tried to follow it in their next films. Movies like Baazigar where Shah Rukh Khan played the negative role, Ajnabee (Akshay Kumar), 1947 Earth (Aamir Khan), Dhoom Series where the antagonist become the main protagonist in the film. In all these films the main protagonist covert into antagonist as per the directions of the scripts. The positive character of the Hero suddenly changes to take the revenge of the wrong things happened with them, and the actor unexpectedly start applying all the negative traits to fulfill their revenge from the villain.

Country like India where these are treated as Gods and Goddesses and cinema consist a big space in the common man's life. Actors like Rajnikanth in Tollywood film Industry is worshipped by the audience (Manoj Kumar R, n.d.). Every year 12th December is celebrated as a big festival because of the birthday of the superstar. He acquired such a position in the hearts of their fans that, if he goes missing from the big screen for the period of 3 years, nobody can challenge his supremacy on box office. But when these stars portray negative role in the screen it also affects the mindset of the viewers. Films like 'Shivaji – The Boss' where Rajnikanth plays the role of a good guy, he faces all the adverse situations against him, stopping him to be a good person, then he acquires the characteristics of an antagonist than he got solution of all the problems. Despite it's a good movie but still it creates a negative impact on the society especially on their youth audience. That if they do anything wrong, they can escape from the hands of the law and never will be caught for their wrongdoings. If we concentrate on Bollywood in 2017 we saw films like Kaabil, Raees, Mom, Bhoomi, Simran and Haseena Parker. These films were totally different in their storylines but one thing in common that the protagonist of the film become the antagonist in the end to take their revenge.

Syd Field ("The Creation of Character–The Character Biography ~ Journalism and Communication," n.d.) comes up with the theory of Film analysis and how to analyze a character, he said there are various ways of characterization and character development in a film few of them are as follows:

1. **Personality trait** of the character where he/she can be shy, brave, selfish, humble etc. They traits are not static, a person who is shy in the starting become outspoken in the climax.
2. **Internal conflict** helps to understand what the character is going through.
3. **External conflict** it is a conflict that occurs between the characters of the film. This conflict is expressed through a fighting sequence or a disapproval in the opinion
4. **Character relationship** What kind of relationship our character will have with all around the plot. He/she must be someone brother, wife, husband, friend etc. But these relationships sometimes stressed out with the development of script.

Character analysis of these films and will help us to understand the reason behind the protagonist negative traits and why they must be villain in the film to take their revenge.

Kaabil ("Kaabil Plot Summary – Times of India," 2017)

Rohan Bhatnagar (Hrithik) is visually-impaired since birth, however he doesn't require anyone helps in day to day works, he is so independent that he ran his daily life smoothly. Rohan is a very decent guy with all the good traits. Even after he is visually impaired still he doesn't consider himself weak in any sense. Then he met Supriya Sharma (Yammi Gautam), she is also visually impaired. After few meetings they fall in love and got married. However, the neighborhood goondas Amit (Ronit Roy) has his bad eyes on Supriya. So, he started stalking the couple.

One day he found Supriya alone at home and raped her with his friend. Couple decided to launch a complaint against them. But because of the political background of the Amit's brother the police didn't support the couple. And Supriya was again raped by the same two guys. Because of the routine humiliation and unable to do anything against it, she decided to commit suicide to stop this disgrace. From here our main protagonist Rohan decided to take the revenge for his loss. From a very generous and humble guy, he changed to an avenging person; he decided to take law in his hands to take his revenge. As he was a good mimicry artist he takes the advantage of his voice and start plotting against the criminals. He started targeting both the convicts one by one and because of his flawless planning; police were unable to reach him. Police was having full doubt on him regarding both the murders (shown as accidents), but in the law of evidences they were unable to reach him.

Raees ("Raees Plot Summary – Times of India," 2017)

The film starts, where a child name Raees (Shah Rukh Khan) lives with his mother in Gujarat. Raees from his childhood had an urge to earn money quickly. So, from the starting as a child he starts smuggling liquor in a dry state of Gujarat. The very famous dialogue of the film "Ammijan, kahti hai ki koi bhi dhandha choota bada nahi hota (My mother said, that there is no such thing called small or big business)". This dialogue justifies all the wrongdoings of the Protagonist in the film. As the Raees grown up, he decided to run his own business and need the help for funds to start it. He tries to take the help from Jairaj (Raees was doing smuggling for him) but ends up with a loggerhead. So, he decides to run his business by his own and went to Mumbai where he met Moosa Bhai (Goon). With the help of Moosabhai and after few struggles Raees became a very well-known face in his area.

In the meanwhile, an IPS officer Majumdar started following Raees to catch for his illegal activities. Raees started facing opposition from political power and his life become upside down. The second half of the film is all the about the chase and running between Raees and Majumdar (IPS). Raees business starts affecting by this, so he went again to Moosa for his help. Moosa agrees for his help but asked him to deliver his consignment. Later, Raees got to know that consignment was carrying RDX and it was used for bomb blast in Mumbai. Now Raees was totally helpless, he realized that there is no escape from this. So, he decided to surrender himself to the police, but Majumdar (IPS) creates a fake encounter and shot Raees. While going through all this Raees as a Protagonist kills lots of people, done lots of illegal things but when he died in the end we feel sorrow for him. Earlier if a bad guy (Antagonist) dies, audience feels victory on screen but now our protagonist consists the bad traits in it and audience is enjoying this formula.

Mom ("Mom Plot Summary – Times of India," 2017)

Devki Sabharwal (Sridevi) is a biology teacher in a school in Delhi, where her step-daughter Arya is her student in the class. Arya doesn't like her step mother she always calls her ma'am, instead of mom. The stress in their relationship was quite visible through their conversations. There is a boy in the class who had a crush on Arya and he writes lewd messages to her. Devki noticed these messages and throw boy's phone out of the class. Now this boy naturally goes against them. Devki loves Arya like her own daughter Priya (Real daughter). Devki husband Anand tries to neutralize the equation between them, but the Arya is so stubborn that she doesn't want to see Devki around her. One day Arya asks his father to go in a party but his father refuses in the first instance. But still she goes to the party on the promise to come home early. In the party the same boy encountered Arya and proposes her, but she denies, which hurt the ego of the boy. Then he planned to kidnap the girl with his cousin and drivers help.

On the night Arya was gang raped by these guys and thrown in the gutter. In morning a passerby calls the police and takes her to the hospital. Devki files a complaint against all the convicts but in the absence of evidences all the charges were unable to prove in the court. This is the real turning point of the film where Devki decide to take the law in his own hands. The famous dialogue of the film was said by all the culprits when they were misbehaving with the girl "Ja Bula Apni Maako (Call your Mother)", was the real strength behind Devki to fight for her daughter Arya. With the help of a spy DK (Nawazuddin Siddiqui) she one by one start plotting against all the culprits and start punishing them for the wrongdoings with her child. On one place she said a dialogue, "Kya kah rahe the, Ja Bula Apni Maako, Le aa gaye uski Maa." She killed all the three convicts and in the last the main culprit Jagan, she killed it with the help of police in the end of the film. In this film a mother is shown with a great conviction to guard his child from all the odds of the world.

Bhoomi ("Bhoomi (2017) - IMDb," n.d.)

Arun Sachdeva (Sanjay Dutt) is a shoe smith and his daughter Bhoomi (Aditi Rao Hydari) is busy with the preparation of Bhoomi's marriage. A guy is having crush on Bhoomi and asks her to marry him, but she denies, which hurts the ego of the boy. Just day before her marriage she was gang raped by the boy she refuses and his 2 other known persons. Next day everything got changed her marriage was broken. Arun files a case against the culprits but in the absence of proper evidences the case was dismissed, and all the culprits were free by the court. Here, Arun and his daughter Bhoomi decides to take the revenge for their insult. And they start plotting to take their revenge. Aditi who looks sweet and stuttering girl in the starting now becoming a tougher girl and turns into an avenging angel.

Simran (Kaushal, 2017)

In this film Simran is not the name of any character in the movie. Praful Patel (Kangana Ranaut) is a 30-year-old divorcee living with her parents in Georgia. Praful works as a housekeeper in a five-star hotel. She lives in a middle-class family where the family is the main critic. She wants to live her life on her own terms without the interference of the family. To escape from all these nagging, she decided to go her cousin wedding in Los Angeles. In Los Angeles she went to casino where she loses all that she had. The goons from which she has taken the financial help now start chasing her and compelling her to return the money back. Praful is now not left with any other options despite bank robbery. She started collecting the amount she needs to pay to the

Goons which was $50,000 with interest. She just wants to get rid from the situation when she realized that she raised the money that she required, she went to her workplace where she put all the money in her locker. But soon she realized that her Hotel manager has stolen her money from the locker, but she can't prove it. In the end, she surrenders herself to the police and accused her manager about that he had all the money she looted from the banks. This is how she takes her revenge from the manager. The film is all about the struggles of Praful but still she manages to be bold and take her own decisions in life. It is said that this film is based on the real story of a lady from Gujarat.

Haseena Parker ("Haseena Parkar (2017) – IMDb," n.d.)

The film roams around the relationship of Dawood and his sister Haseena Parker (Shraddha Kapoor). Haseen came into limelight when Dawood left the Mumbai in 1993 after Mumbai Bomb blasts. In the family of 12 children lives in Dongri with their cop father, who was well known for his honesty. But his son starts working for contract killings and money extortions. But after the Mumbai Blast police founds the involvement of Dawood, so he has to leave the country, but he wants someone very trustworthy who can operate his empire in Mumbai. The film runs in the court room where every time with the court proceedings, movie goes into flashback with every question and answers round. In this film it was depicted that Haseena and his family go through all this because they were linked with Dawood. But it's actually a one-sided story because the evidence in real says that Haseena was using the name of Dawood and became the Appa (Godmother) of Nagpada area in Mumbai. Haseena who was depicted a shy and innocent girl in the starting of the film became a fearless girl and shows in the role of godmother taking the ruling position of the Nagpada area. Every single decision about that area was taken by her in the name of Dawood.

Conclusion

As we gone through all these 6 selected films, we noticed various major points to be discussed in these above films. Despite these were good entertaining films but still they create negative impact on the viewer's especially on youth. Earlier cinema depicts that truth and honesty always wins. The positivity of the hero always compels the villain to defeat. But now as per the changing scenario and the experiments of the new coming directors, they portray their main protagonist with all the negative traits so that the protagonist will take his revenge in by hook or by crook. These heroes are shooting on the cops, killing people without any fear of law, as if there is no law in the country. This kind of attitude is very much attracting the new generation youth. Day by day with the increase of such kind of depiction of Heroism on the screen is creating more violence in the society. Threating, bulling, physical and verbal abuse, stealing is very commonly found in the society. Recent movies are showing a new type of physical abuse and torture which is affecting the young minds. According to a study child who were violent films or shows are more prone to adapt criminal minds. We must accept this truth that today's directors are choosing those scripts which are very bold, or we can say that more violent and vulgar in their approach to increase their box office collection ("Villains are new Heroes of Bollywood Movies," 2017). Bollywood overused the formula of revengeful parents in Bhoomi, Mom, Maatr like films in 2017. In all these three films parents take the law in their hands and take their revenge in a very terrifying and bold manner.

REFERENCES

Indian Film Industry, Film Industry India. (n.d.). Retrieved from http://www.indianmirror.com/indian-industries/film.html

July 7th, 1896 - Indian Cinema is Born. (n.d.). Retrieved from https://www.mapsofindia.com/on-this-day/july-7-1896-indian-cinema-is-born

Grant, A. (2011, January 2). Welcome to Bollywood! Retrieved from https://www.thoughtco.com/what-is-bollywood-3549901

Topic: Film Industry in India. (n.d.). Retrieved from https://www.statista.com/topics/2140/film-industry-in-india/

Bollywood, Pollywood, Tollywood, and More - Film Industry Nicknames Around The World. (2017, April 25). Retrieved from https://

www.worldatlas.com/articles/film-industries-around-the-world-with-hollywood-inspired-nicknames.html

http://shodhganga.inflibnet.ac.in/bitstream/10603/97263/9/09_chapter3.pdf

Mahajan Sagar Bhaskar Ranjana* et al. (IJITR) INTERNATIONAL JOURNAL OF INNOVATIVE TECHNOLOGY AND RESEARCH, Volume No.4, Issue No.2, February - March 2016, 2844 – 2851. 2320 –5547 @ 2013-2016 http://www.ijitr.com All rights Reserved. Page | 2844 Recent Genre Based Categorized Comparisons of Bollywood Movies Through Radar [accessed Nov 02, 2018].

Eight Character Roles. (2011, May 3). Retrieved from https://timstout.wordpress.com/graphic-novel-writing/eight-character-roles/

When Lead Actor Played Antagonist's Role too in a Bollywood Film. (2018, July 6). Retrieved from http://mywordsnthoughts.com/myworld/2016/10/when-lead-actor-played-antagonists-role-too-in-a-bollywood-film/

Manoj Kumar R. (n.d.). Why Rajinikanth is Thalaivar of the masses. Retrieved from https://indianexpress.com/article/entertainment/tamil/rajinikanth-birthday-4978420/

The Creation of Character-The Character Biography. (2015, November 29). Retrieved from https://wecommunication.blogspot.com/2015/11/4-creation-of-character.html

Kaabil Plot Summary - Times of India. (2017, January 27). Retrieved from https://timesofindia.indiatimes.com/kaabil-plot-summary/articleshow/56800302.cms

Raees Plot Summary - Times of India. (2017, February 3). Retrieved from https://timesofindia.indiatimes.com/raees-plot-summary/articleshow/56948865.cms

Mom Plot Summary - Times of India. (2017, July 9). Retrieved from https://timesofindia.indiatimes.com/mom-plot-summary/articleshow/59513613.cms

Bhoomi Movie Review {3/5}: Watch Bhoomi for Dutt. He's from that era of larger-than-life heroes who get you to whistle even when he is killing people. (2017, September 22). Retrieved from https://timesofindia.indiatimes.com/entertainment/hindi/movie-reviews/bhoomi/movie-review/60781575.cms

Kaushal, S. (2017, September 15). Simran movie review: KanganaRanaut shines in a self-indulgent, chaotic film. Retrieved from https://www.hindustantimes.com/movie-reviews/simran-movie-review-kangana-ranaut-adds-life-to-hansal-mehta-s-film/story-4qTpViPAAlTIdDysuCS0rK.html

HaseenaParkar Review {2/5}: This crime drama fails to offer an insight into Haseena's life whatsoever as an individual, beyond her infamous identity as Dawood's sister. (2018, April 2). Retrieved from https://timesofindia.indiatimes.com/entertainment/hindi/movie-reviews/haseena-parkar/movie-review/60784661.cms

Villains are new Heroes of Bollywood Movies. (2017, December 31). Retrieved from https://livewithstyle19.com/2017/11/20/villains-are-new-heroes-of-bollywood-movies/

17

Alluring yet Mysterious: Representation of Femme Fatal in Hindi Noir Films

Neema Negi

Emergence of Noir Genre

Film noir is a French word usually depicts the "Dark Cinema". The term firstly used by French Critic Nino Frank in 1946. The era of 1940' and 1950's of American Films is usually deeming a Film Noir genre. Film noir is also a specific period of Film History of German Expressionism and French New Wave. It is characterized by cynicism and pessimism and set with an oppressive world of crime and corruption. It's visualistic style and bleak thematic content makes it different genre. If talk about the feature of Noir film the protagonist is mainly disillusioned, friendship is difficult and innocence cannot survive in such a world.

In styles the films are black, use of shadows, fog bound and smoky spaces. Some of the most prominent directors of film noir included Orson Welles, John Huston, Billy Wilder, Edgar Ulmer, Douglas Sirk, Robert Siodmak, Fritz Lang, Otto Preminger, Henry Hathaway and Howard Hawks. Films like *Odd Man Out* (1955) and *The Third Man* (1949) shows this style and thematic outlook. Noir films had many characteristics certain films shows the flashback, the burden of the past the character was living. Sometimes these flashback crimes narrated in different scenes.*The Double Indemnity* (1944) is the perfect example of such narrative. Women played a major role in the terms of noir film, these women is femme fatal means killer or (deadly women). These femme fatal were the wildly ambitious, sexy, crooked, selfish, mysterious, double crossing irresponsible, manipulative women and do whatever to accomplish their purpose.

According to Dirks (n.d) mention in his article that the character type of femme fatale was derived from the anti-heroine vamps of early cinema, such as Theda Bara in *A Fool There Was* (1915). She was first introduced as an evil temptress with her character name of Vampire, and she spoke her most-famous line of all: Kiss me, my Fool. Flappers in the Roaring Twenties, helped along with the popularity of *It Girl Clara Bow*, and the German film *Pandora's Box* (1929) with Louise Brooks as the iconographic and erotic femme fatale, also contributed to the archetypal development of the character.

Another significant root of Noir Genre arrived out from German Expressionism. In the historical perspectives, the emphasis is on the noir films emerged in Hollywood and beyond including India during 1940s, 1950s and 1960s which is considered as classic period of film noir. The trend towards film noir in the post-war period is often seen as having been influenced by the influx of immigrant filmmakers from Central Europe and disillusionment caused by the Second World War. It has also been suggested however that it was economically driven by the cutbacks in sets and lighting made during the war and more feasibly the desire to produce low-budget movies with good percentage profit margins. Certainly there is a strong sense in which these films, both in terms of cinematic style and bleak thematic content, echo German Expressionist film of the 1920s, a movement that may also be seen as having been influenced by the traumatic experience of the First World War. As mentioned, the film noir is a style of filmmaking discovered by a French critic, based on German Expressionism and made in the United States. Obviously, these were non-American filmmakers, mainly from Germany who fled to America after the troubled Nazism. However, they reached in America when the nation was facing the ill-fruits of World War-I and the Great Depression.

A reference is invited from the paragraph on Culture and society in the Great Depression from Britannica website that says - For Americans, the 1930s will always summon up images of breadlines, apple sellers on street corners, shuttered factories, rural poverty, and so-called Hoovervilles (named for President Herbert Hoover), where homeless families sought refuge in shelters cobbled together from salvaged wood, cardboard, and tin. It was a time when thousands of teens became drifters, many marriages were postponed and engagements were interminable birth rates declined and children grew up quickly, often taking on adult responsibilities if not the role of comforter to their despondent parents. It was a time when the number of women in the workplace actually increased, which helped needy families but only added to the psychological strain on the American male, the traditional breadwinner of the American family.

Definition of Film Noir

Describing film noir is always been hard because of its exposition category. Many Scholar says that it's not a film genre it's a tone, style, mood and point of view of film. The Encyclopaedia Britannica elaborates that it's a style of Filmmaking characterized by elements such as cynical effects, stark lightning effects, frequent use of Flashbacks, intricate plots and existentialist philosophy.

According to Gaines (2011) mentioned in his article define Noir film "One of the sub-genres that defined classic American crime and detective movies was film noir, a style that was pervasive in detective films of the 1940s and 1950s. Film noir arose during the post-World War II period in the United States as a generation that fought in one of the most brutal conflicts the world had ever seen returned home to a changed America where jobs were scarce and the national mood seemed darker and more cynical than during the war itself'.

According to New Oxford American Dictionary the Noir is; "A genre of crime film or fiction characterized by cynicism, fatalism and moral ambiguity."

As Martin (1997) defines—Classic film noir was Hollywood's-dark cinema of crime and corruption, a genre underpinned by a tone of existential cynicism, which stripped bare the myth of the American Dream and offered a bleak nightmare vision of a fragmented society that rhymed with many of the social realities of post-war America. Martin is commenting on socio-economic conditions in the US that prompted to make this style of filmmaking.

According to Hirsch (1982, p.21) further defines Film Noir, is a descriptive term for the American crime film as it flourished, roughly, from the early forties to the late fifties. It embraces a variety of crime dramas ranging from claustrophobic studies of murder and psychological entrapment to more general treatments of criminal organizations. In range of theme and in visual style, it is both varied and complex, and in level of achievement it is consistently high, film noir is one of the most challenging cycles in the history of American films. Film Noir is one of Hollywood's only organic artistic movements, defines film noir foundation and continue the elaboration further as:

Beginning in the early 1940s, numerous screenplays inspired by hardboiled American crime fiction were brought to the screen, primarily by European émigré directors who shared a certain storytelling sensibility highly stylized, overtly theatrical, with imagery often drawn from an earlier era of German-expressionist cinema.

Noir Cinema in India

In Hollywood these noir genre were made during the Depression following the World War II but in India the noir genre came after

Post Independence era that portrayed corruption, politics, crime unemployment, bureaucracy and nepotism. As crime and criminals is one of the base for noir Films. In the era of 40's and 50's many films were made on crime and corruption *Kismet* in (1943), *Baazi* (1951) and *Kaala Bazaar* (1960). Most of the Indian filmmaker of those eras were exposed to many Hollywood films and aware themselves with the surroundings of different Cinema. Indian Filmmaker made noir films but they featured these elements of noir unknowingly. The Hollywood film *The Invisible Man* (1933), a horror movie, directed by James Whale is considered as classic noir. Hindi films like *Mahal* (1949), *Woh Kaun Thi* (1964) and *Kohra* (1964) strongly reflect the noir elements.

The first noir film of Hindi Cinema was *Baazi* (1959) and then Gurudutt film *Taxi Driver* (1976), *House no. 44* (1955) and *Jewel Thief* (1967) made in same style. Then in the era of 50's the noir films were made by different filmmakers but less in numbers. *Jaal* (1952) was a noir film by Gurudutt remake of Italian Film Director *Bitter Rice* (1949). The journey till continues 70's and film like *Deewar* (1975) based on the life of Haji Mastan a gangster of Mumbai. In the late 80's films like *Tezaab* (1988), *Parinda* (1989) where the protagonist unfortunately coddle in the crime business due to their social conditions are considered in this category. In those eras the central character indulges in the business of crimes because of its circumstances that intentionally came to Mumbai to earn bread but involve forcibly in this tacky business.

In the 20th century Ram Gopal Varma introduced the film *Satya* (1998) which got critically acclaimed and the new genre Mumbai noir came into fore. Following that Company (2002), *D Company (2005), Sarkar (2005)* made by Ram Gopal Varma. Then Sriram Raghvan appears to be only filmmaker who actually revive this noir genre in contemporary Hindi cinema He used certain elements of noir in his films which seems he's much inspired from Hollywood noir genre. His films like *Johnny Gaddar (2007), Ek Hasina Thi (2004),* and *Andhadhun (2018)* strongly portrayed the character of femme fatal. All these films presented stark noir elements like betrayal, greed, temptation, strangeness, sexual motivation, brutality and other peculiarities close to noir movies. This was added with socio-economic and polito-cultural background peculiar to Indian society.

Representation and Characteristics of Femme Fatal in Hindi Noir Film

Allen (1983) states, "femme fatal is a woman who lures men into danger, destruction, even death by means of her overwhelmingly seductive charms". The femme fatal is a combination of glamour and sensuality with a self-motivated ambition and self interest is one of the powerful figures represented in a classical Hollywood Cinema. In Hindi Cinema femme fatal is mostly characterized as a Vamp. Their steamy look, the sizzling dance moves who dominated Indian Film Industry in 60's and 70's even call them sultry babes and nasty vamps. They lured heroes flirted with them drank liquor, smoked and did everything that considered taboo and always on power with main villains. Fearless Nadia, the first lady in the era of 50's who ruled the Bollywood with her arrogance and bold Avtar.

Another popular character Lalita Pawar, who ruled the silver screen almost three decades, was always portrayed as wicked Sasuma. Bindu and Aruna Irani from her sizzling dance moves to cruel mother-in-law and sister-in-law were seen conspiring against protagonist. Helen was the quintessential of the 70's. She played westernized unliberated characters and bagged all the item numbers during that era. In the era of 80's Praveen Babi and Zeenat Amaan were modern and urbanized heroines in films like*Hare Rama Hare Krishna* (1971) and *Deewar (*1975). As the Bollywood brought to a change the concept of vamps changed completely.

In the 90's heroines like Sridevi, Kajol, Urmila Matondkar played a negative role and without hesitation played a character of villainess shades. Early 2000 Priyanka Chopra and Bipasha Basu played sultry women and scandalize the good man in *Aitraaz* (2004) and *Jism* (2003). They experiment with the characters still there like Vidya Balan in Ishqiya (2010) played a manipulative women and Mahi Gill lovelorn women explores the grey shade of women's characters in *Saheb, Biwi and Gangster* (2011). According to Mazumdar (2007) says the heroine of Hindi Film was the site of virtue and Indianness while Vamp always seen as home breaker who displays wanton sexuality on the screen. In filmic term she says their sexual displays are always seen in bars, casinos, often followed by sexual relations with criminals. Rekha in *Ittefaq* (1969) starts an illegal affair with a police officer preferring to kill her husband than to break up with her lover. Rekha poses a naive wife but in the end Director shocked us with the original character of Rekha. Neeta (Ravina Tondon) in *Aks* (2001) is a more complex character. She played a character with maturity particularly while displaying her love and confusion.

According to Sharma (2007), there are three types of prostitutes. These women sometime indulge in the business of prostitution willingly or unwillingly because of their socio economic condition and later get associated with the world of crime. Character of Nina (Geeta Bali) in film *Baazi* (1951) and Kamini played by Wahida Rehman in *CID* (1956). As shown in Hindi Films, the entity of Femme fatal is against the norms of the society. They usually do the unethical things which are bound to bring more the woman a sense of guilt at some point of life.

The femme fatal mostly attack directly on traditional womanhood and the nuclear family. They deny playing a role of dutiful wife and a responsible person and sometimes use her sexual attractiveness to gain independence and for their motives lead up to any bad work. In Vishal Bhardwaj *7 Khoon Maaf* (2011) Priyanka Chopra killed her all the husband and keep marrying in search of truc love. She doesn't want to compromise with things which make her uncomfortable and which do not match with her desire. Again in the same way the character of Priyanka Chopra in *Aitraaz (2004)* married to an old tycoon for his money, she tries to seduce the much-married Akshay Kumar and when she fails, all hell breaks loose. As earlier she refused to get married as marriage is confining and a detriment to her career.

In *Gupt* (1997) Kajol Played a serial killer who finished off everyone who stood in the way of her true love and herself. In the same way the recent film of Sriram Raghvan *Andhadhun* (2018) Tabbu played the femme fatal as she was in extra martial affair and killed her husband, at once she was shy, then susceptible and then cruel and finally killed everyone whom she found suspected. Sriram Raghvan always played better with the characters of femme fatal and perfectly bring out the best of it, as in *Ek Hasina Thi* (2004) where Urmila Matondkar avenge herself on the hero who had pushed her admitting a crime for which she was imprisoned. Another Femme fatale Rimi in *Johnny Gaddar* and Simi in *Andhadhun* is the perfect portrayal of modern representation who can do anything to live their life in their own terms Filmmaker Sriram Raghvan had frequently used red lipsticks, mysterious and dark outfits to reflect Mini's and Simi's indirect association with blood and her dangerous desire which is a major characteristics of femme fatale. Now the representation of femme fatal is completely different they are no more vamps in truth more than that, they are lead protagonist running for money and power and cross the confines and do whatever which make them happy.

Conclusion

Femme fatal is a dangerous woman who is alluring and mysterious at the same time. She's is beautiful, intelligent and capable of getting men to do what she wants. They are more popular now days because of their non traditional role and the major thing is that they are now playing a lead protagonist. Though Bollywood films and actors have evolved from the age of the vamps the unparalled glamour poise but the elegance of the yesteryear vamps will always be missed.

REFERENCES

Allen, V. M. (1983). *The femme fatale: erotic icon.* Troy, N.Y.: Whitston Pub. Co.,.

Dirks, T. (n.d). *aMC Filmsite.* Retrieved from Filmsite.org: http://www.filmsite.org/femmesfatales.html

Gaines, J. (2011, Novemebr). *Library Inspirin*

Hirsch, F. (1982). The Dark Side of the Screen: Film Noir. *Journal of the University Film and Video Association*.

Martin, R. (1997). *Mean Streets and Raging Bulls: The Legacy of Film Noir in Contemporary American Cinema.* Scarecrow Press.

Mazumdar, R. (2007). *Bombay Cinema: An archive of the City.* Minnesota Press.

Sharma, K. (2007). *Indian Social Structure and Change.* rawat publications

Websites

https://libguides.aquinas.wa.edu.au/c.php?g=582968&p=4076698

http://www.whatisnoir.com/

https://en.oxforddictionaries.com/definition/noir

PART 5
Film Analysis and Criticism Evaluation

18

Indian Art Cinema: The Sinking Ship

Sudhanshu Maheshwari

Introduction

Mainstream and art are two prominent style of cinemas in India. But what was the reason that mainstream cinema overtook the space occupied by art cinema? Why art cinemas fail to garner mass support? Why art cinema fails on Indian box-office?

These are some popping questions which are always debated upon but we are unable to reach to any conclusion. The researcher tries to accelerate this debate between art and mainstream cinema and tries to understand the importance of this cinema and also the reasons of its diminishing impact in present scenario.

The researcher will also try to understand the fact that why still majority of Indians are not relating and connecting with this parallel cinema.

The researcher will also analyse, if the rigid censor board is stopping the Indian directors to per sue this cinema.

What is Art Cinema?

Basically art cinema is different from mainstream cinema and focuses on a particular target audience. Majority of times these kind of films are made on serious issues and also raises the alarming issues of the society. They are symbolic in nature and generally have good social messages. It has been observed that art cinema is more relatable to intellectuals and urbanised population who want realism and logic. If we analyse it in Indian perspective than, art films are made on experimental basis. Basically today also directors are not ready to take risk of making art films as it is seen as loss making project.

Anurag Kashyap, Bimal Roy, Ketan Mehta, Mahesh Bhatt are some rare example who tried and some are today also trying to establish the Indian art cinema among the masses.

Objective

The researcher feels bad when a highly critically acclaimed film flops at the box office. Today personality battle can be witnessed at every level of Indian cinema and the only victim in such situation is art cinema, the true content and a noble story. The key to success at box office rests in some individuals hand and rest are deprived of that commercial success. We will try to go deep in this scenario and figure out the real problem and solutions to it.

The research will try to create an optimistic environment for art cinema in India and to strengthen it, researcher will attach certain case studies of films which were not associated with mainstream cinema but had a lasting impact on society. And as it is said we have to dig deep into history to understand the present situation, so researcher will study the impact of art cinema and its relevance at different period of time.

Review of Literature

The researcher while making this research paper analyse certain articles, blogs of different people to strengthen its perspective. Following material were read by the researcher:

1. ***"Indian Art Cinema" by Soumya Venugopal in Youth ki Awaaz:*** This article highlighted the basic difference between mainstream and art cinema. It also highlighted

the recent trends related to development of parallel cinema in India.

2. ***Art Cinema in India by Hrishkesh Somani:*** This article focused on the golden history of Indian art cinema and also discussed the issues related to this style of filmmaking.

Finding and Inferences

According to above result 63% of population feels that Indian cinema is not given importance in India. This indicates that researcher and his target audience is on the same page and both understand the diminishing situation of Indian art films.

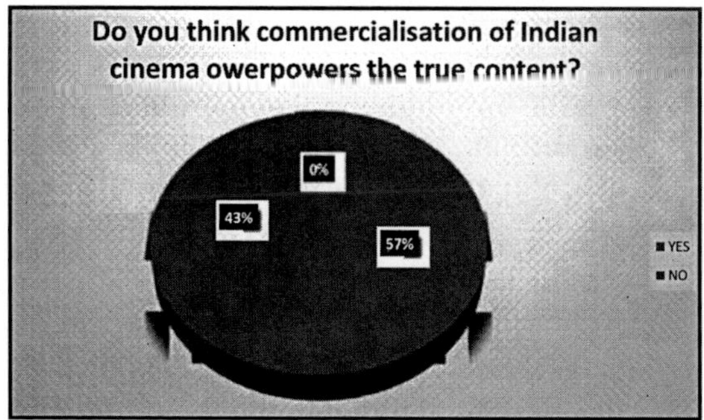

According to the above result 57% of people feel that commercialisation of Indian cinema overpowers the true content. This shows that people are aware of the fact that the real power or key to success in Bollywood is in the hand of few people and the true content is neglected.

According to above result 47% respondent will buy a movie ticket even if there is no known actor. This was a close contest as 53% people said they will not buy a movie ticket, so majority lies here. The researcher feels that "yes" percentage would have been even low if rural population would have been taken into consideration.

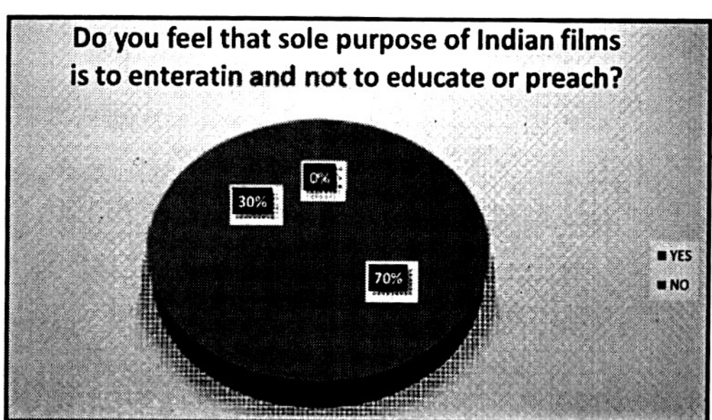

According to above result, 70% of respondent feels that the sole purpose of Indian film is not to entertain but also to educate and preach. This highlights the difference between the approaches of audience of urban and rural to some extent.

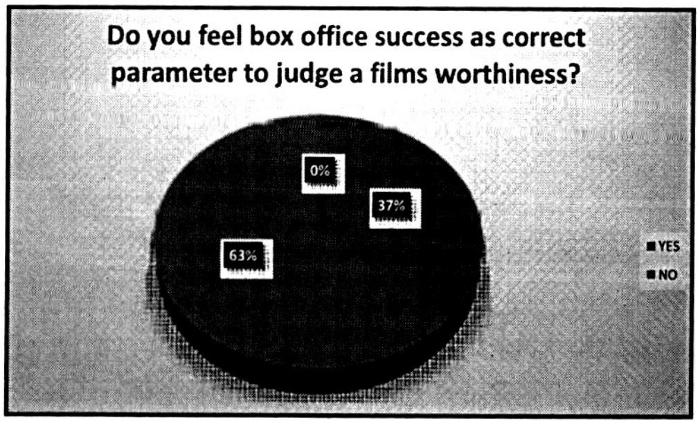

According to above result 63% respondent feel that box office success is not the correct parameter to judge films worthiness. Only 37% see box office success as ethical parameter. This shows that to some extent people are changing and are also trying to judge films worthiness through other angles too.

According to above result whooping 80% respondent perceive that strict rules of CBFC discouragers the filmmakers from making art film. Researcher perceive this as anger of general public towards the functioning of CBFC because in recent times it has been in controversy. Researcher also understood that this was not only restricted to art films but was also related to mainstream cinema.

According to above result, 50% respondent want art films to be made tax free and same number of respondent don't want this to be implemented. People against this action felt that this will create more disparity between art and commercial films. On the other hand people in support felt this will motivate directors to make more art films thus creating a positive environment in favour of art films.

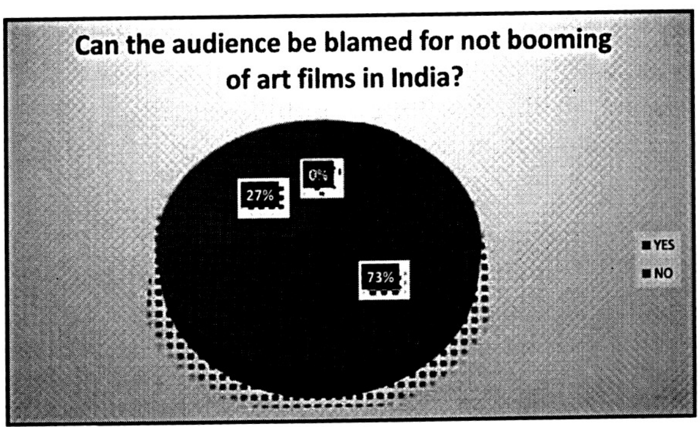

According to above result 73% of people felt audience at general should be blamed for not booming of art cinema. When researcher asked the reason for this tough stand, it was understood that people have created a comfort zone for themselves which they do not wish to cross. Basically they love a particular kind of cinema.

According to above result 67% of respondent feel that releasing of art films on Netflix will be more profitable. For researcher this was an expected response because majority of generation in present scenario are consuming videos on digital platform. People in against of this said that this will even restrict more the reach of art cinema as people in rural area or small city are not using Netflix.

According to above result only 33% respondent said that filmmakers should stop making art films. 67% of individual want art films to be made which shows that parallel cinema enjoys a good support among the intellectuals and urban population. Researcher deliberately asked this question in straight forward manner because this reveals the actual perception of people towards the art cinema in India.

Survey Analysis

After conducting this survey, researcher concluded that people as a whole do not have problem with art cinema. When we observe questions ranging from 2 to 5, it is clear that people are concerned about the present situation of art films in India. For instance 63% respondent feel that box office success is not the correct parameter of judging films worthiness. This is a startling fact because we live in a world where money is everything and we enjoy seeing that which film broke which record. So if 63% respondent feel it as not correct parameter than this showcases that audience is sensible enough to judge between a good and bad film.

Secondly 67% respondent want art films to be made in India, which again showcases that if director will take risk, the audience will whole heartedly welcome the art film.

Thirdly this survey also raises question on the functioning of CBFC because 80% of individual feel that strict rules of CBFC discourages filmmakers from making art films. But according to researcher, we cannot solely hold CBFC responsible because that body make the cut which they feel can stir a controversy in society or can affect the social harmony. So primarily the public as a whole should also become liberal and free from preconceptions. This perspective brings the researcher to question 8 of the survey, according to which 73% people believe that the audience itself is not letting Indian art cinema boom. This is true to some extent because films are said to be mirror of society and if audience start demanding for more logical and content driven films than filmmakers have to make such films to sustain in market.

Notable Case Studies

Do Bigha Zameen

Do Bigha Zameen, directed by Bimal Roy is seen as the best film when we talk about art cinema or parallel cinema. The film raised the issue of farmers beautifully and showed the struggle of a farmer to save his "Do Bigha Zameen". The story revolve around a farmer named Shambu. He owns a two acre land in village but is shocked to learn that the local zamidar Harnam Singh is willing to construct a mill in the village which will also lead to the acquisition of his two acre land. When Shambu protests, he is given a time frame of three months to repay the loan he took from Harnam. Now Shambu with his son Kanahiya goes to Calcutta for living. Shambu leaves his wife Parvati and his ailing father alone. Now Shambu become a rikshaw puller in Calcutta and Kanahiya starts polishing shoes. But as earning is not enough, Kanahiya starts stealing and gets indulged in pick pocketing. Learning this Shambu beats Kanahiya and teaches him lesson. Now worrying for their husband and son, Parvati comes to Calcutta where she is harassed by an individual. When she run from there she is hit by a truck. Accidentally Shambu is on the same street and take her wife to hospital. Now Shambu spends all his spending to cure her wife and Kanahiya sees this as lesson taught to him by god for stealing. Than as all the spending his over Shambu cannot retain his two acre land and a mill is constructed there.

So in this Bimal Roy dictorial there was no big sets, neither an artificial world was created, but then also it won first filmfare award, and Bimal Roy won National Award for best director. Film was also shown on 7th Cannes Film Festival.

Saaransh by Mahesh Bhatt

Saaransh is another good example when we think of art cinema. This movie was directed by Mahesh Bhatt. This film dealt with ultimate truth of life i.e. "Death". Its simple story also focussed on the way an individual should live his life.

The story revolve around retired teacher Pradhan and his wife Parvati. Their son died in New York after which they both live a lonely life. Parvati guru told her that there would be a rebirth of his son in this house. After this they give one room of the house on rent and a girl named Sujata comes to live there. Sujata is an aspiring actor and has a boyfriend Vilas. Sujata becomes pregnant but Vilas want her to go through abortion. But Parvati perceives that child as her own child as her guru predicted of this earlier. Now Pradhan is on goal to save that child and to fight the corrupt system. Like this the child is saved and Sujata and Vilas live a happy life. Then they both leave Pradhan house which lead to a trauma for Parvati as she perceives their son as her own. But then Pradhan explains her the importance of life and ask her to learn to handle such ordeals.

Now this epic tale of Mahesh Bhatt won Filmfare award for best acting, best story, and best art direction.

Conclusion

The researcher when decided to work on this topic was concerned about the future of Indian Art Cinema. He wished that that these films should not be made as no one gives respect to this style of filmmaking. But when researcher critically analysed the situation and conducted a survey, it was found that people were aware about the challenges faced by Indian art cinema and they also wish to expand its reach to new heights.

After commercialisation, the film scenario changed completely and big budget films become a trend. But today also film on social issues can be made in an entertaining way. Movies like Padman create awareness and earn revenue on same time.

So striking a balance between art and commercial cinema is necessary if we have to cater to a larger audience and have to sustain the rich legacy Indian Cinema as a whole.

19

Effect of Watching 'A' Certified Movies on Children: A Study

Smriti Bajaj

Introduction

The history of cinema in India extends back to the beginning of the film era. The Indian film Industry is the 2nd oldest in the world. Following the screening of the Lumiere and Robert Paul moving pictures in London (1896), animated photography became a worldwide sensation and by mid-1896 both Lumiere and Robert Paul films had been shown in Bombay

The Cinema of India, colloquially known as Indywood consists of films produced in the nation of India. Cinema is immensely popular in India, with as many as 1,600 films produced in various languages every year. Indian cinema produces more films watched by more people than any other country; in 2011, over 3.5 billion tickets were sold across the globe, 900,000 more than Hollywood.

The Central Board of Film Certification (CBFC) (often referred to as the Censor Board) is a statutory censorship and classification body under the Ministry of Information and Broadcasting, Government of India. It is tasked with "regulating the public exhibition of films under the provisions of the Cinematograph Act 1952". Films can be publicly exhibited in India only after they are certified by the Board, including films shown on television. CBFC India is considered to be one of the most powerful film censor boards in the world due to its strict ways of functioning.

Films are certified under 4 categories. Initially, there were only two categories of certificates – "U" (unrestricted public exhibition) and "A" (restricted to adult audiences). Two more categories were added in June 1983 – "U/A" (unrestricted public exhibition subject to parental guidance for children below the age of twelve) and "S" (restricted to specialised audiences such as doctors or scientists). In addition to these certifications, the board may also refuse to certify.

- **U (Unrestricted Public Exhibition)**

  Films with the U certification are fit for unrestricted public exhibition and are family friendly. These films can contain universal themes like education, family, drama, romance, sci-fi, action etc. Now, these films can also contain some mild violence, but it should not be prolonged. It may also contain very mild sexual scenes (without any traces of nudity or sexual detail).

- **U/A (Parental Guidance for children below the age of 12 years)**

  Films with the U/A certification can contain moderate adult themes, that is not strong in nature and can be watched by a child under parental guidance. These films contain moderate to strong violence, moderate sex scenes (very little traces of nudity and moderate sexual detail can be found), frightening scenes or muted abusive and filthy language.

- **A (Restricted to adults)**

  Films with the A certification are available for public exhibition, but with restriction to adults. These films can contain heavily strong violence, strong sex (but full frontal and rear nudity is not allowed usually), strong abusive language (but words which insults or degrades women are not allowed), and even some controversial and adult themes considered unsuitable for young viewers. Such films are often rectified for TV and video viewing, which doesn't happen in case of U and U/A certified movies.

- **S (Restricted to any special class of persons)**

  Films with S certification should not be viewed by the public. Only people associated with it (Engineers, Doctors, Scientists, etc.), have permission to watch those films.

  Additionally, V/U, V/UA, V/A are used for video releases with U, U/A and A carrying the same meaning as above.

- **Refusal to certify.**

  In addition to the certifications above, there is also the possibility of the board refusing to certify the film at all.

Guidelines for Certification

✓ anti-social activities such as violence are not glorified or justified

✓ the modus operandi of criminals, other visuals or words likely to incite the commission of any offence are not depicted; scenes

✓ showing the involvement of children in violence as victims or perpetrators or as forced witnesses to violence, or showing children as being subjected to any form of child abuse

✓ showing abuse or ridicule of physically and mentally handicapped persons; and

✓ showing cruelty to, or abuse of animals, are not presented needlessly

✓ pointless or avoidable scenes of violence, cruelty, and horror, scenes of violence primarily intended to provide entertainment and such scenes as may have the effect of de-sensitising or de-humanising people are not shown

✓ scenes which have the effect of justifying or glorifying drinking are not shown

- ✓ scenes tending to encourage, justify or glamorise drug addiction are not shown
- ✓ scenes tending to encourage, justify or glamorise consumption of tobacco or smoking are not shown
- ✓ human sensibilities are not offended by vulgarity, obscenity or depravity
- ✓ such dual meaning words as obviously cater to baser instincts are not allowed
- ✓ scenes degrading or denigrating women in any manner are not presented
- ✓ scenes involving sexual violence against women like attempt to rape, rape or any form of molestation or scenes of a similar nature are avoided, and if any such incidence is germane to the theme, they shall be reduced to the minimum and no details are shown
- ✓ scenes showing sexual perversions shall be avoided and if such matters are germane to the theme they shall be reduced to the minimum and no details are shown
- ✓ visuals or words contemptuous of racial, religious or other groups are not presented
- ✓ visuals or words which promote communal, obscurantist, anti-scientific and anti-national attitude are not presented
- ✓ the sovereignty and integrity of India is not called in question
- ✓ the security of the State is not jeopardised or endangered
- ✓ friendly relations with foreign States are not strained
- ✓ public order is not endangered
- ✓ visuals or words involving defamation of an individual or a body of individuals, or contempt of court are not presented. EXPLANATION: Scenes that tend to create scorn, disgrace or disregard of rules or undermine the dignity of court will come under the term "Contempt of Court'' : and

- ✓ national symbols and emblems are not shown except in accordance with the provisions of the **Emblems and Names (Prevention of Improper Use) Act, 1950 (12 of 1950)**
- ✓ The Board of Film Certification shall also ensure that the film
- ✓ Is judged in its entirety from the point of view of its overall impact; and
- ✓ Is examined in the light of the period depicted in the films and the contemporary standards of the country and the people to which the film relates provided that the film does not affect the morality of the audience
- ✓ The Board shall scrutinise the titles of the films carefully and ensure that they are not provocative, vulgar, offensive or violative of any of the above-mentioned guidelines.

Enforcement: Since 2004, censorship is rigorously enforced. There have been reported instances where exhibitor's staff – the booking clerk who sold the ticket, the usher who took minors to the seat, the theatre manager and the partners of the theatre complex – were arrested for non-compliance with certificate rules.

Objectives

1. To find effects on children watching A certified movies.
2. To find the reasons for parents to take their children for watching A grade movies.
3. To study behavioural effects on children after watching A certified movies.
4. To study parent-children relationship after watching adult content.
5. To study the intensity of crime committed by children after watching A certified movie.
6. To study the reasons for censor board to give any movie A-grade certification.

7. To study whether certification by censor board should be optional.

Hypothesis

Parents found their children to be more friendly with them after watching A certified movies, their reason to take them along to watch movies above their age allotment is that today's children are much more intellectual.

Review of Literature

Vickey Lalvani a journalist from Times of India reported on May 14, 2013 that theatre owners cry foul over families bringing their children to watch film with sex/intimacy and violence. Parents also insist that their internet kids are smart enough to deal with it. Theatre owners trying to avoid children to enter, but most of the times they are accompanied by their parents.

According to a news in TOI on May 14, 2013 due to not being allowed to watch a movie with kid, parent painted fake moustache on a boy hardly 12.

According to journalist Niharika Lal on June 9, 2018 reported that despite of being told several times parents bring their children to watch A certified movies and then argue if not given entry saying who is the parent you or us, my child will sleep in the middle or where should I leave him/her with then?

According to journalist Nivedita Mookherji of DNA India reported on April 16, 2010 that soon in India films will be rated as U, 12+, 15+, A and S. If the Cinematograph Act of 1952 is repeated then I&B Ministry had prepared draft Cinematograph Bill 2010, which refers to a multiple rating strategy. Which will be inline to international norms.

According to an article in The Indian Express on September 11, 2015 by Shubhra Gupta he wrote "in the age where everything is just a download away things need to be dealt with more caution".

According to an article in The Economic Times on August 12, 2017 by Vasudha Venugopal govt. sources said with Nihalani's exit it will bring in reforms in film certification starting with putting in place recommendations of the Shyam Bengal Committee Report.

The Hollywood reporter's Nyay Bhushan on November 8, 2017 reported that controversial censor boards chief Pahlaj Nihalani by parson Joshi as since appointment in 2015 he had unleashed many a controversies over his demands for cuts in a film.

Analysis

The research results show that most of the people like to watch movies occasionally, generally with their friends in multiplex. Also, mostly viewers check the certification of the movie. The results also show that parents aren't comfortable to watch A certified movies with their children. They even don't allow them to watch it with their friends.

Few questions were asked regarding the acceptability by the parents and parents who are comfortable for the reason they believe that today's children are much more tech savy and they can easily get things available on internet. Few results also show that parents found a changes in their children. Among which the most common change was children shared a friendly bond with their parents.

It was also seen that majority of the viewers are with the decisions of censor board to make necessary changes or cuts in the movies wherever it is required.

Conclusion

The 1952 Cinematograph Act sets out the structure of censorship as it stands today. veryone, from the chairperson down to the advisory panel members, is a government appointee. And every government at the Centre has taken advantage of this, staffing the CBFC with party loyalists eager to make cuts and deny certificates to films critical of the establishment. It is not just the content of film that is regulated, with all areas of film culture coming under scrutiny. Cinema as a medium has an immeasurable influence in its ability to reach masses, influence viewpoints and shape culture, especially in India. Entertaining, challenging, informational, and critical, films can send either overt or covert messages with considerable impact on its audiences.

REFERENCES

https://asiasociety.org/india/events/censoring-cinema

http://www.filmreference.com/encyclopedia/Academy-Awards-Crime-Films/Censorship.html#ixzz5WHYktne1

https://www.livemint.com

20

Film Analysis through a Web of Networks: A Paradigm Shift on Writings about Regional Films

Manish Prakash

Introduction

Since centuries, there have been presence of cinema in the society and it has great potential to change a person's life. Since the invention of the moving images back in the 1895 by Lumiere brothers it has always had its shock value. It entertains us yet mesmerises with its use of the creative language which no other medium can offer. It has a deep impact on the minds of the people. Undoubtedly, it leaves a certain impact on us which can't be described in words. The very purpose of the cinema is to entertain yet it comes with a message which has great significance in our life.

It has been more than a century since the arrival of the first film but still it has made its indelible mark in the psyche of the people. Cinema since its arrival in the twentieth century has seen a lot of changes as the time progressed. The films of different countries hold their own value as comes with their own narratives. The films of France, Italy, Germany, America, England, China, Korea, Iran, India or any other country differ from each other yet each one of them have their own significance. The American films or the films made in Hollywood have the intrinsic quality attached with it which is more technically sound and replete with the special effects whereas films made in France, Italy or Germany have a meaning in their narratives which is more realistic in nature.

The cinema of India which saw the light of the day since the first film which released in the theatres, *Raja Harishchandra* (Dhundiraj Phalke,1913) was more of devotional in nature. With time, the genre changed from mythological films to social films to comedy to drama interspersed with each other. This in a way makes a significant change in the narrative of the Indian cinema. People who wrote about the film or the ones who gave the review of the films also changed with the times. The whole network of film analysis changed from time to time. In the similar vein, it was more of a transition of film reviewers from print medium to broadcast medium to the cyber medium.

Regional Films and its Analysis

In the contemporary times, regional films have gained a certain momentum with respect to its reviews in different news portals as they have a storyline which is completely different from a regular mainstream film. With the emphasis on some of the regional gems like *Sairat*, *Natsamrat*, *Village Rockstars* in the recent times, the film writing has changed for the better. To begin with, *Sairat* (Nagraj Manjule, 2016) which is a story about two lovers who belong to different castes in one of the villages of Maharashtra and hardships they face once they decide to get married and ultimately are killed in the end hold a certain significance as it bypassed the binary of a mainstream film and came out trumps with not only critical acclaim but also with huge financial profit at the box office.

The film was written and reviewed on almost every single platform and was given a certain feel where it was criticised for its portrayal of the caste dynamics in the hinterland and the violent end it showed. On every platform whether in the national dailies or news channels or on the web, it faced a certain heat because of its narrative which was based on the honour killing. The after life of the film became interesting as it started dwelling in the symphony of the various writing on the social media and different other platforms. The context seemed relevant as India was in the transition phase where it was grappling with number of cases related with the honour killing or the inter-religion marriages in different parts of the country and the film became a catalyst in this whole new movement. Thus, creating an atmosphere where everyone interested in the films started penning down their thoughts on the film. The web-portal like Scroll.in, Firstpost, Huffington Post, Caravan magazine came with their opinions on the film.

In the same year, *Natsamrat* (Mahesh Manjrekar, 2016) another gem from the Marathi film industry was written a lot for its provoking theme and the lead actor's conflict with life. There were a number of opinions on several platforms which published on the areas of arts and popular culture. The film talked about the life of a thespian who retires from acting and the life he leads after dividing his property with his children. It had a powerful message for the young audiences who treat their parents or the old ones in a bad manner.

This film was talked about a lot in the mainstream media and the web-portals which completely changed the discourse around the film. The very essence of the film lied in the message it wanted to convey which became a ploy for the writers to pen down their opinions on the film. In the following years there were yet few instances when regional films were on top of the minds of the film be it films from the Malayalam film industry, Bengali film industry or the north eastern frontiers. The north eastern frontier was represented by one of the youngest filmmakers of Assam, Rima Das who single handedly crafted this film and is a sheer joy to watch.

The films talks about what we left behind and the significance it has in our life. *Village Rockstars* (Rima Das, 2017) is a film which gives a new direction to the Indian film industry and is worthy of being nominated as India's official entry for the Academy award. It transports us in a different zone which can be realized once we watch the film see the latent potential it has. Film critics across platforms have talked about this right from the mainstream media to the web portal and the likes of Anupama Chopra who has given a special attention on her film review platform, *Film Companion*. This is quite praiseworthy where a film which belongs to regional arena has a strong place in the media which only caters to the commercial pot-boilers in the recent times. There is a long road ahead for the regional films which make their mark purely on the basis of their sincere storytelling.

Anna MM Vetticad one of the major film critics of the recent times has penned her opinion on the subtitling in the regional films where she mentions that "most producers lack the vision to see that subtitling makes their films accessible to non traditional audiences which could translate their stars into becoming more familiar and thus more attractive to audiences and producers outside their home turf over time which in turn would lead to more inter-regional exchanges of acting talent, more pan-India audiences for all Indian films and ultimately a better spread of all languages outside states in which they are usually spoken" (Vetticad, 2016). This in turn sets the tone for the regional films which become popular outside the state it is released and make their mark outside it.

Film Analysis of the Yore and the Shift

Since the first film of the world was made, it was written and talked about and there was word of mouth publicity and it had a deep impact on the psyche of the people. Although, the films directed by Lumiere brothers in 1895 was nothing but a shock to the audiences as they had for the first time seen something which was unusual. Earlier, they had seen an image which was still but now it was moving and it had its own significance and shock value attached with it which left them in awe of it.

Film reviews have a long history and its inception itself was with the people associated with the journalism or the film conscious people. With the passage of time, it has changed drastically as technology slipped in and the reviews published in the newspapers started waning and this shift which is inevitable due to the onslaught of technology in the recent times. There have been so many instances when films had an impact because of the reviews written by so many film critics who publish themselves in the newspapers. There have been tremendous transformation because of the technology but the film and its review have changed for the better.

Earlier there were merely one sided effort from the critics who used to publish their reviews but nowadays due to a plethora of opinions on different platforms, it is very difficult to be content with only one review as people tend to look at many reviews which are published elsewhere before watching any film. Despite several reviews people usually turn to theatres for the entertainment. The mall culture have simply changed the cinema going culture as it's the leisure time which is spent there and people flock to the theatres when in the mall. There have been many instances when people go to the theatres to watch a certain film but end up watching another because of the reviews they have read or seen.

The films and its reviews might be similar or different depending on the way films are received or promoted and the role of the producers, distributors and exhibitors play a significant role in it. There is a marked shift because of the commerce attached with it. After the advent of globalisation in the 1990s, there is another angle which is attached with it and majority of the channels and newspapers succumb to it. There is no denying the fact that a certain amount of pressure has been attached to the film reviewers and people respond to it accordingly.

Thus, writing the review of a film quite interesting in current scenario. Sangita Gopal in her book refers to the "liberalisation of the 1990s completely transforming India's economic and cultural landscape leading to the two major factors; urbanisation and the rise of the middle classes". (Gopal, 2011). This in turn leads a situation in which people from across India have been empowered to use the technology and write their opinions on the platforms they are comfortable with. The very idea of the middle classes have changed and they have started spending a notable amount of their time in the weekends in the malls thus watching films in the multiplexes.

There is a complete transformation in the way these people have been using the visual medium for their benefit. They get empowered by their participation in the various activities on different platforms because of the change in technology. The art and craft of the whole film business has changed and similarly its reviews. Notably, the whole gamut of information on the film has shifted and a person who even has a sheepish idea about the film can pen down their thoughts with the help of a number of technology. With this, a number of regional films have seen the light of the day and directors and producers have been benefitted from it. Although a film like *Baahubali* could not garner rave reviews yet it raked in moolah at the box-office which is testimony to the fact that not all reviews matter as there are certain films which come with a package which appeals to the audiences. There have been a several anecdotes about the film and its review but ultimately it's the audiences who decide which film to watch and not. There are various factors involved which decide the fate of the film despite its reviews. So, here I argue that the film reviews can be a pre-cursor for the success of a film but that is not the only factor for the smooth run of a film despite a number of views on several platforms altogether.

Conclusion

Any film has its own shelf life and it undergoes a lot of scrutiny by the film critics all across the world yet it maintains its essence despite several opinions on it. In the recent times, a film and its life increases manifold as so many people write on it and there is a complete dissection of its narrative, music, performance etc. Irrespective of its analysis, a film makes its mark in our minds even if it did not have a good run at the box-office or has not got thumbs up from the critics purely on the entertainment quotient which is still undisputed in today's world.

REFERENCES

Gopal, S. (2011). *Conjugations: Marriage and Form in New Bollywood Cinema.* Chicago: THe University of Chicago Press.

Vetticad, A. M. (2016, May 20). The diary of a frustrated Indian film buff. *Business Line*.

Manovich, Lev. *The Language of New Media.* New York: MIT Press, 2001.

Tapscott, Don. *Grown Up Digital.* New Delhi, New York: Tata Mc Graw Hill, 2009.

Verdi, Jyotika. *The Cinematic Imagination.* New Delhi: Permanent Black, 2003.

Jenkins, Henry. *Convergence Culture: Where Old and New Media Collide.* New York and London: New York University Press, 2006.

Fenton, Natalie. *New Media, Old News: Journalism and Democracy in the Digital Age.* London, Los Angeles: Sage, 2010.

Don Tapscott, Art Caston. *Paradigm Shift: The New Promise of Information Technology.* London: Mc Graw Hill, 1993.

Vetticad, A. M. (2016, May 20). The diary of a frustrated Indian film buff. *Business Line*.

Castells, Manuel. *The Rise of the Network Society: The Information Age - Economy, Society and Culture.* Sussex: Willey- Blackwell, 2010.

21

Through the Freudian Lens: Zindagi Na Milegi Dobara

Deepika Dhawan

Director Zoya Akhtar's film 'Zindagi Na Milegi Dobara' introduces the concept of three inseparable childhood friends who despite their differences get along well. Not just get along well, they also enjoy the time with each other and hold the moments spent with each other very dear to their hearts.

The film portrays the human mind as explained by Dr. Sigmund Freud, originally a neurologist and the father of psychoanalysis. In Freud's Iceberg Theory, Freud broke down the mental structure into 3 parts: Conscious (above the water surface; everything we are aware of), Unconscious (part of iceberg below the water surface; larger than conscious) and Preconscious (the plane of awareness between the unconscious and the conscious).

Id works on the 'Pleasure Principle'. It makes up most of the Unconscious part of the mind and it demands immediate gratification. It develops in a person right after birth. The Ego, of which our perceptions, thoughts and judgements are part of, seeks long-term gratification as opposed to the Id's immediate gratification. It works on the 'Reality Principle'. The Superego develops around the age of 4 years. It is our moral compass and conscience. It represents the values of the society. The Superego works on the 'Perfection Principle'.

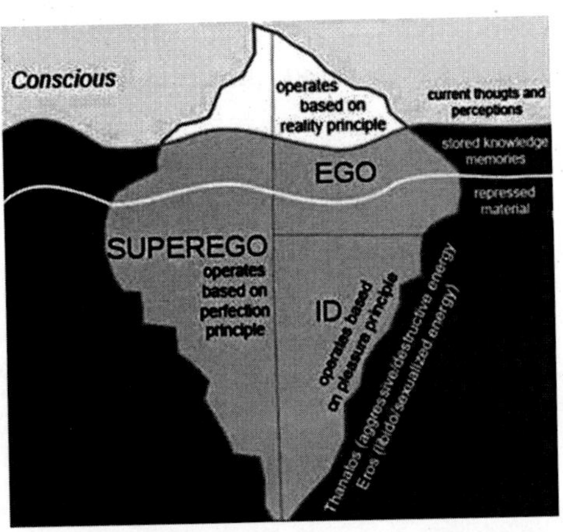

The image shows the 'Iceberg Theory' by Dr. Sigmund Freud explaining the Id, Ego and Superego amidst the Unconscious, Preconscious and the Conscious.

This film is actually a reflection of how the human mind works. The three characters Imraan, Kabir and Arjun represent the Id, Ego and Superego respectively. Through the story, the film attempts to explain how the mind works in conflict and in harmony.

Imraan: The Embodiment of 'Id'

Imraan, played by Farhan Akhtar, is a 'free-spirited' person who is not essentially a long-term planner. He likes to do things spontaneously. His actions are clearly based on the 'Pleasure Principle', like the 'id'. Just like Id, he believes in 'living in the moment' and pursues 'immediate gratification'.

Despite his mother telling him to stay away from his biological father who had not accepted his mother after he found out that she got pregnant, Imran still goes ahead and meets him. He believes in quickly satisfying his needs. Imran is not a person who tries and pretends to be perfect. He doesn't believe that he should do something to get an approval from other people. He simply does things to please himself.

Imraan doesn't seek long-term gratification. Even while he tried to ask a girl out, it didn't matter to him that she didn't speak his language and there was a communication barrier. All he wanted to have was a good time and gratify his physical needs from that relationship. This is a typical 'id' phenomenon.

Imraan also ignores logic. During a road trip, irritated with Arjun's repetitive phone calls from work, he snatches his cell phone and tosses it out the car. He doesn't think twice and acts swiftly without measuring the consequences.

Morality is a weak point for Id. Likewise, Imraan is not good with handling situations that require good moral behaviour. Like the Id, Imraan behaves selfishly. He has an innate behaviour of satisfying himself first and then thinking of anything else.

For Imraan, there is no practical thinking. He loves to get lost in his own thoughts, write poetry and have multiple varied perspectives. He does not believe in traditions or conventional way to deal with things. He is an explorer and a risk-taker.

The Id is just a collection of urges and has no real awareness. Hence Imraan doesn't really fear anything. Even if he is aware of an incoming challenge, he bounces back with aggression. The id doesn't know how to deal with peace. It only behaves and represents the carnal desires of the human.

Kabir: The Carefully Decisive 'Ego'

As the peace-making 'Ego' between the Imraan and Arjun, Kabir is the pragmatic force that neither seeks perfection nor really cares about satisfying the urges. The ego only observes and understands the surroundings. It understands what the Id wants and what are the social norms. The ego thinks about how to make peace between the two. The ego does not believe in extremities. It just focusses on making rational and realistic decisions.

Kabir, the character played by Abhay Deol, is a sensible and fun-loving person who is very dependable. He will still help out his friends even when he himself is going through some tough time emotionally. Internally, he faces a dilemma with his 'I-didn't-even-propose' marriage to his fiancé Kalki Koechlin. On one hand, this whole setup of him proposing Kalki made everyone in their families happier than ever. On the other hand, Kabir never really wanted to ask Kalki to marry her.

While fighting this emotional battle within, he tries to keep Imraan and Arjun at peace and the trio hangs out happily. But since they all are fighting their emotional battles, Imraan and Arjun obviously lock horns now and then because of a past issue between them.

The id and superego are always on a battle to control the behaviour. So the ego's job is to mediate between the two. Similarly, Kabir used to be in the middle of Imraan and Arjun's fights all the time and like the ego, he could choose whose side he wanted to be on. So like the id, if Imraan was given more support by Kabir, it sometimes turned out to be inappropriate and if Arjun was given more support by Kabir, the situations turned out to be more about rigid perfection.

As the representation of ego, Kabir was more realistic and balanced as compared to Imraan and Arjun. From reuniting both of them to planning the whole trip that satisfies all of their plans, Kabir acts as a mental will of the group. Kabir relentlessly tries to keep the atmosphere light when there is a conflict. He also drifts between Imraan's spontaneous and carefree personality and Arjun's uptight behaviour.

Arjun: The Socially-righteous 'Superego'

The Superego, as Hrithik Roshan, is the polar opposite of id. It is the moral compass of the human mind. It is concentrated on the ideals of the world and looking towards success and aspirations. It is what we call the 'conscience'. It provides a sense to differentiate clearly between right and wrong. Like the id and unlike the ego, the superego is not realistic. Basically, a set of moral lessons that we have learnt from parents, society and organized religion.

Arjun is the personification of the superego. He is a workaholic and completely enslaved to the extent that he carries his laptop and answers all his official calls on a holiday trip. Tracing back to the early death of his father and the residual debt left by him, Arjun confesses that the only dream in his life is to earn money and retire at the age of forty.

He is often seen to be stridently bragging about price tags and comes out as a man completely consumed by his superficial needs, because of which he lost his girlfriend in the past. But later, experiencing the magnificence of the underwater world, he discovers happiness in things beyond work and money, further triggered by Laila's take on the same.

The Superego demands more requirements that are so severe that the person could never live up to them and he would suffer constant feelings of guilt. Likewise, Arjun has built a web for himself that makes him prioritise work over spending quality time with his loved ones. This being completely opposite to Imraan, Arjun learns that he has been missing out on the 'joy of living'.

Arjun strives to achieve perfection. He has planned everything and aspires to be extremely successful. He is cautious against making any mistakes. Arjun is not a risk-taker and he does not do things spontaneously. He prefers planning and security in life. He is the kind of person who faces difficulty in loosening up at a vacation and living the life to the present. For him, time and life are all about fulfilling materialistic desires and working hard for them. He doesn't believe in embracing experiences and pausing life a bit.

Getting along Well

Freud believes that a mentally healthy person has a strong ego, keeping the id and the superego balanced because if they became imbalanced, mental illness would be the result. Anxiety is a result of the id and the superego fighting for dominance or an existence of a moral dilemma.

Imraan's character exemplarily motivates the audience to not let your inner demons consume you, despite the endless number of times life pins you down. Since Imran's character is like 'be in the moment', he embraces the differences unlike Arjun. Imraan does not crave for perfection and is happy with what he is doing. He doesn't have high aspirations and high morals to hold onto and lives uninhibited.

Though there is a lot of emotional conflict within Kabir and his role as a peace-maker, he himself changes by the end of film. Sometimes, our ego prefers one more than the other. This is exactly what Kabir kept on doing. He valued Kalki's and their families' happiness too much more over his own, in regard to his decision of marriage.This is a perfect example of when we give more value to what the society wants us to do and do nothing about how we really feel. This is an emotional dilemma that every human being goes through at some point in their lives.

The film shows Arjun (the superego) adjusting to the bigger-than-life and life-threatening challenges by Imraan (the id). Whereas Imraan also accepts that gaining happiness from the gratification achieved is more important than going on adventures all the time. He realises the importance of satisfaction and evolves towards stability.

BIBLIOGRAPHY

Nayar, R. (Ed.). (2016). Cultural Studies in India. London: Routledge.

Bhugra, D. (2008). Psychoanalysis in Hindi cinema. ActaNeuropsychiatrica, 20 (02), 96-97. doi: 10.1111/j.1601-5215.2008.00275.x

How The 'Zindagi Na MilegiDobara' Characters Inspire Us To Do More And Be More | Youth Ki Awaaz. (2018). Retrieved from https://www.youthkiawaaz.com/2014/06/zindagi-na-milegi-dobara-characters-inspire-us/

id, ego, & superego. (2018). Retrieved from https://www.youtube.com/watch?v=WRtItnRRV1M

Psychoanalytic film theory. (2018). Retrieved from https://en.wikipedia.org/wiki/Psychoanalytic_film_theory

Surendran, V. (2018). Why we love Zindagi Na MilegiDobara. Retrieved from https://www.indiatoday.in/movies/bollywood/story/four-years-of-zindagi-na-milegi-dobara-282482-2015-07-15

This psychoanalysis of 'DilChahtaHai' will blow your mind | The Express Tribune. (2018). Retrieved from https://tribune.com.pk/story/1062229/this-psychoanalysis-of-dil-chahta-hai-will-blow-your-mind/

22

Film Review: Elements of Film and Style of Writing

Dr. Ambrish Saxena

Review writing involves critical assessment of a piece of literature or a work of art, like a book, theatre performance, music concert or a movie. Film review is a niche area which requires a distinct approach and understanding on the part of the reviewer. Many newspapers and magazines publishing film reviews hire experts for reviewing new films for them. Film reviewing is a work of journalism rather than of academic criticism. Still, only a reviewer with an in-depth knowledge of cinema and the film craft can come out with impressive piece of writing.

Format of Film Review: Can there be a Uniform Pattern?

Most of the reviewers follow a prescribed format while writing about films. It includes name of the film, prominent actors, settings (time and place) and type or genre (comedy, adventure, drama etc.) in the first paragraph, plot summary of the film and at least 5 events covering the entire scope of the film without revealing the end in the second para, discussion on one or more aspects of the film like acting, direction, editing, costume design, set design, music songs in the third para. The reviewer has to be specific and can cite some examples from the film in the fourth para. This is to be followed by the overall reaction to the film including the opinion of the reviewer on the quality of the film having recommendation for potential viewers in the fifth para.

But the question remains; can there be a fixed format for writing film reviews? Is it not upon the reviewer which aspects of the film he or she wants to cover and what kind of writing he/she want to follow? This paper tries to find answers to such questions by collecting film viewers' opinion on some selected reviews. These reviews and viewers' opinion on them is expected to provide vital input with regard to film reviewing.

Collection of Viewers' Opinion based on Selected Film Reviews

This researcher took into consideration three film reviews which were written by this researcher himself during three consecutive years i.e. 2016, 2017 and 2018. Review of Pink was written in September 2016, review of Newton in September 2017 and the review of Manto in October 2018. These reviews were posted on social media receiving applauds and appreciation in the form of comments and hundreds of like.

As part of the study, these reviews were made available to a select group of viewers and their opinion was sought on which elements of film need to be covered in a review and what should be the appropriate style of writing in a film review.

Pink Pinkpink: Review of Pink Film [Film Review in September 2016]

The concept of liberty propagated by libertarian philosophers like Jefferson and Mill in the later part of 18th century talked about freedom of choice and the primacy of individual judgment. This concept prepared ground for the establishment of democracy in the West, and encouraged newly independent countries of Asia and Africa to go for constitutional democracies post Second World War. The mix of equality and freedom led to women's movements in more liberalised world in the second part of 20th century.

The feminist movement raised issues like reproductive rights, protection against domestic violence, sexual harassment and sexual violence, and right to have equal pay and maternity leave. The movement made its impact in India too like in other parts of the world. Despite the fact that India has a patriarchal society which is essentially feudal in character, the voice for women's rights made headway in political, social and cultural spheres.

Indian films have also been raising the issues associated with the pride and dignity of women striving for their due status in the society. PINK is the latest addition in redefining womanhood, and the quest of women for leading a life of their choice with conditions unattached. This is a story of three girls coming from diverse background but united on one ground i.e. desire to live a normal life like an ordinary human being but assertive enough to thwart any interference in their way of life.

The film strikes very hard on the orthodoxy of virginity of women, and pleads in unequivocal terms that a woman (including prostitute and wife) has absolute right over her body. It makes a mockery of the stereotypes that women living alone (not with parents), wearing short clothes, consuming alcohol, partying with friends, remaining out till late hours and showing overt behaviour at public places are always bad in character; and that is why they fall prey to men's urge.

PINK hammers on the hypocrisy of Indian society, and exposes our double standards. It also exposes our regional biases, highlighting the demeaning of North Eastern natives at the hands of superior North Indians. The story and screenplay is good and despite few missing links, the film compels the viewers to think. The filmmakers have played wise by incorporating Amitabh Bachchan in the drama, keeping the commercial success in mind. Piyush Mishra has posed a grave challenge to Bachchan senior in manoeuvring. In any case, it is a must watch film.

NEWTON – A Journey to Explore Roots of New India [Film Review in September 2017]

I had seen the promos of NEWTON and what I could make out that the film touches upon the electoral system in India. Further, I came to know that the plot of the film revolves around the mystified issue of Naxalism or Maoism. So, I decided to watch NEWTON.

And, I must confess that this is one of the best films I have ever seen. I have been following Naxalism from the days of Charu Majumdar and Kanu Sanyal to Nag Bhushan Patnaik and Vinod Mishra; and I have been witnessing all its manifestations from PWG to MCC. But, the way Naxalism has been depicted in NEWTON is stunning. Without naming Salwa Judum, the 'forced' transfer of tribals from their villages to 'safe heavens' in urban shelter homes has been described. Towards the end, we see on the screen mining activities on the leveled forest land. Superb narrative….

Whether NEWTON is about Naxalism or 'unrepresentative' democracy? Or both? Or subsidiary issues are more important than the apparent major issues of Maoism and Election? What exactly are the issues – right of tribals on forest land, education of tribals, the subjugation of tribals by the political class, miserable living conditions of tribals, the highhandedness of security forces, and so on? I believe that everything has been bundled, leaving it to the viewers to receive what each one of them wants to receive. In fact, when I was coming out of the cinema hall after watching the film, I overheard that every viewer had his or her own take.

NEWTON is a commentary (you decide if it is a sad commentary) on India's electoral system. Academically, I have worked a lot on India's electoral reforms, but I was astonished to see how election related issues unfold in this film. Whether casting vote is merely ceremonial or it carries some meaning if you would have never heard about contesting candidates? Whether casting vote is a matter of choice or compulsion under coercion? Whether motivating electorates to cast their votes and doing everything possible to make sure that all the votes are cast will change the face of the society or it will remain a farce in the wake of abject poverty and backwardness? Polling booth in the ruined building of a school; is it education versus democracy?

NEWTON raises questions but no handy answers. The Director Amit Masurkar has left the task of finding answers on the viewers; though this process can take you to soul-searching. Despite dealing with a ferocious subject, there is no repugnance or ghastliness in this film. It may be the reflection of Iranian cinema. It is alleged that NEWTON is plagiarized from the Iranian film SECRET BALLOT, though Amit Masurkar denies the charge. What to say of copying, NEWTON is not even inspired from any film, says Amit.

For me it is a film rooted in Indian society, and it gives shocks to elite urban class of multiplexes but very softly and gently. Using dark comedy to emphasize on real serious issues requires a kind of acumen which the director Amit Masurkar and protagonist Rajkumar Rao evidently possess. Throughout the screening, I found everybody in the cinema hall laughing, despite the fact that the film was grim and grey mingled in its concept and plot. Words are short to admire such craft of storytelling.

MANTO: A Biopic of Saadat Hasan Manto [Film Review in October 2018]

I know the literary genius Saadat Hasan Manto for almost 35 years through his short stories and analytical write ups on his unusual life and his impact on literature, politics and society. I have done the dramatic adaptations of his stories by the titles **"Toba Tek Singh"** and **"Khol Do"**. As theatre director, my theatre group in Varanasi "Gokul Arts" made several performances of these plays in many cities during 1980s and 1990s. The central character in "Toba Tek Singh" was played by Chittaranjan Giri, an NSDian known for his award winning and internationally acclaimed films ***The Man Beyond the Bridge*** **(2009)** and ***Lathe Joshi*** **(2016)**. You might also be remembering him in ***Gulaal*** **(2009)** and ***Mangal Pandey: The Rising*** **(2005)**. My adaptation of **"Khol Do"** was also performed by the students of Vivekananda Institute of Professional Studies (VIPS) with an award in "**Anugoonj**", the annual festival of Guru Gobind Singh Indraprastha University, Delhi, in the year 2005. The play was directed by Prince Shadwal, now a filmmaker with number of films like ***Tanu Weds Manu, Pappu Cant Dance Saala, Dum Maro Dum, Force and D Day*** to his credit. The central character of Sakina was played by Aman Deep Kaur.

The point proved. Saadat Hasan Manto has always been alive in the hearts of scores of rational mindsets and youthful youths who do not feel comfortable in this feudal and duplicitous society. He is also an icon even in Pakistan for all freedom loving and rational minds. Manto's social recognition has really never been an issue not only in partitioned India and Pakistan but also in undivided India. Though his political recognition was always an issue as he had no access to political dispensation in pre-Independence India. Pakistani leadership woke up lately by issuing a postal stamp on him in 2005 and honoring him posthumously with Nishan-i-Imtiaz, the top civilian award in 2012. Indian leadership is still in slumber which has deepened in recent years. Manto's literary recognition has been an issue always; during his life time his was never acknowledged bigger in stature as compared to his contemporaries Ismat Chughtai, Krishan Chander and Rajinder Singh Bedi. Even Progressive Writers Association failed to stand by his side while he was facing onslaught from all around. Faiz Ahmad Faiz also refused to accept his writings as literature.

The life of Saadat Hasan Manto had different colours and shades with highest degree of sensitivity. His courage to call dark as dark was exceptional and his attitude to say no to anything which was unconvincing and irrational was astonishing. This would have obviously fascinated Nandita Das when she decided to make a film ***Manto*** on the life and work of Saadat Hasan Manto. In this 112-minute biopic released last week, she has focused on the writer's life mainly between 1946 and 1955, his Bombay days, his Lahore days but skipped Delhi days. The film is a classical work by Nandita Das who feels that "Manto is relevant today as he went beyond the religious and national identities which are diving us, not just in India, but the world over. You interchange the religion in his stories and they would still work. He did not spare anyone. Manto gives me a perfect excuse to respond to what is happening today when identity politics is being played out everywhere".

As a film enthusiast and critic, I agree completely that a film particularly a biopic carries the filmmaker's point of view. No filmmaker can create an all-inclusive film with the exception of Manmohan Desai, Yash Chopra and the like. In a biopic the most important colour of the life of the concerned personality and the most significant contribution of that person should be the central theme. The film ***Manto*** succeeds in portraying Manto's character with conflicting shades of rudeness and arrogance on one hand and honesty, pride and sensitivity on the other hand. Though I feel there may not be a conflict among the above traits since the natural outcome of extreme honesty and sensitivity is non-compromise and least tolerance to wrongs leading to arrogance. But, the film slogs on the other aspect i.e. the most significant contribution of the writer Manto. By all accounts, you would agree that as an individual and as a writer he was not conformist, he was not communal, he did not believe in religious identities and he even discarded national identities following partition of India. In the film ***Manto***, this aspect of his personality and work has been subdued by the whole debate on obscenity and morality. The second half of the film is more or less devoted to this debate only.

The film ***Manto*** devotes considerable time to the trial that Manto had to face for being *fahaash* (risqué) writer. He was even convicted for that. The agony of Manto was the result of Indian/ Pakistani mindset that does not find anything wrong in the sexual exploitation and rape of women but one who is raising voice against this by creating gory scenes in flushy language so as to give shock to his readers is punished for obscenity. The trial of Manto happened for his short story "**Thanda Gosh**t" and the film ***Manto*** also creates a scene in the film based on this short story. But, I feel the filmmaker missed out the real take away from this short story and the trial i.e. the brutality and the torture faced by women during partition as part of religious persecution. Even in **"Khol Do"** (the film carries of scene based on this short story as well), Sakina's sexual exploitation by *rajakars* (Muslim volunteers) could have been used to underline the victimization of women also by the people of her own religion.

The climax of the film comes sudden though doing it in the backdrop of short story **"Toba Tek Singh"** was appropriate. The viewers would have felt contended to find the filmmaker highlighting the futility of nationality based on religious identities. Manto wrote this short story to prove the absurdity of Partition of India. This point has also been raised by historian Ayesha Jalal, Manto's grandniece, in her book "The Pity of Partition: Manto's Life". The sub-continent is again witnessing polarization on religious grounds that Manto had opposed all his life. We need to be beware of this phenomenon if we have watched ***Manto***. That will be our real take away from the film.

And, I must mention in unequivocal terms that Nawazuddin Siddiqui is an actor par excellence. Nandita Das could never had a better choice.

Analysis of Film Reviews as Per Opinion of Viewers

The responses of film viewers incorporated in this study has brought some interested input regarding film reviews. The same is analysed here.

1. **First person approach:** The personal approach of the film reviewer is important in writing his/her piece on any new film. This enhances receptivity of the intended message.
2. **Knowledge of reviewer:** Film lovers reading the review should be reassured of the knowledge and understanding of the reviewer. If the reviewer succeeds in establishing his/her authority as an expert, reliabilityof communication is bound to increase.
3. **Opinion rather than information:** Film goers are interested in the opinion of the reviewer so that they can

decide whether the film under review is worth watching or not? They are not much interested in basic information about the film which they believe they will get in any case.

4. **Priority regarding film elements:** The readers are interested in knowing about the following compartments of the film in order of preference.
   - Story/theme or subject
   - Actor or actress
   - Music and songs
   - Director
5. **USP of the film reviewed:** While reading a review, film lovers' quest is to find out the most fascinating or motivating area of the film. Finally, the USP of the film leads a film goer to cinema halls.

Conclusion

The approach of film lovers regarding film reviews has changed on many count. The readers of review are not interested in information, they are interested on informed opinion of the expert. They expect an analytical piece in the film review which can give them clarity of thought about the film. Film goers appear choosy and they want an opinion if the film is worth watching. Style of writing matters and a personalised approach of the reviewer makes an obligatory impression.

List of Contributors

1. **Yogita Swami** is PhD scholar in the School of Media and Communication at Manipal University, Jaipur. She has done film appreciation course from FTII, Pune. She been a practicing journalist and anchor in various television channels including Jaipur Doordarshan.

2. **Shruti Sharma** is pursuing 2nd year (Semester-3) in Bachelor of Journalism and Mass Communication at Chandigarh University, Gharuan (Punjab). She is a cinema enthusiast and wishes to pursue higher studies in the same subject.

3. **Gurwinder Singh** is PhD research scholar (UGC-JRF) in the Department of Journalism and Mass Communication, Punjabi University, Patiala.

4. **Nitya Dhingra** is PhD Research Scholar (ICSSR), Department of Journalism and Mass Communication, Punjabi University, Patiala.

5. **Kanika Arya** Assistant Professor at Dhyanasadhana College, Thane, Mumbai University. She has more than 8 years teaching experience and 2 years industry experience. Cinema studies is her core functional domain.

6. **Muskan Sidana** is Assistant Professor in the Department of Journalism and Mass Communication, CT Institute of Higher Studies, Jalandhar. She has done B.A. (Journalism and Mass communication) and M.A. (Journalism and Mass communication) from Doaba College, Jalandhar, affiliated to Guru Nanak Dev University, Amritsar. Her research interest lies in Mass Communication and Public Relations.

7. **Samiksha Sharma** is final year BJMC student at DME Media School, Delhi Metropolitan Education, Noida, affiliated to GGSIP University, Delhi.

8. **Dr. Vikrant Kishore** is an academic, filmmaker, photographer, author and a journalist; he has more than 25 documentaries and corporate films to his credit. Currently working at Deakin University as Senior Lecturer in Screen and Design, he is the Course Director for Film, Television and Animation. A recipient of prestigious IPRS Scholarship (Australia), Dr. Kishore was a short-term fellow at the "Karl Jasper's Centre, Cluster of Excellence", Heidelberg University, Germany. He has been a jury member of various film festivals. He is the author of the book "From Real to Reel: Folk Dances of India in Bollywood Cinema", published by UNESCO-Apnieve. Recently, he has directed a 12-part web-series – It's My Desi Life for SBS Hindi, Australia

9. **Mohd. Kamil** is Assistant Professor at Delhi Metropolitan Education (DME), Media School Guru Gobind Singh Indraprastha University, Delhi. He has worked with*The Times of India* where his stories had been published at both state and national level on regular basic. He has cleared the CBSE-NET examination in 2015-16 after which he switched to academics.

10. **Annu Sangwan** is students at K R Mangalam University, Gurugram. She is interested in media academics and research.

11. **Dr. Manasvi Maheshwari** is Assistant Professor in K R Mangalam University, Gurugram. She has been in media industry and academics for more than a decade. She has worked at Vivekananda Institute of Professional Studies and JIMS Vasant Kunj of Guru Gobind Singh Indraprastha University, Delhi. She has keen interest in research and has presented papers in national international seminars and conferences.

12 **Kritika Sati** is UGC NET qualified Assistant Professor at DME Media School, Delhi Metropolitan Education, affiliated to Guru Gobind Singh Indraprastha University. She is post graduate in Mass Communication from Guru Jambheshwar University of Science and Technology, Hisar, Haryana. Before joining DME, she worked in public relations industry for over a year.

13. **Nidhi Suryavanshi** is journalism student at India Today Media Institute (ITMI), Noida, Uttar Pradesh, India. She is a research enthusiast with special leaning towards world cinema.

14. **Kush Kalra** is Assistant Professor at DME Law School, Delhi Metropolitan Education, Noida. He has authored several books and holds Limca Book Record for record number of publications in his name in a year. He is an avid writer and participates in national and international conferences.

15. **Dr. Radhika Mehta** is working with JIMS Rohini as Assistant Professor. She has experience of more than 10 years in academics. She has presented several research papers in national and international seminars, many of these works have been published in national and international journals. She holds M.Phil and PhD in Mass Communication.

16. **Divya Khera** is working in JIMS Rohini as Assistant Professor. She teaches French language and Personality Development and is also pursuing Diploma in French from Delhi University. She is post graduate in Mass Communication from GJU Hisar and has more than 5 years teaching experience in addition to industrial experience.

17. **Anand Kumar. V** is practicing advocate at Delhi High Court and has his own law firm AP Legal Chambers. He also keeps a tab on Bollywood films. Over the years, he has developed a habit of watching films with a completely different angle and has expanded his interest in world cinema. He particularly appreciates parallel cinema and loves unorthodox way of filmmaking and narrative styles. He regularly writes about films and film personalities in his blog.

18. **Shikha Sharma** is Assistant Professor in School of Journalism and Mass Communication in K.R. Mangalam University, Gurugram. She has more than seven years' experience in media academics. She has been working as a freelancer and has directed various short films. She is pursuing PhD in cinema studies.

19. **Neema Negi** is pursuing PhD in Hindi Cinema from Dev Sanskriti University Haridwar, Uttrakhand. She completed her masters in Journalism and Mass Communication and specialization in Advertising from Doon University, Dehradun. Her focus of interest lies in Indian Cinema; she has completed the one month Film Appreciation course in 2015 from Film and television Institute of India.

20. **Sudhanshu Maheshwari** is student at India Today Media Institute, Noida. He interested in research in varied areas.

21. **Smriti Bajaj** is final year BJMC student at DME Media School, DME Noida affiliated to GGSIP University, Delhi.

22. **Manish Prakash** is Assistant Professor in the Department of Mass Communication and New Media, Central University of Jammu, Bagla (Rahya-Suchani), Jammu and Kashmir. He specializes in Cinema Studies, New Media, Contemporary Issues in Media, Online Communication, Cinema and Society, Media and Popular Culture. He has around 5 years teaching experience and is simultaneously pursuing PhD from JNU, Delhi.

23. **Deepika Dhawan** is studying in Apeejay Stya University, Gurgaon. Earlier, she was working at Delhi Metropolitan Education. She is a Mass Media graduate from I P College for Women, Delhi University and has done her PG Diploma in Advertising from Apeejay Institute, Dwarka. She also holds a postgraduate certificate in Market Research and Data Analytics from MICA, Ahmedabad. She has worked in advertising at Innocean Worldwide India.

24. **Dr. Ambrish Saxena** is an accomplished media professional, educator, trainer, researcher, author, anchor and political analyst. He has worked at different media platforms ranging from theatre, puppetry, print, radio, television to films, before switching over to media academics. He has played a long inning in active journalism having worked with various newspapers. He has academic association with more than 20 universities which include 4 central, 5 state and 9 private/ deemed universities. He has 27 books to his credit as sole author, main author, chapter writer and editor. He has a long list of research papers presented in national (17) and international (26) seminars/conferences. He has extensive international exposure having visited China, Australia and the United States in his academic pursuits.

Index

Aarakshan 149

Age of the Respondents 103

Agree Disagree 12, 13

Analysis 203

Analysis and Interpretation 93

Analysis of Film Reviews as per Opinion of Viewers 225

Appropriation 83

Arjun The Socially-righteous Superego 215

Bajirao Mastani (2015) 121

Behl, A. Chaudhary, M (2011) 57

Bhoomi 173

Bibliography 20, 28, 86, 217

Biopics 89

Bollywood 17

Bollywood Film and the Musical 66

Bollywood Song and Dance Continuation of a Larger 74

Cast and Crew of Kanchana Sita 156

Caste and Communal Conflict 149

Central Board of Film Certification 147

Character relationship 170

Characterization of Rama - Ethical Dilemma Pers 162

Climax 163

Collection of Viewers' Opinion 219

Content analysis 18

Content Analysis 25, 103

Content AnalysisTable 1 Synopsis of the films 110

Covert Advertising 24

Critic's Complaints and the Director's Response 159

Critical Acclaim 159

Criticism and Critical Acclaim 159

Data Analysis and Findings 25

Data Analysis and Interpretation 18

Data AnalysisSurvey 103

Defining Bollywood Song and Dance Sequences 64

Definition of Film Noir 180

Dialogues 158

Difference on the Basis of Video 58, 60

Director G. Aravindhan 155

Dirty Picture 149

Discussion and Analysis 119

Dissecting Director's Classic 160

Emblems and Names (Prevention of Improper Use) Act 201

Emergence of Noir Genre 178
Enforcement 201
Era of Diaspora 47
External conflict 170
Extreme Violence 149

Film Analysis of the Yore and the Shift 208
Film Analysis through a Web of Networks A Parad 205
Film censorship 146
Film Review Elements of Film 218
Finding and Inferences 189
Findings and Results 50
First person approach 225
Folk Dance 62
Footnotes 87
Format of Film Review 218
Freedom of Expression 137
Freedom of Speech and Expression 135
Freudian Lens Zindagi Na Milegi Dob 212

Gehlawat, A 57
Getting along Well 216
Guidelines for Certification 199
Gulaal (2009) 222

Haider 149
Haseena Parker 174
History of Indian Cinema Music 54
Hypothesis 43, 202

Iceberg Theory 213
Impact of Biopics on Audience 90
Importance of Film Censorship 148
Imraan The Embodiment of 'Id' 213
Indian Art Cinema 188
Indian Cinema 8
Indian Cinema and Covert Advertising A Study of 22
Internal conflict 170
Introduction Multiplexes 8
Introduction of Biopics in India 90

Jacob, L (2002) 57
Jodhaa-Akbar (2008) 120
Journals 29
Journey of Punjabi Cinema 43
Judiciary and Freedom of Speech and Expression 137

Kaabil 170
Kabir The Carefully Decisive 'Ego' 214
Kamasutra 148
Knowledge of reviewer 225

Lathe Joshi (2016) 222
Links 21
Literature Review 31, 118, 128
Location 158

Main Body of Paper/Argument 129
Malayalam Cinema 154
Man Beyond the Bridge (2009) 222
Mangal Pandey The Rising (2005) 222
Manish Prakash 230
Manto 223, 224, 225
Meaning of aesthetic 143
Meaning of applaud 142
Meaning of blasphemy 142
Meaning of celluloid 144
Meaning of denigrate 142
Meaning of depict 142

Meaning of foist 142
Meaning of fraternity 142
Meaning of genre 144
Meaning of nausea 143
Meaning of petitioner 143
Meaning of preamble 142
Meaning of revocation 143
Meaning of unhindered 142
Methodology 11, 128
Methods 146
Mom 172
MSG 149
Multiplex Oriented Indian Cinema 8
Multiplexes and Indian Cinema 9
Murder 148
Muskan Sidana 227

Narration 161
Nativity 160
Negative portrayal of a popular figure or an 149
New Bollywood Music/Remake Era 55
Noir Cinema in India 181
Not in Favor 12, 13, 14
Notable Case StudiesDo Bigha Zameen 194
Novelty 161

Objective 11, 188
Objective and Methodology 118
Opinion rather than information 225
Origin of Indian Cinema and Period Dramas/Films 116

Paanch, 150
Padmaavat (2018) 123
Parzania 149
Personality trait 170
Pink Pinkpink Review of Pink Film 219
PK 143, 148
Plot 156
Politics 150
Priority regarding film elements 226
Problem with Period Drama/Films 117
Prologue to the Making of Kanchana Sita 155
Promotional trends 17
Punjabi Films Post-Partition 45

Rachel Dwyer 168
Raees 171
Ramayana 153
Reason 14
Refusal to certify. 199
Regional Films and its Analysis 206
Religion 148
Remake Version 58, 59
Reports 21, 29
Representation and Characteristics of Femme Fatal 183
Research Design 102
Research Methodology 18, 25, 38, 43, 93
Research Objectives 38, 92
Result and Discussions 112
Review of Literature 10, 91, 100, 188, 202
Rockstar 150
Role of Biopic Films in Promoting Sportsmen and 99
Role of Folk Dance in Bollywood Cinema 76

Saaransh by Mahesh Bhatt 195
Samiksha Sharma 228

Sexuality 148
Shruti Sharma 227
Significance of the Study 56, 92
Simran 173
Singers Turning Actors Era 48
Smriti Bajaj 230
Sudhanshu Maheshwari 230
Suggestions 141
Survey 102
Survey Analysis 193
Syd Field 169
Symbolic Elements 24

Technical Elements 24
Tim Stout 168
Toba Tek Singh 222, 225
Transition of Romance in Hindi Cinema from 'Swiss 30
Turning Point 46

UA - Parental guidance 147
Universal 147
USP of the film reviewed 226
Utilisation of Indian 62

Websites 186
What are Period Drama/Films? 116
What is Art Cinema? 187
What is Cinema? 146
Working Definitions of Key Terms 24